Alasdair MacIntyre

Alasdair MacIntyre is widely recognised today as one of the most significant philosophers working in the English-speaking world. His intellectual impact has not been confined entirely to the world of philosophy for, unlike many technically minded philosophers, MacIntyre has avoided separating the issues of both general philosophy and moral philosophy from the social and historical context in which they are embedded.

This study seeks to set before a largely non-philosophically minded social science readership something of the social and cultural significance of MacIntyre's work. It does this by first outlining the main political and cultural influences that have shaped the outlook of MacIntyre's writing. The most important of these influences are undoubtedly, on the one hand, Christianity and, on the other, the Marxist tradition, as well as the broad intellectual inheritance of the classical world. This book argues that it is out of these traditions that MacIntyre has produced his radically distinctive critique of contemporary liberal societies. The book then examines the significance for the social sciences of MacIntyre's elaboration and restatement of an Aristotelian critique of the moral culture of modernity. MacIntyre's work is shown to be deeply connected to the historical narrative of social change presented by Karl Polanyi, and this work is shown to be more plausible than some contemporary critics would allow. MacIntyre's characterisation of modernity, as being based around an unfounded managerialist culture and a rhetorically emotivist moral discourse, is seen to reveal the potential of a critical social science based on Aristotelian moral categories.

Peter McMylor lectures in Sociology at the University of Manchester.

Alasdair MacIntyre

Critic of modernity

Peter McMylor

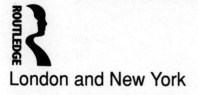

London and New York

First published 1994
by Routledge
11 New Fetter Lane, London EC4P 4EE

Simultaneously published in the USA and Canada
by Routledge
29 West 35th Street, New York, NY 10001

Typeset in Baskerville by
Ponting–Green Publishing Services, Chesham, Bucks
Printed and bound in Great Britain by
T.J. Press (Padstow) Ltd, Padstow, Cornwall

British Library Cataloguing in Publication Data
A catalogue record for this book is available from the
British Library.

Library of Congress Cataloging-in-Publication Data
McMylor, Peter, 1958–
    Alasdair MacIntyre: critic of modernity/Peter McMylor.
        p.   cm.
    Includes bibliographical references and index.
    1. MacIntyre, Alasdair C.–Contributions in philosophy
and social sciences.   2. Philosophy and social sciences.
I. Title.
B1647.M124M38   1993
192–dc20   93–3490
                                                    CIP

ISBN   0–415–04426–X
           0–415–04427–8 (pbk)

Contents

Contents

Preface

This is not a book written by a philosopher, although it is about someone who for most of his academic life has carried that official designation. Nor is it to be understood as being in any way a substitute for reading MacIntyre's diverse writings. The substance of MacIntyre's work lies in the detail of the argument on the printed page. No summary can do justice to the richness and complexity of his later books especially. As a sociologist who lacks the particular academic skills of a philosopher I can only say in justification for having written this text that what interests me about the work of Alasdair MacIntyre is its intent and potency as social criticism, albeit sharpened by the analytic bite of philosophical rigour. MacIntyre is, in the very best sense of the word, a moralist: the limitations and the impoverished quality of life under contemporary liberalism are his real concern and he is consequently too important a writer to be left only to the philosophers. This is particularly the case given the rather complacent consensus emerging within Anglo-American sociology on the enduring value of liberalism, even when decked out in fashionable French or German conceptual clothing.

MacIntyre's work contains so many substantive issues, as well as numerous hints and asides that merit the attention of a sociologist, that it is impossible to follow up more than a few of them within the space of a book of modest size. I would very much like to have attempted to connect MacIntyre to a rich vein of American social criticism in particular. The writers who MacIntyre clearly has much in common with, at least in relation to their perception of the ills of liberalism, are figures like Richard Sennett, Christopher Lasch and, above all, Philip Rieff. The omission of Rieff is a particular misfortune, because in recent years MacIntyre has made particular reference to his work on our therapeutic culture, as a basis for understanding contemporary western society. I hope to remedy this omission elsewhere.

In the course of writing this book I have naturally incurred a number of intellectual debts. The most obvious of these is to Huw Beynon, who supervised my PhD thesis from which this book in part derives. Without Huw's patient and wise advice nothing would have been produced. I would also like to thank Richard Brown and John Maguire for their encouragement when I began to write. As is obvious from the text, Scott Meikle has been an important influence on what follows, but is unlikely to be very happy about the result and bears no responsibility for any of the conclusions drawn from his work. Lastly, I would like to acknowledge the support of many friends and colleagues who, frequently without realising it, make many things possible.

Peter McMylor
Manchester 1993

Part I

MacIntyre – Christianity and/or Marxism?

Chapter 1

Christianity and Marxism
Acceptance and rejection

The first book ever written by Alasdair MacIntyre was entitled *Marxism: An Interpretation.*[1] It begins with the following words:

> The division of human life into the sacred and the secular is one that comes naturally to Western thought. It is a division which at one and the same time bears the marks of its Christian origin and witnesses to the death of a properly religious culture. For when the sacred and the secular are divided, then religion becomes one more department of human life, one activity among others. This has in fact happened to bourgeois religion ... Only a religion which is a way of living in every sphere either deserves to or can hope to survive. For the task of religion is to help see the secular as the sacred, the world as under God. When the sacred and the secular are separated, then the ritual becomes an end not the hallowing of the world, but in itself. Likewise if our religion is fundamentally irrelevant to our politics, then we are recognising the political as a realm outside the reign of God. To divide the sacred from the secular is to recognise God's action only within the narrowest limits. A religion which recognises such a division, as does our own, is one on the point of dying.[2]

Here we see presented to the world for the first time many of MacIntyre's familiar themes and concerns: the anxiety about the division and fragmentation of everyday life in relation to a great moral scheme and an absolutely distinctive certainty that this is a modern 'bourgeois' phenomenon. But what is perhaps most useful about seeing this very early passage is in the entirely theological character of its analysis. Anyone looking at

MacIntyre's work must not only be struck by the remarkable consistency of his intellectual preoccupations but that in many respects he has turned full circle and in his later work returned to the theological issues and concerns that he began with. This is correct, yet also greatly to oversimplify, for the long journey of movement and return has been an enormously enriching one.[3] However, the initial use of theological language is important even if we only note the original motivation that lies behind his sustained critique of western societies.

It is also the case that the theological nature of MacIntyre's stance is an essential conditioning factor in understanding his initial relationship to Marxism. In what follows, I will begin by charting MacIntyre's original characterisation of Marxism and Christianity and then examine his later partial rejection of both, but noting what he felt was always crucial to retain from each in his sociological understanding of western societies. It will I believe prove fruitful to examine in some detail MacIntyre's first sustained piece of argumentation, as well as his other early essays, so that we can begin to appreciate his relatively early theoretical sophistication and as an indication of the powerful and original vision that inspired his early and later work. It would, of course, be foolish to deny development and any discontinuity in MacIntyre's thought, but I am convinced that an excessively 'textual' approach, i.e. one that ignored the very particular values and dispositions present at an early stage of his intellectual formation, would miss something vital about the nature of his later thought. I shall emphasise, at first, the strong religious and theological nature of the original analysis (long out of print) in order to bring out both the continuity and the contrasts with the later and more 'sociological' analysis of the revised edition.

CHRISTIANITY AND MARXISM: THE ORIGINAL POSITION

Why did MacIntyre choose to begin his intellectual career with a book on Marxism? The answer lies in his view that Marxism is one of two really serious attempts to provide a clear rival world view to Christianity in the modern world, the other being positivism. Marxism is seen by MacIntyre as the more important of the two because of positivism's rather limited appeal, being largely limited to intellectuals who have had little interest in trying to provide a wide-ranging and popular positive account of the nature of religion itself. Marxism, in contrast, has a very clear and powerful account of the nature and function of religion within its own theoretical terms of reference, the key point being for MacIntyre that 'Marxism envisages the whole of human life in terms that explicitly deny the God-given character of the world'.[4] But what makes Marxism most paradoxical is that Marxist theory and hence Marxist atheism has religious roots.

How can this paradoxical claim of MacIntyre's be understood?[5] In essence it lies in the continual instability and tension within the Christian tradition between Church and state, sacred and secular. This tension is the result of the fact that it was the established political and the old religious authorities that had Jesus killed and in so doing helped create a religious community that was for some time independent of the state and very often persecuted by it. But the Church did recognise the authority of the state as a power that was granted by God but separate from the Church. All political orders are sinful and stand in need of Christian judgement, but for the Church to identify itself too closely with any one particular order will lead it into failure and sin, as God is reduced in this process to the God of one limited and inadequate human order. It follows from this as MacIntyre suggests that

> This means that one of the fruits of the gospel may be an anticlerical secularism and an atheism that rejects false gods. The gospel itself is atheistic where any god other than the one true God is concerned. Where he is not preached, atheism may be the surviving fruit of the gospel.[6]

Marxist atheism becomes then an almost necessary and even potentially a protective doctrine for Christianity, or at least for a Christianity that has become forgetful of the need for a full and rigorous negative theology, which ought to prevent the Church succumbing to the idolatry of identifying God with whatever images a particular society, at a particular time, has of him. But MacIntyre is prepared to argue, at this stage, that at least in part Marxism's critique of religion rests on a mistake, the mistake that it inherits from eighteenth-century rationalism which is all too ready to identify the superstitious representation in religion with the nature of the mythical dimension itself. The error, he suggests, lies in the assumption that mythical thought is failed scientific thought, that it is 'would-be science distorted by human needs and emotions'.[7] Instead MacIntyre wants to suggest that myth is attempting something different from science, in that it attempts a total picture of the world, albeit from a necessarily limited or partial view from within that world which means that a stretching of language via metaphor is crucial to myth. It follows from this, that unlike science, which seeks to separate out the emotive element from questions of cognition, myth prizes the connection between description and evaluation:

> For myth and science both select certain facts as significant: they differ in their criterion of significance. A metaphysics is a rational myth. A superstition is a myth without the control and criticism of reasoning. A religion is a myth which claims both a foundation in history and to point beyond itself to God.[8]

For MacIntyre at this stage the weakness of Marxism, like that of eighteenth-century rationalism and certain versions of modern positivism, is that it mistakes religion for myth pure and simple. Marxism seeks social and indeed functional explanations of religion on the assumption that these will exhaust its meaning. But MacIntyre acknowledges the great advantage Marxism has over Christianity in view of its emphasis on science and the importance accorded to scientific method. Interestingly enough, he suggests the real advantage enjoyed by Marxism in relationship to science lies not in easier acceptance of science's ability to explain the world, for Christianity can justly claim to have encouraged the contemplation and understanding of the world, but rather the distinctiveness lies in Marxism's understanding and celebration of the active use of technique in relation to the manipulation of the material world. Modern science, MacIntyre suggests, urgently raises through the question of technology, the issue of power, an issue he believes Christians have all too often evaded by using the imagery of the servant as an apparent model for the renunciation of power. This will not do, he says, for the Christian is 'a sinner and yet justified, always . . . in a tension between the power of God in Christ and the powers of this world'.[9] Marxism, of course, has had a long engagement with the issue of power and its relationship to technology. This makes it very important for MacIntyre, who sees Marxism as a secularism formed by the Gospels committed to justice, and so charged with theological significance.

MacIntyre makes a strong theological claim to connect what he perceives as important in Marxism with Christianity. He does this by deriving five social and political principles implicit within Christianity from Jesus' account of the last judgement in Matthew 25: 31–5. These principles were:

1 That not only individuals but whole societies were to be redeemed 'and before him shall be gathered all the nations'.
2 There are real forces of evil at work in the world which generate real pain and suffering and because of a lack of pity or compassion.
3 It is the business of God to judge, not of man here and now to distinguish sheep from goats.
4 It is the task of human beings to show mercy in practical ways in order to set some limit to the lack of mercy in the world – 'I was in prison and ye came unto me'.
5 In this world we meet God in the shape of those in need and we can never know for certain when we are being so confronted.

For MacIntyre it is clearly in the area points 3 and 4 that Marxism presents its strongest challenge to Christianity, precisely because its stance and overarching imperatives are so close to that of the Gospels.[10]

When examining the differences in the two books MacIntyre wrote concerning Marxism and Christianity, one is bound to be struck very forcibly by one thing: that although in many respects the books are quite distinct, when it comes to the internal account of Marxism as a theory or doctrine, they differ hardly at all and in fact are virtually a word for word transcription. It seems therefore that what changed in the intervening fifteen years was not any significant shift in MacIntyre's understanding of the nature of Marxism as a body of thought, although there clearly is a shift in the significance that MacIntyre attaches to the truth status that Marxism is presumed to possess. What appears to happen is that in the second text all direct references that appear to endorse a Christian theological position are removed and replaced by a form of sociological analysis which is distanced from both Christianity and Marxism, but seeks to examine the cultural significance of both, a significance that is seen as vitally important, but also, in some respects, no longer available. I explore this sociological moment in MacIntyre's thought below. However, the picture of MacIntyre's intellectual development is further complicated by the fact that in the intervening years he produced essays of a clearer and perhaps more conventionally Marxist nature and, as is well known, was a member of the International Socialists (IS), one of the more intellectually open and creative of the Far Left groups.[11] We will have occasion to address these essays in Marxist philosophy shortly.

It seems clear that what impels MacIntyre towards Marxism, as it is to do a later generation of so-called Liberation Theologians,[12] is in the Christian commitment to practise and to encounter God in the world, amongst the poor. This sets up an ideological and often institutional tension, which as MacIntyre argues refuses 'the identification of outward religion with inward righteousness' as 'just the source of that self-righteousness of religious believers which leads them to withdraw from the world for which Jesus died and to see the Church not as a community that redeems the world but rather as a fixed community of the redeemed'. To escape this danger means to turn to the secular world as a place of religious significance, 'This is the search of Hegel's philosophy'.[13] It is precisely this leap into the embrace of the secular which MacIntyre will later see as ultimately damaging for Christianity as a distinct current within society, a topic we will explore below.

The importance of Hegel lies in the way he injects into a historical understanding issues and concerns that ultimately have their source in theological concepts.[14] Hegel's three key concepts: 'self-estrangement', 'objectification' and 'coming to one's own', are all seen by MacIntyre as the projection on to a historical narrative of a Christian account of the Fall, the sinfulness of the world, and the process of redemption. 'Self-estrangement' is seen as a description of the Fall. It appears both in relationships between human beings and as internal to the mental life of a person. Human beings fail to live up to the moral law that they themselves create; this itself is a marker of the selfishness and egoism in the life of society and results both in conflict and a bad conscience. This process of 'self-estrangement' from the products of one's own thought and behaviour produces what Hegel calls 'objectification', the failure to recognise the world as a product of a person's own thought and actions, and this failure of recognition is clearly the hallmark of the developed theory of the alienation of subject and object.

But, for Hegel the crucial move in the escape from this situation is the coming to see and understand one's homelessness in the world. The way back is seen as being through self-knowledge, an act that Hegel calls 'appropriation' or 'coming to one's own'. This process of the growth of self-knowledge is what Hegel takes the substance of human history to be about, the gradual emergence of human freedom out of slavery. For Hegel, of course, religion and in particular Christianity are a transitional phase to be transcended by the emergence of a purer recognition of the nature of freedom in reason, i.e. as philosophy which in overcoming religion would also reveal its truth in the reconciliation of the finite and the absolute, as prefigured in the doctrine of the incarnation, as the unity of man and God in Christ. MacIntyre's account of Hegel is rather distant and external in the sense that he seems to see the work as providing a rich new vocabulary of transcendence and redemption,[15] rather than as a system of thought to be completely accepted. MacIntyre is happy to accept the Marxist critique of the Hegelian system, seeing Hegel as a representative bourgeois in its heroic phase of overthrowing the remnants of feudalism, but who is ultimately idealist in substituting ideas and concepts for material reality.[16]

MacIntyre proceeds to rehearse the now familiar root of Marx's thought through the Left-Hegelians and Feuerbach, in an admirably clear and sympathetic manner. This, it is important to remember, was no mean achievement in 1953, when in Anglo-Saxon philosophy circles the attitude to Marxism, in an increasingly Cold War climate, had been set a few years earlier by Popper's harsh dismissal.[17] Feuerbach like Hegel is seen by MacIntyre to be trying to fulfil Christianity in secular terms. Religion is seen to have arisen for Feuerbach by a process of the objectification of the human essence, so religion in reality is a massively distorted projection of the fundamental reality of what it is to be human. Christianity is a vision of humanity, but humanity as a loving community. Theological language about a powerful, loving God is in reality a projection of humanity's deepest needs. So religion must be humanised to overcome the processes of objectification which have produced such a gulf between humanity and the real human essence. But the question then arises as to how this process of necessary humanisation is to be achieved. The answer to this question once again raises for MacIntyre the limitations of this Left-Hegelian critique when compared with Christianity, as he puts it:

> both of them (Hegel and Feuerbach). . . see the path to our redemption as through hard thinking. This is an illusion that the Bible does not share. Feuerbach could say that 'Politics must become our religion', but he thinks of politics as an affair of rival theories. . . Thus Feuerbach loses his grip upon the Biblical doctrine of man in a way in which Marx, who exposes his illusion at this point, does not.[18]

Christianity is like Marxism in being a form of praxis, i.e. a unity of theory and practice and hence tying thought or commitments of a morally imperative kind to actions in the world. Hence it could never be purely idealist in outlook. MacIntyre then begins to tell the perhaps overfamiliar story of Marx's move from Hegel's philosophy to politics and political economy. He insists that Marx remains true to the spirit of Hegel's intentions even when he attempts to supersede Hegel's own philosophy. MacIntyre presents this point with a clarity which would be hard to surpass:

> But even in his formulation of this problem of how to pass beyond Hegel, Marx remains a Hegelian. For when he sees the Hegelian philosophy as the final synthesis in thought of the ideal, and sees it over against its antithesis, the real material of the nineteenth century, and then attempts to realise the former in the latter: when Marx does this, what else is he doing but initiating a new phase of Hegel's own dialectic?[19]

MacIntyre then moves on to deal with Marx's task of producing a critique of the actuality that Hegel had thought effectively realised the ideal: the Prussian state. Marx, of course, had little difficulty in showing that the Prussian state was not an expression of a free society, it lacked a democratic form to express the popular will and engaged in anti-democratic practices like censorship. MacIntyre places considerable emphasis on the

Feuerbachian element in Marx's critique of Hegel, for ultimately what is wrong with the modern state is its failure to
accord with the real nature of man as a social being in society.
Marx modifies Hegel on the basis of the Feuerbachian concept
of an essential human nature. This notion of an essential
human nature will play an important role in MacIntyre's later
Marxist essays on the nature of morality under modern
capitalism.

   From the realities of the Prussian state, Marx is soon made to
face the grim general reality of the emerging industrial capitalism of his epoch, in terms of his personal acquaintance with
Frederick Engels and in Engels's writing on the state of the
working class in England. It is this that impels Marx into a much
deeper analysis of political economy than he had hitherto
attempted. In this process he is trying to discover how philosophy can be turned into an instrument of transformation, in
order to realise the real or essential nature of human beings.

   MacIntyre then goes on to elaborate on the themes of
alienation and estrangement that are developed and concret-
ised out of Hegel's philosophical system by Marx in his analysis
of political economy. MacIntyre first notes the general nature of
Marx's account:

> When man as a worker becomes himself a commodity, he is
> fundamentally alienated, estranged from himself. Under the
> form of labour, man sees himself as a commodity, as an
> object. Hence as labour he objectifies, externalises his own
> existence. A consequence of this is that life becomes not
> something which he enjoys as a part of his essential humanity,
> but rather merely an opportunity to a living, a bare physical
> subsistence. . . Thus to be human is to be estranged. But
> when man is a being divided against himself, able to envisage
> himself as a commodity, he breaks the community of man
> with man.[20]

MacIntyre then reveals the specifics of Marx's analysis. Labour
is the root of the process and private property the end result,
Marx is in effect writing the substantive history of this Hegelian
story of alienation and estrangement. What Marx finds in the
political economists is a grasp of the process by which under the
system of private property the satisfaction of human needs is
forced into the form of selling one's labour. Any question of a

national or even a human interest as having values in their own
right is eliminated in favour of questions of revenue and profit.
The working-class interest becomes relegated to a question of
the necessary costs of production. The division of labour in
society can raise the overall level of wealth whilst rendering
work less and less a free expression of human nature. The result
of this is that money, which ought to be a means of human
existence, becomes its end and the result of this is as MacIntyre
puts it: 'it is money, the abstract form of man's estrangement,
which rules society.'[21]

Before going on to examine the significance that MacIntyre
gives to these writings of Marx, it is worth dwelling for a
moment on the actual significance of MacIntyre's intellectual
achievement in this work. For again it is worth reminding
ourselves that this book, *Marxism: An Interpretation*, was written
in 1952 (finished in October of that year) and within a relatively
limited amount of space, there is a discussion of almost all the
themes of the early Marx that will a few years later dominate the
thinking of the New Left, a New Left that MacIntyre will play a
substantial role within. Clearly MacIntyre is writing at an early
stage and at a time when, in the Anglo-Saxon world, the
understanding of Marxism is dominated by, on the one hand,
orthodox Stalinist Communist interpretations (Stalin is still
alive at the time MacIntyre is writing), and, on the other, by
numerous disillusioned Cold-War polemics. It is I believe very
difficult for anyone to regard the work, whatever one's view of
its religious content, as anything other than a brilliant presentation and anticipation of much of the best humanistic Marxist
scholarship of the next decade or more.[22]

Clearly then MacIntyre sees Marx's achievement as principally
consisting of being able to give a more exact historical and
material form to the account of human estrangement that is to
be found in Hegel's work. It follows on from this that at this
stage, MacIntyre is able to celebrate this analysis, in terms of
Marx having been able to give a fuller expression to the forms of
Christian thought he inherits from Hegel. MacIntyre even goes
so far as to claim that Marx is actually more faithful to the spirit
of the Gospels than Hegel; he suggests that Marx:

is far more Biblical than Hegel both in the concreteness and
in his seeing the proletariat, the poor, 'the least of these' in

the parable of the sheep and the goats, as those who bear the
marks of redemption. In the Gospel riches mark estrangement: men who possess them are possessed by them. It is only
the poor who can enter the Kingdom. If they would do so, the
rich must become poor. What Marx did. . . was to translate
the judgement of Jesus on all antitheses of rich and poor
into an immediate judgement upon the capitalist society of
his own day.[23]

One may wonder at the wisdom of such a straightforward
identification of the nineteenth-century proletariat with 'the
poor' of first-century Palestine, given the specificity of Marx's
analysis of capitalism, but it is at the least a very suggestive
parallel. Indeed it may be more than just suggestive when we
consider that the theologian, Nicholas Lash, in commenting on
Marx's theory can argue that

the idea of the *last* revolution . . . is quite clearly mythological or symbolic in character, rather than descriptive of
any historical revolution that would or could occur. It is
mythological because, central and indispensable to its construction is the concept of a proletariat defined in Hegelian
terms, as existing in 'pure negativity' . . . because no social
class has ever existed, or could ever exist, in 'pure negativity'
it would seem impossible for there ever to occur, within
human history, a social revolution the agent or agents of
which were devoid of *all* 'particular' interest.[24]

This is a rather ironic turning of tables, by a theologian, on
Marxism, but there is little doubt that many, including some
Marxists, would today agree with this view.[25] But for MacIntyre
what is most important about Marx's identification of the
proletariat with redemptive transformation consists in the
moral quality of his historical judgement, ultimately based on a
vision that allows the overcoming of alienation that as MacIntyre
says it 'would be impossible without his vision of what man
ought to be'.[26] It is the grounding of this 'ought' of moral
judgement, that will be at the centre of MacIntyre's future
preoccupations, and an issue to which we shall have to return.[27]
    In the original work MacIntyre proceeds by applauding Marx
for the powerful originality of his *Theses on Feuerbach* with the
emphasis on practice as a criterion of truth and the concomitant

emphasis on material transformation. There then follows a cogent account of *The German Ideology*, presented as a fully worked out account of Marx's materialism with full historical backing. Here MacIntyre, in the original work, claims to see a change in the nature of Marx's analysis between the earlier work and *The German Ideology* – a distinction he appears unwilling to sustain in the revised edition. In essence MacIntyre claims that in *The German Ideology* Marx makes a quite fundamental move from having been a prophet to being a theorist. By a prophet, MacIntyre appears to mean those elements in Marx's thinking that have their roots in Hegel's thought such as the issues of alienation and estrangement, which of course he argues are of Christian origin. He is not suggesting that the real content of these concepts is missing from this later work but rather that it is present in the analysis of the concrete context of the social division of labour. MacIntyre suggests that Marx is claiming empirical confirmation for his understanding of history. This is a claim to have moved towards creating a science, a science that will be predictive. This is not an intellectual position that MacIntyre will feel able to sustain and presumably this is why a number of pages are removed in the revised edition.[28] It seems to me that there is rather more going on in the production of the revised edition of the book than the removing of Christian commentary that the author could no longer accept or feel publically comfortable with.[29] MacIntyre is claiming at this point that Marx is now giving up the moral perspective on capitalism and communism in favour of science, 'Marx does not uphold communism as what ought to be, but simply as what will be'.[30] MacIntyre's later work of the 1950s will suggest such a distinction is untenable and unjust to Marx, but in his criticism of what he takes to be Marx's scientism he points the way towards positions that he will later develop more fully. In the first place MacIntyre notes that the attempt to claim 'scientific' status for Marxism creates a problem for any philosophy that claims to be a philosophy of action. How can a philosophy designed to motivate behaviour fail to involve moral criteria of choice and judgement. A theory deprived of a compelling moral imperative will become one more tentative empirical hypothesis capable of a fickle rejection, as any evidence will always be susceptible to other interpretations. But most importantly MacIntyre raises an objection to the implications for Marx's theory in this supposed positivist move, namely what might be briefly summarised as the dangers of reductionism and economism. MacIntyre makes these criticisms of Marxism in the following interesting and, perhaps, prescient way,

> by restricting man's estrangement to his social and economic distress, Marx has abandoned the search for wider forms of human alienation which might menace the course of man's coming once more to his own. This lays Marx's theory open to the danger of objectification, of failure to recognise other forms of estrangement which will mislead it and give to it categories of thinking which will falsify Marxist experience.[31]

We are close to the heart here of the early MacIntyre's fundamental attitude to Marxism, for despite the sympathetic nature of his exposition, he does, in fact, articulate a religiously inspired critique of this tradition. As we shall see, I do not think it wholly implausible to argue that much of the fundamental structure of that critique remains a vital presence in much of MacIntyre's thought right through to the present. It is, ultimately, the clear-sighted appropriation by Marx of the inherently critical moralism of the Christian tradition, that gives Marxism its strongest appeal for MacIntyre. It is a turning of Christian morality against its own society and indeed against its own ostensible representatives. The powerful moral logic of such views has attracted many Christian thinkers to savagely radical moral and cultural critiques of societies that they saw correctly, as decreasingly Christian, even in a formal sense. It is this situation that famously led Kierkegaard to his furious denunciation of the conventional Christian morality of his day; to his denouncing of apparently Christian virtues like prudence, hallowed for the most part throughout the Christian tradition, because of the instrumentalisation of this virtue in a hypocritical way by a thoroughly bourgeois society.

MacIntyre argues that Marx was from the outset preoccupied by questions that by their very nature share a common intellectual and spiritual territory with religious and metaphysical systems. These are questions which are only abstractly defined as concerning human estrangement, alienation and the hope for reconciliation: the substantive nature of these concerns are issues such as material want, starvation and hunger, pain and cruelty, the purpose that may or may not lie behind individual and corporate human life, and the possibilities of a changed condition that may resolve these real material and frequently tragic problems. There can be little doubt that Marxism when it has made its strongest claims has operated on terrain that is filled generally by theodicies.[32] In so far as religion has always sought to provide intellectual satisfaction through generating meanings and interpretations concerning the purpose of pain and death, so Marxism's compelling account of the meaning and the long-term purpose that underpins human history, has provided a, perhaps, tragic rationalisation of human pain and suffering as humanity supposedly moved towards its goal. But as MacIntyre could quite clearly see from the very beginning, Marxism is dealing with dimensions that most certainly lie outside the field of the sciences. What, at this stage, worries him about Marxism is its claim to a scientific certainty about matters which are always to some extent debatable and contestable, as he put it:

> Morality is always to some degree ambiguous, metaphysics a commitment that can never be fully justified. The tragedy of Marxism is that it wished to combine the scope of metaphysics with the certainty of natural sciences. It was therefore forced on the one hand to reject religion, since it claimed a scope as wide and authentic as that of religion, and on the other hand to oversimplify all questions of technique in order that they should conform to the initial pattern to which Marx had bound his thinking. This in turn involved Marxism in a form of human alienation, to which it has itself too often been blind, but of which its history is the clearest exposition. For human thought, human rationality always tends to be too abstract, and not to allow for the independence of those structures which man in society has created. There is an unpredictability here which is not to be overcome by more human cleverness but only by a greater humility, by a greater recognition of the limitations of human thought and action.[33]

The importance of this passage is that, apart from the clear anxiety about the positivistic element in Marxism, it prefigures what will come to be MacIntyre's central claim about social science methodology. This is his profound scepticism about attempts to eliminate moral and evaluative features from programmes in the social sciences, in order that they should conform to what many took, in the fifties, to be the natural science model.[34]

We should pay especially careful attention in the above passage to the quite shrewd sense of Marxism as an ideology competing against other ideologies with similar scope and range, i.e. religion, and its necessity to clear the ground of potentially competing loyalties. MacIntyre is here turning Marxism's critique of ideology back on itself, as he quite clearly sees the dangers of a reification within Marxism. He displays an almost Adornoesque sensitivity to the dangers of identity-thinking as the particular is subsumed under general concepts, and human particularity is threatened by a false totalisation. Here MacIntyre's Christian humanism and its sense of finitude, expressed as the Christian virtue of humility, provides a sure defence against the dangers of a totalitarian Stalinist Marxism and a valuable inoculation against the later anti-humanist (and strongly atheistic) structuralist Marxism.

MacIntyre is rare among philosophers, at least as a professional group, in formally recognising the socially located particularity and self-interest of intellectuals and theorists. The point could be made more firmly about Marxism, that one of the most important aspects of it, and an aspect most often ignored, is that it is above all an intellectual product, which, of course, means that it is produced by intellectuals. Once viewed as an ideology, whatever else it may be, Marxism must come under the same shadow of suspicion that it has cast over all other belief systems: a suspicion that behind the promise of human emancipation and a freedom from the illusions of ideological systems there lurked yet another set of special interests seeking wealth and power. The most cogent advocate of this view has been the American sociologist Alvin Gouldner, who pointed to a rather curious anomaly in Marxist theory, which consisted of its inability to account for the existence of middle- and upper-class revolutionary intellectuals. Their existence seemed to suggest either a capacity for a pure and unmediated 'reason' (a product of education) able to transcend the limitations and distortions that economic class interests, or else raise the possibility that these intellectuals were in some way furthering a set of objectives that might even be described as 'class interests'.[35]

In some respects Gouldner, being a professional sociologist, has an advantage over MacIntyre, for whatever the dangers of sociological reductionism, of which MacIntyre is all too well aware, it remains true that the bold social contextualising of ideas provides powerful clues for interpretation. MacIntyre for all the careful attention he pays to historical and social context remains still somewhat reluctant to push the sociological dimensions of his understanding far enough. The difficulty is, that it is hard to do more than one thing at a time. The careful delineating of ideas, in this case Marxism, almost inevitably leans even the most self-conscious of accounts towards an internalist reading of a body of thought. This must lead to a sober recognition of the inevitability of some disciplinary boundaries, whilst still acknowledging the urgent necessity of going beyond them. The implication from Gouldner's work would point towards the necessity of a sociology of intellectuals, with a clear sense of group interests, as opposed to a perhaps looser contextualising sociology of knowledge.

In essence MacIntyre argues that Marxism has religious roots in that it gains its vision of the good life of peace and reconciliation from Christianity, mediated by Hegel, but makes it historically concrete. But inherent in this theory of Marxism is a tendency to objectification. This is a product of combining an aspiration for science and truth-telling myth, i.e. religion. In the process the crucial theological move associated with the via negativa, i.e. that important statement about the fundamental nature of reality may only be possible by excluding positive terms and that sometimes the best we can do is use extended metaphor instead, is lost. So Marxism makes the move from a general orientation, to a clearly defined programme to end alienation here and now, via a specific organisation that accepts certain statements as transparently true. It clearly remains the case that all of Marxism is not invalidated by the presence of positivist elements: MacIntyre makes an explicit contrast between the early Marx of *The Paris Manuscripts* and the Marx of *The Communist Manifesto*.[36] The possibility must be held open of Marxism as 'prophecy' or analysis, contributing to a general emancipatory project for humanity. It is this conception that seems to inform some of the essays of the later 1950s, and which form, as we shall see, a crucial bridge to later historicist critique of moral thought, especially as embodied in the book *After Virtue*. It is to these essays and their relationship to the later work that we now turn. MacIntyre's changing attitude to religious belief will be charted in a later section.

In 1958–9 MacIntyre published his path-breaking essay 'Notes from the Moral Wilderness I' in the journal *New Reasoner* produced by a group of Marxists who had broken with the British Communist Party over the invasion of Hungary in 1956. In this essay his problem is essentially: does the reality of evils of Stalinism mean that the only viable option left is that of liberalism. As he puts it 'a position we are all tempted into is that of the moral critic of Stalinism'.[37] In answer he deploys what is to become a typical MacIntyre technique: the use of the idea of a range of characters who represent a variety of moral positions but who like the characters of a novel are not necessarily fixed but may represent moments in the development of an individual's consciousness. In this case the characters are the Stalinist, the revisionist, the moral critic, etc.

In *After Virtue* these characters are replaced by the manager, the therapist and the aesthete. They, like the above, are representative figures but also elements of our own consciousness.

What is the weakness in this revived liberalism? It is principally an appeal to moral principle (and what follows echoes through all MacIntyre's work): 'the fragility of their appeal to moral principle lies in the apparently arbitrary nature of that appeal. Whence come these standards by which Stalinism is judged and found wanting and why should they have authority over us?'[38] The moral (liberal) critic seems to have won independence from the Stalinist bureaucracy, i.e. leaving the party 'freed' the critic from an organisation that had, albeit for wicked purposes, institutionalised belief. The moral critic, MacIntyre argues, has exchanged this conscious dependence for an unconscious one, a dependence on the prevailing liberal culture of the west. This liberalism turns out to be the flip side of Stalinism. Stalinism identifies what is morally right with what *will* be the outcome of history. The individual, including his or her moral position, is predetermined by history: 'The "ought" of principle is swallowed up in the "is" of history.' On the other hand, the moral critic effectively removes himself from history, becoming a 'spectator'. Principles are invoked as valid but quite external to the actual course of historical events. 'The "ought" of principle is completely external to the "is" of history',[39] i.e. to what is actually happening or what is likely to happen. This is described by him as the prevailing liberal ethos:

> For it is of the essence of the liberal tradition that morality is taken as autonomous . . . it is the doctrine that moral principles can have no non-moral basis. Our judgements on specific moral issues may be supported by the invocation of more general principles. But in the end our most general and ultimate principles, because they are that in terms of which all else is justified stand beyond rational justification. In particular, by any appeal to facts historical or otherwise.[40]

It follows that the hallmark of liberalism is the arbitrariness of moral judgement. For the moral critic condemns Stalinism on the basis that he or she chooses values to condemn it, i.e. the facts of Stalinism are confronted with a set of moral principles. From this it is possible to discern the likely social role of the radical critic in western society. It is expected that there will be protesting minorities on particular issues. Radical public protest, especially by intellectuals, can be viewed as the critic, exhibiting his or her self choosing a set of private values, embodying and reinforcing the arbitrary and abstract nature of western pluralism.

Is there an alternative to this arbitrariness which does not involve accepting Stalinism or something equally repellent? MacIntyre suggests at this stage that there is, and that it lies in a return to a more authentic Marxism. This naturally means rejecting the then widespread Stalinist versions of the theory, which meant seeing historical developments as the product of simple objective laws and a rigid division between the material basis of society and its politics – cultural superstructure. Marxism, he argues, is not about the creation of a socialist material base, created by force or manipulation, upon which will arise a socialist superstructure. The two, argued MacIntyre, will be created together or not at all, and in the process any version of a means–end morality is rejected.

He states that:

> the economic basis of a society is not its tools, but the people co-operating using these particular tools in the manner

necessary to their use, and the superstructure consists of the social consciousness moulded by and the shape of this co-operation. To understand this is to repudiate the ends–means morality for there is no question of creating the economic base as a means to the socialist superstructure. Creating the basis, you create the superstructure. There are not two activities but one.[41]

MacIntyre then goes on to show us how Stalin's economic version of Marxist theory of conceptualising historical change in terms of positivistic laws led to a severing of Marx's economic theory from his concept of human nature, with disastrous consequences. He states bluntly:

Marx inherits from Hegel a conception of the 'human essence'. Although human life at any given moment is not a realisation of this essence, because human life is always limited in ways characteristic of the basis of a given form of society.[42]

He continues that capitalism, for Marx, creates the possibility of realising human potential in new ways but that this realisation must never be interpreted as an abstract law, standing over and above human beings and independent of human will.

It is this that points us towards MacIntyre's third way. It suggests a Marxist theory, which regarded history as providing a basis for standards, but without making the process automatic or devolving it from human choice and commitment. MacIntyre is involved here, as so often later, in trying to transcend the liberal distinction between human nature and morality, that is, in constructing a relation between 'what I am, what I can be, what I want to be and what I ought to be'.[43] MacIntyre is arguing for a Marxist naturalistic basis for morality. In his claim that 'morality expresses the most permanent and long run human desires,'[44] we can see the embryo of his view developed in *After Virtue* that it is necessary to revive the role of the virtues as guides for 'untutored human nature', in enabling the realisation of a human telos. In 'Notes from the Moral Wilderness', it is even possible to discern the same structure of argument as found in *After Virtue* concerning morality and the pursuit of human purposes, the Greeks, the Bible, the medieval world are all commended for keeping 'the connection (broken by liberalism) between the moral life and the pursuit of what men want,'[45] whether in the notion of the pursuit of philosophy (Aristotle) or as God offering to meet your desires (the Bible), or God meeting your desires by fulfilling your nature (Thomist synthesis of Aristotle and the Bible).

It is Marxism, for MacIntyre at this point, that performs the feat of restoring this pattern of thought lost to liberalism. Marxism is a bridging theory. For most of human history, long-run desires cannot achieve fulfilment, humanity fails to understand its real, long-term needs and desires. That is until the possibility of doing away with class society and the creation of real human community becomes possible.

This Marxist view suggests that morals are necessary to protect these long-term desires, or the end of our natures, but in the present they seem to lose their point and then morals become objectified and alien to us. With morality objectified or standing above us, so desires become wild and anarchic. At this stage of MacIntyre's thought, capitalism seems to both heighten this division but also to create the material conditions to resolve it. He suggests

> capitalism provides a form of life in which men rediscover desire in a number of ways. They discover above all that what they want most is what they want in common with others; and more than that a shared human life is not just a means to the accomplishment of what they desire, but that certain ways of sharing human life are indeed what they most desire.[46]

MacIntyre finds in his Marx no trace of a means–ends morality characteristic of Stalinism, but the notion of a *real* but developing essential human nature. He interprets this to mean that human conduct is not merely to be judged by its effectiveness in bringing communism closer, but that in your behaviour now, you to some degree embody the human nature which communism will fully realise.

This is MacIntyre's third way and clearly it depends upon the reality and plausibility of Marx's essentialist notion of human nature and Marxism as a general theory of this nature's development in history. Whatever MacIntyre's views now, this remains a possible resolution to the problem of liberalism. Were it possible to update such a view of Marxism it would promise a most powerful challenge to liberalism.

What, then, has been MacIntyre's response to his loss of confidence in a Marxist resolution to his dilemma? He has principally deepened and extended his critique of liberalism both philosophically and sociologically and surveyed the philosophical and cultural resources of the past for an alternative to Marxism. None the less he remains committed to the fundamental diagnosis of the *New Reasoner* piece. In the preface to *After Virtue* he quotes from the essay a critical remark about the then revisionist communist Leszek Kolakowski: 'One cannot revive the moral content within Marxism by simply taking a Stalinist view of historical development and adding liberal morality to it.'[47] He reaffirms his view that leaving Stalinism, by turning to the liberalism, which Marxism had originally emerged to criticise, is not good enough, 'since I continued, and continue, to accept much of the substance of that criticism, this answer was not available to me.'[48] So is there a non-liberal alternative?

After Virtue is his answer. MacIntyre tells us that this work arose out of an attempt to write two books, one on the fate of morality in the modern world and another on the philosophy of social science. In the process he discovered that the arguments of one book required the arguments of the other.[49]

After Virtue begins with a 'disquieting suggestion'. MacIntyre develops the view, present in all his work, that in modern liberal society, the moral basis has fragmented. It is not that we are confused over particular moral questions but rather we have lost the basis for understanding what a coherent moral argument is. This is because our moral vocabulary has lost the institutional framework and shared conceptual understanding, which originally provided it with meaning and persuasiveness. With moral vocabulary ripped from its context, we are left only with the fragments of the originally meaningful moral scheme. The fragments are used, or referred to in everyday life, so we continue to act as if there continued to exist an overarching moral framework within which to relate to one another. In practice we have a marked tendency to appeal to different bits of the fragments, hence our difficulty.

The cultural and intellectual response to this situation is the emergence of emotivist ethics, in which arguments about values are considered to be nothing more than statements of individual preference; argument tends to become a species of rhetoric which makes a person's feeling present to the world; so they can exhibit the choosing of a position – as we see in the following definition, the moral critic has resurfaced in a new guise:

> Emotivism is the doctrine that all evaluative judgements and specifically all moral judgements are *nothing but* expressions of preference, expressions of attitudes or feeling, in so far as they are moral or evaluative in character . . . factual judgements are true or false; and in the realm of fact there are rational criteria by means of which we may secure agreement . . . But moral judgements, being expressions of attitude or feeling, are neither true nor false and agreement . . . is not to be secured by any rational method . . . It is to be secured if at all by producing certain non-rational effects on the emotions or attitudes of those who disagree with one. We use moral judgements not only to express our own feelings and attitudes but also precisely to produce such effects in others.[50]

It is crucial to grasp that MacIntyre is not claiming that this philosophical theory is very widely accepted, although its emergence in the late nineteenth century and early twentieth century is not without significance. Indeed in his *A Short History of Ethics*, he pointed to several powerful critics of the view.[51] But rather the point is that something very much like emotivism is, in fact, institutionalised and operational in a society like our own.

This is indeed central to the whole of MacIntyre's approach and provides the justification for his importance, for social theory, for he argues that moral philosophy, including emotivism:

> characteristically presupposes a sociology. For every moral philosophy offers explicitly or implicitly at least a partial conceptual analysis of the relationship of an agent to his or her reasons, motives, intentions and actions, and in so doing generally presupposes some claims that these concepts are embodied or at least can be in the real social world.[52]

The link between the theory and the practice can be seen to be provided in this case by nothing less than Weberian sociology, which also places values beyond argument, and focuses on a discussion of means. Therefore neither emotivism nor Weberian sociology are mere theory, but simultaneously an analysis of, and the embodiment of contemporary life.

The point can be made clearer, if we look at the difficult example of nuclear weapons. In a public arena without shared moral criteria, the debate over the possession and use of nuclear weapons has some peculiar features. There are, of course, many grounds for opposing nuclear weapons, some pragmatic and tactical, but others take a more 'moral' form. It is the latter form that concerns us here.

Many, although by no means all, people who oppose nuclear weapons on 'moral' grounds, do so because they are members of communities that MacIntyre describes as bearers for the traditions of the virtues. They tend to oppose the possession and use of nuclear weapons, on the grounds – which have a long pedigree – that the *intention* to kill vast numbers of people in a war, is immoral. Such an intention was and is a central part of current nuclear strategy, given the targeting by the west of Russian cities. Clearly such an objection could be rooted in the abstract moral principle of the 'moral critic', but groups within the opposition do also rest their claim on the existence of a shared human nature, which is not being realised by such an intention. This would be the position of certain kinds of humanist; certainly the Christian tradition of the 'just war' forbids the intention of killing civilians for this reason; certain kinds of socialist and anarchist would have similar grounds for opposition. This is the structure of the early (Marxist) MacIntyre's argument as in, for example, the value to be found in the bravery of the deaths of the 'good' communists, displaying something of the potential of human nature whose realisation is communism.[53]

How does the state respond to such claims? Its apologists do not normally make a direct appeal to moral principle as would the liberal critic. It is normally conceded that the use of nuclear weapons would be a truly appalling thing, but that the missiles must remain targeted. This is because bureaucratic organisations, on this view, operate on an implicit means–ends morality. Such forms can have no concept of the *intention* to do something as being evil. A modern bureaucratic state's only relevant criterion is effectiveness; that this particular threat to exercise nuclear weapons has proved to be effective: 'there has been no war for 40 years in Europe'. The ends are chosen, there can be no intrinsically evil means, only means that would fail or whose use would jeopardise the ends. Means are not internally related goods to ends, they are but a medium for attaining what is wanted.

Emotivism is embodied then in bureaucratic forms, and in the process the distinction between manipulative and non-manipulative forms of behaviour becomes critically blurred. Bureaucratic organisations, private or public, are involved in a competitive struggle for scarce resources, to put at the service of predetermined ends. Managers have to use their resources towards achieving those ends as effectively as possible. About the ends, of course, no reasons can be given in the actual practice of managing. The manager is one of MacIntyre's key characters in our moral drama and his theorist is Weber. For, as he puts it:

> Weber's thought embodies just those dichotomies which emotivism embodies and obliterates just those distinctions to which emotivism has been blind. Questions of ends are questions of values, and on values reason is silent, conflict between rival values cannot be rationally settled. Instead one must simply choose between parties, classes, nations, causes and ideals.[54]

If the manager obliterates the manipulative/non-manipulative distinction at the level of the organisation, the therapist obliterates it at the personal level. The manager treats ends as given and is concerned principally with technique, how to transform the resources at his/her disposal into a final product, e.g. investment into profits. The therapist also has a set of pre-determined ends, to which to apply technique. Mental illness, frustration, dissatisfaction, etc. are to be transformed to create 'healthy', i.e. self-directed, organised contented individuals. But neither manager nor therapist can meaningfully argue about the moral content of ends.

If Weber is the theorist of the manager, then for MacIntyre, Erving Goffman gives us the therapeutic vision of society. The therapeutic self in Goffman is a spectral self that flits from role to role, being

> no more than a 'peg' on which the clothes of the role are hung.[55]

But the 'I' has not disappeared in Goffman, rather it stands over and against each of its roles. Its sense of 'freedom' seems to reside in its relative indifference to any particular role and an awareness of the ultimate contingency of each situation.

It is out of these two key figures that the culture of what MacIntyre terms 'Bureaucratic Individualism'[56] is discernible: the manager grounded in organisational effectiveness, the therapist in the sovereignty of the individual as free self. In so far as both characterise moments in our lives, moral debate becomes histrionic, an assertion of ungrounded, unshared assumption; success in such roles takes the forms of conversion or manipulation rather than rational persuasion.

MacIntyre argues that this position emerges for both institutional and intellectual reasons. The fragmentation of a shared system of argumentation (his pre-Enlightenment unity) occurs, for institutional reasons, because of the secularisation of the state, the fragmentation of religious and cultural organisation (the Reformation and growth of Nation States), the emergence of new economic and social forces. But this change is also a change in what is accepted as a viable argument.

In philosophy, the response to the breakdown of shared understanding, was, in the hands of figures like Hume and Kant, to seek to ground ethics in the individual. Kant sought rational principles that any individual could accept, whilst Hume and many others in the eighteenth century sought to ground morals in human passion. But for MacIntyre it is what their thought has in common that is more important, i.e. the negative features of their argument. These features explain why the attempt to find in philosophy what had been lost in religion failed because

> reason for him [Kant] as much as for Hume, discerns no essential motives and teleological features in the objective universe available for study by physics . . . what is true of them is true also of Diderot, of Smith and of Kierkegaard. All reject any teleological view of human nature, any view of man having an essence which defines his true end.[57]

In other words they reject what the earlier MacIntyre had noticed as crucial to Marx, as a way of overcoming the alternatives of liberalism and Stalinism.

In essence, MacIntyre argues that without some teleological

framework, in which the concept of the virtues is at home, we are forced in our culture, to ground morals in the individual. A position that may well lead to the adoption of a Nietzschean perspective: the assertion of our individual morals and desires through the power of the will. This is the dark side of emotivism: a self that has no criteria external to it, will impose itself on reality, perhaps by subtle manipulation, perhaps by rhetoric, but perhaps also by force!

If the cultural strength of emotivism is that moral conclusions cannot be derived from factual premises, it follows that only factual claims are open to communal or public verification. MacIntyre will not accept this. *After Virtue* has a principal purpose in attempting to reconnect the two, via a return to a form of Aristotelianism.

Aristotle is important for MacIntyre for two reasons. The first is that his is a form of thought that has proved itself as capable of providing the intellectual basis of at least three different cultures. Ancient Greece, the Arab Islamic Empire and medieval Europe. The second reason lies in the teleo-logical nature of Aristotle's arguments. For an emotivist culture can only arise when in both theory and practice, the distinc-tion between man as he happens to be and 'man-as-he-could-be-if-he-realised-his-telos'[58] is rejected. Aristotle derives con-cepts of purpose and intention from factual premises, and so doing heals this gap.

It is these issues of purpose and intention that are involved in MacIntyre's arguments concerning the social sciences. for the Fact–Value split only applies in this arena, if we are committed to producing universal laws of predictability, based upon certain versions of what natural scientists do. Doing this means stripping the social sciences of references to purposes and intentions. But if we reject such a view, as MacIntyre contends that we should, and view human action and indeed the whole of human life in a teleological framework, then it becomes less difficult to move from facts to morals and norms. MacIntyre's intention seems to be to construct the social sciences, as versions of *practical reason*, not seeking universal laws, but as producing value-laden guide-lines for human communities.

Aristotle then serves duty in filling the gap in MacIntyre's scheme that Marx's own teleology of human nature and history once filled. But MacIntyre has clearly lost faith in essentialist metaphysics. For he rejects what he sees as Aristotle's 'meta-physical biology'[59] but paradoxically it is precisely a revival in metaphysical realism that has allowed a regeneration of a version of Marxism premised upon Aristotle's (cum Hegel's) metaphysics. Such a view would, in effect, fulfil the promise of the young MacIntyre.

The core of MacIntyre's arguments is that Aristotle avoids abstract moral imperatives bearing down on recalcitrant human nature – as in versions of the Kantian and more general Protestant tradition – by the employment of practical reason as embodied in the tradition of the virtues; the virtues being settled dispositions, acquired by practice, which enable us to behave in ways that allow us to flourish, in human practices and pursue the good life. Virtues are to be used in cooperative human activity, i.e. in practices, carried out according to stan-dards of excellence characteristic of those practices; examples would include painting, sports, musicianship, farming. Missing, significantly, from MacIntyre's account of such practices are most forms of modern work organisation. While work was still tied to the household it could be seen as a vital part of a human practice sustaining various communal forms of life, but when

> work moves outside the household and is put to the service of impersonal capital, the realm of work tends to become separated from everything but the service of biological sur-vival and the reproduction of the labour force, on the one hand, and that of institutionalised acquisitiveness, on the other. *Pleonexia*, a vice in the Aristotelian scheme, is now the driving force of modern productive work. The means–end relationships embodied in such work – in a production line, for example – are necessarily external to the goods which those who work seek.[60]

Modern capitalism is a form of institutionalised life that can be destructive of the virtues, marginalising and relegating them to small areas of human activity.

It is the concept of a practice that enables MacIntyre to keep Aristotle's teleology, without his so-called metaphysical biology. Practices find their place in life shared with others, but the role of the virtues is not limited to distinct practices. MacIntyre argues that virtues sustain individuals and communities in very different situations and practices. Life is perceived as narrative, in which virtues enable subjects to fulfil both short-run and long-run intentions with relative harmony and as such make for the 'unity of a single life'.[61]

This unity of a single life is naturally connected with that of other lives, both now and in the past, via the complex tissue of responsibilities, roles and commitments that I share in. So the narrative order of my own life is part of a variety of communal narratives, and indeed, of moral traditions. It is in that context that MacIntyre attempts to answer the problem or question, what is the end of human life to be? 'To ask "what is the goal for me?" is to ask how best I might live out that unity [of a life P.M.] and bring it to completion.'[62] It is to view the life of an individual and community as a narrative quest, a narrative quest that pursues *the* good. But what is *the* good? Briefly and inadequately – we pursue the problem in the final chapter – MacIntyre believes the good is to be found in the looking for it. We start to look for the good in the social and moral particularity that we inherit from the past, family, town, profession, nation, class, etc. This means that pursuit of the good is always in part a communal enterprise, developing further, or even rebelling against what we inherit. Though clearly MacIntyre believes that a total rebellion, or repudiation of the past, is impossible and in so far as we think it is we suffer from painful liberal individualist delusions.

Ultimately, then, MacIntyre's teleological framework is a perspective on human life, and human community as *story*. This, then is the strength and perhaps the weakness of the mature MacIntyre. The rejected Marxist naturalistic essentialism, is replaced by an Aristotle stripped of his naturalistic essentialism and replaced by notions of narrative unities. But, as MacIntyre argues, the culture of 'bureaucratic individualism' minimises practices with a narrative teleological structure guided by the pursuit of goods internal to practices. Compared with Marxist essentialism, such a structure must seem fragile indeed, but clearly narrative elements cannot be eliminated from human life, as they constitute a part of human consciousness, so MacIntyre places his hopes on our ability to build upon these elements, in the formation of human communities.

CULTURAL CHANGE AND THE 'SOCIOLOGICAL' MOMENT

So far we have examined the origins and the broad outline of MacIntyre's essentially moral critique of modernity. Now I will return to examine an earlier phase of his work, what I have called the sociological moment of his analysis, or more precisely a sociological and historical analysis, of moral and religious change. Here I am concerned with a series of writings from the mid-sixties, especially two short books: *Secularisation and Moral Change*, published in 1967 and *The Religious Significance of Atheism*, published in 1969, and their relationship to his later work.[63] Here MacIntyre deploys a range of philosophical, cultural and sociological conceptualisations in order to make sense of the changing context of religious and non-religious understandings in western liberal societies.

The first move MacIntyre makes in what might seem a set of standard philosophical essays on theism, is to establish the difference in social context between the debate today about belief and one a century ago. As almost always in MacIntyre's work it is the holding in tension of the relationship between the internal content of argument and the surrounding social world that is vital for the development of the position. In this case MacIntyre begins by questioning just how serious the issue of belief and unbelief is for the protagonist of both positions. He notes the real psychological significance that the debate about belief in God had for a considerable number of Victorian intellectuals like Henry Sidgwick and Matthew Arnold and wonders why, although the issue is discussed, it seems to make so little impact in the present. He attempts to get at the problem by examining the logical structure of contemporary theism and suggests that this can only be understood when it is realised that in entering the modern world theism had to face two successive crises, firstly in the seventeenth century and secondly in the nineteenth. However, before establishing the nature of these crises he insists on establishing the specific uniqueness of the modern situation in relation to religion.

For MacIntyre, at least the MacIntyre of the mid-sixties, this uniqueness is defined in relationship to science. In seeing science as a distinctively modern attribute he finds himself faced with the challenge of the then very fashionable work of

Claude Lévi-Strauss and in particular his modern classic *The Savage Mind*. In this work Lévi-Strauss argues that the neolithic revolution with its medicines, tools and relatively advanced food production all required a deep study of nature. This was, of course, an attack on the French tradition of anthropology established by Lévy-Bruhl which viewed the primitive mind as irrational and prelogical. In contrast Lévi-Strauss was suggesting that in reality the so called primitives were as scientific as we are. This is because the approach of the primitive and the modern just reflects two approaches to nature, one very close to the material world, the other at one remove from it. MacIntyre is quite firm, however, in arguing that in his intricate mapping of the primitive systems of classification, Lévi-Strauss is mistaken in suggesting that what primitive people were doing was anything like the same sort of activity as modern physics. The reasoning behind this position is essentially a Popperian view of science. He appears to reject all attempts at the sociologising of science as a practice because he claims they miss the main issue, 'the essence of science consists not in the theories advanced at any one time but in the capacity to transform and replace those theories'.[64] Utilising Mary Douglas' *Purity and Danger* with its conception of dirt as 'matter out of place', i.e. a way of coping with disorder, MacIntyre suggests that this furnishes us with a 'photographic negative' of Karl Popper's view of the practice of science. This, MacIntyre claims, establishes the difference between the primitive and the modern, for

> Primitive man acknowledges the existence of the anomaly, of the exceptional, of that which constitutes a counterexample to his conceptual generalizations, only in order to outlaw that anomaly; and he thus avoids having to revise or reformulate his prevalent beliefs. The scientist, however, accepts anomalies and exceptions as a basis for either abandoning or revising the theories which he has hitherto accepted.[65]

It is no doubt true that this view could well be contested by anthropologists on theoretical and empirical grounds,[66] but it remains an interesting and revealing move on MacIntyre's part: in the first place it highlights his insistence on the uniqueness and specificity of the modern, and secondly, his commitment to a developmental conception of rationality and an opposition to relativism; an opposition which he maintains in his later writings even when he is prepared to concede the truth within, and the inevitability of, a certain version of relativism, seeing it contributing to the historical grounding of the development of rationality.[67]

What then were the specific problems that science and modernity presented to traditional theism, as it entered the modern world. The first crisis that we referred to above took the predictable form, given MacIntyre's reading of the nature of prescientific cultures, of a crisis of refutability. Could the claims of religion be treated like any other set of claims and be subjected to the test of being falsified. It would seem that in this situation, religion, and its intellectual representative theology, had two options: firstly it could present itself as a hypothesis like any other body of knowledge, and in the context of the eighteenth century reformulate itself as a Deist first cause of natural phenomena, or, secondly, it could refuse to adjust to this situation and cut itself off from the secular intellectual disciplines. If the first strategy is followed then it leaves itself open to a simple intellectualist dismissal around the issue of why anyone should bother speculating about the supposed first cause of reality. If the second strategy is followed, then the relationship of theological thought to the wider intellectual world becomes acute, as MacIntyre puts it, 'theology then becomes a realm apart, a discipline which legislates for itself and which disowns the current badges of intellectual legitimation; its links with general culture are necessarily weakened.'[68]

The second crisis is really an intensification of the first, as the techniques of critical and refutable science were applied to the study of history, and hence the great historical claims of Christianity were to be judged by the same modern cultural standards. MacIntyre argues that there were three fairly distinct responses to this rather more widespread intellectual crisis. The first was the adoption of a self-conscious intellectual atheism. But MacIntyre goes on to ask an interesting question of this atheism,

> In which God is it that they disbelieve? In Russell's case it is the God of Newton's *Scholium*; in Sartre's case it is the God of Leibniz's *Theodicy*. The answers are characteristic: the God in whom the nineteenth and early twentieth centuries came to disbelieve had been invented only in the seventeenth century.[69]

The significance of this point for MacIntyre lies in the fact that this type of atheist was, even in the nineteenth century, rather unusual. The serious ex-Christian atheist was rare compared with the great number of secularised non-believers for whom all the issues surrounding belief had little or no meaning. It is this latter condition that MacIntyre sees as characteristic of contemporary liberal societies and that this indifference is a most significant fact about them, the implications of which go far beyond the question of religious belief itself. We will explore this issue below, but before doing so we must examine the other options available to those facing the crisis of theism.

The second response is the path of rejecting any attempt to adapt theism to modern modes of apparently scientific assessment. The version of this view that MacIntyre focuses on in the work under discussion has essentially a liberal theological form: it insists that religious concepts are unique and address a fundamentally distinct arena of life, which has its own specific forms of validation; the most extreme version of this view we know how as Wittgensteinian fideism. MacIntyre notes that slogans suggesting that all utterances had a unique logic of their own were happily adopted by theologians, and led them to be very tolerant of contradictions and even, perhaps, incoherence, as the use of concepts like Kierkegaard's idea of 'the absurd' reaches a point of making religion logically invulnerable to criticism.[70] MacIntyre notes that culturally this can mean theologians playing down the differences between denominations and even religions. However, MacIntyre's stay in America has inevitably reminded him that a non-liberal response was possible. In a later discussion of the role of Scottish philosophy and theology in shaping the intellectual life of early nineenth-century America, he says of John Witherspoon – evangelical theologian and president of Princeton University – that,

> It was Witherspoon's contention that the findings of moral philosophy are not merely consistent with Evangelical Protestantism: they are a kind of prologue to it. None the less they can and ought to be defended on their own independent rational grounds. And it was Witherspoon who ... laid the basis for a cultural alliance between moral philosophy and the Protestant religion which in the first part of the nineteenth century partially defined moral consensus in America.[71]

The crisis of this conception of theism provoked not a liberal withdrawal to the margins of academic and intellectual culture, but rather something like a militant rejection of the whole culture of intellectual life. As MacIntyre went on to point out,

> The consequences for American political culture in the longer run have been dramatic. Moral philosophy, having lost its key place in the curriculum, lost its social influence. Evangelical Protestantism was fated to become systematically isolated from intellectual life, and its leadership fell to the largely uneducated ... A confrontation between a liberal intelligentsia whose abstract principles can appeal to no foundations recognised by most of their fellow-countrymen and a mindlessly militant Evangelical minority, portrayed in their own rhetoric as a Moral Majority, has been a long time in the making.[72]

The third response is to attempt to maintain the connection between Christian orthodoxy and the wider secular culture. But how is the connection maintained when the sceptical assumptions of that culture are so deeply embedded that close connection would seem to lead inevitably to secularisation even if the outward forms of religious practice are maintained. It would seem that the only viable response for someone in this position is to attack the dominant culture as wrong or false. The figures who MacIntyre refers to in this context are T. S. Eliot, at least in his social and political writings, and the Tractarians, but we could also add the work of writers like C. S. Lewis and G. K. Chesterton. The popular response to such writers, MacIntyre notes, should give us warning not to paint the dominant liberal culture in too homogenous a way, for as he says of Eliot's work,

> The self-conscious cultural atavism of Eliot is not just a plea for a lost past; it is in part a plea for those elements in the past still embodied in the present, for an identity that we can now neither fully recover nor yet quite disown.[73]

It would, I think, be difficult to resist the view that among the names of those who wish to mount a culture critique, in the attempt to preserve a living connection between faith and culture, we should now add the name of one Alasdair MacIntyre. MacIntyre may not care for the reactionary company of an Eliot, but there can be little doubt that the tradition of the Aristotelian virtues that he defends is a process of defending a connection between a past which he feels can be still alive in the present. This should not be seen as a criticism for there are only a certain limited number of positions it is possible to take up within modernity, in relation to older institutions, practices and ideologies. In response to the criticism and the praise he received for his most influential work, *After Virtue*, MacIntyre has acknowledged the importance of seeing what is still a real and potentially viable instructive presence from the past. It has become clear to him since the writing of *After Virtue* that this is no mere literary or academic exercise but that he has, in a sense, been writing to an audience beyond the bounds of standard philosophic discourse and beyond the bounds of the academic community, as he says of the response to the book:

> I have had in the form of letters, even occasionally of telephone calls, a quite extraordinary response from members of those communities whom I identified as heirs of the tradition of the Virtues . . . not only in the United States but also in Spain and in Italy, some intellectuals, some not all so . . . thus I have some assurance that what I articulated was not just something thought by me, but something thought and felt by a large number of people who recognise themselves as unable to be heard saying what they really mean in modern societies.[74]

To speak for those who find themselves unable to speak for whatever reason, perhaps, in this case, because they were unable to characterise the nature of the cultural situation in which they found themselves, is no slight achievement. However, to get into a position to be able to so speak has been a complex and intellectually arduous journey, involving as it does a mixture of historical reconstruction and philosophical argument. It is clearly the case that such a journey was only possible to attempt once a thorough grasp of what the real nature of the situation was. For it seems certain that the MacIntyre of the sixties did not believe that the position of an Eliot was really viable, at least as it was on offer then. MacIntyre could see that by the middle of the twentieth century the debate about theism had lost the central place it had had in nineteenth-century intellectual life and in this process the content of what was meant by theism had itself changed. In essence MacIntyre is pointing out that questions which had once been principally issues of belief in factual statements about Christianity, had in the hands of mainly liberal Protestant theologians, been turned into matters of choice, 'the leap of faith' and even into an issue of the utility of belief. As he puts it: 'Theists are offering atheists less and less in which to disbelieve. Theism thereby deprives active atheism of much of its significance and power and encourages the more passive atheism of the indifferent.'[75]

As almost always in MacIntyre's accounts of social change we find a skilful weaving of the process of intellectual change with a keen eye for its relationship to wider social processes. The retreat of the substantive content of theism in theology and philosophy is related to, but not reduced to, a sociological account of the wider process of secularisation in which an environment develops which fosters what he terms 'passive atheism'. Fundamentally MacIntyre's sociological account, in *Secularisation and Moral Change*, of the changing nature of religious belief is rooted in the familiar processes of industrialisation, urbanisation and social differentiation, based upon the capitalist division of labour, as he puts it,

What I in fact want to suggest is that the distinctive forms of urban working class life in the industrial city, as they came into being, and as they are to be contrasted with, for example, working class life in the domestic industries of the eighteenth century or in the earlier and smaller commercial city, marked a distinct change so far as religion is concerned. What urbanization of the Industrial Revolution meant was the destruction of the older forms of community, in many cases rapidly, and in particular the destruction of those features of them to which religion had given symbolic expression.[76]

MacIntyre suggests that this occurs because of three related processes. In the first place there is the loss of an apparently unalterable natural order, which sets easily comprehensible limits to all human activity regardless of social rank. Secondly there is the sharp break in the continuity of the social order which had appeared to mirror the natural order in its fixity. Thirdly, and finally, the break-up of shared norms common to all ranks in society and frequently vindicated by reference to religious belief. In the interesting case of England, with which at this point MacIntyre is still mainly concerned, this did not mean the immediate disappearance of religion, rather a new and complex, but clearly perceived, class-based division of labour providing the basis of a moral and religious differentiation. Gradually it seemed that each social class and, perhaps fractions within classes, began to become associated with particular religious denominations, with Anglicanism being retained by the upper classes, whilst Methodism and a variety of non-conformist sects prospered amongst the urban middle classes and indeed among a small but significant minority of the working class, alongside the Labour Churches of the 1890s. The presence within one society of these partially overlapping, partially competing, religious frames of reference, inevitably, in the context of the wider class compromises of English society, prevented any one religious form symbolically representing the whole of society. Crucially this emerging liberal culture was not only not open to any religious absolutism, but for the same reason was unprepared to accommodate to the totalising claims of Marxism. The English working class was not interested in advancing the claims of one way of life over another but in making a material accommodation with employers, which in certain respects mirrored the political and religious accommodation already achieved in that society.

A SOCIAL THEORY AS NOSTALGIA?

The charge of nostalgia has regularly been brought against MacIntyre over this argument and the later presentation of a similar case in *After Virtue*.[77] In essence the claim involves the view that MacIntyre is operating with a simple Gemeinschaft and Gesellschaft distinction between pre-capitalist and capitalist societies, the former possessing organic unity which the latter rapidly loses. In reality MacIntyre was always aware of the dangers of too easy a contrast between these social worlds; in *Secularisation and Moral Change*, he qualifies the point himself when he states, 'The homogeneity of pre-industrial life is, of course, easily exaggerated, but the sharpness of the transition from the values of pre-industrial society to the values of life in the Industrial Revolution can scarcely be exaggerated.'[78]

The whole issue of the contrast between traditional and modern societies is dealt with in a more sophisticated and nuanced way in *After Virtue*. Here MacIntyre is quite explicit

about the difficulty of using contrasts between past and present
that rely on the older sociological models of organic unity
versus differentiation. He says of the medieval world,

> Of all the mythological ways of thinking which have disguised
> the Middle Ages for us none is more misleading than that
> which portrays a unified and monolithic Christian culture
> and this not just because the medieval achievement was also
> Jewish and Islamic. Medieval culture, insofar as it was a unity
> at all, was a fragile and complex balance of a variety of
> disparate and conflicting elements. To understand the place
> of the theory and practice of the virtues within it, it is
> necessary to recognise a number of different and conflicting
> strands in medieval culture, each of which imposed its own
> strains and tensions on the whole.[79]

MacIntyre's entire argument in this work is based on an analysis
of the role of the virtues in a whole range of non-modern
societies: Homeric Greece, classical Greece, the so called
heroic societies of northern Europe and the medieval world.
Crucially, some of these societies are descended from one
another and the values they inherit from diverse sources are
frequently in considerable conflict with one another. So Stauth
and Turner's statement that . . . 'medieval Europe was not
made up of a set of coherent nation-states each with its own
unified morality and religion. Rather we have to imagine
medieval civilisation as a collection of oases surrounded by a
waste land of pre-literate pre-Christian and oppositional cultural movements'[80] is, while probably rather overdrawn, by no
means incompatible with MacIntyre's picture of these societies.
Indeed it could be argued that MacIntyre's sense of the conflicts and contradictions of medieval societies is sharper than
this rather crude sociologising of a division between upper-
class, or, town-based Christian culture, and rural paganism; for
he suggests that the paganism of the heroic societies survived
and continued to inform the practices of the upper classes of
medieval Europe and that in some respects the Church had to
come to terms with this.

MacIntyre's argument is fundamentally misconstrued if it is
assumed to rely upon a seamless organic moral unity lodged in
the past. What is really at stake in his argument is an attempt to
delineate what is distinctive about modernity itself. MacIntyre is

not claiming that past societies were not full of conflicting views
that could not or would not be reconciled with one another,
e.g. Jewish and Christian communities in medieval Europe. But,
rather that these views were embodied in communities, perhaps
competing communities, that within themselves shared a common conception of what the pursuit of the good life was, or,
inherited from the past other conceptions of pursuit of the
good life that were in contradiction with other such conceptions, e.g. the Pagan warrior values of heroic society with the
Christianity of the early Middle Ages. However, what all these
forms had in common was an ability to link the individual via a
socially defined role with the pursuit of human goods, as
MacIntyre puts it in *After Virtue*:

> in much of the ancient and the medieval worlds, as in many
> other premodern societies, the individual is identified and
> constituted in and through certain of his or her roles, those
> roles which bind the individual to the communities in and
> through which alone specifically human goods are to be
> attained; I confront the world as a member of this household,
> this clan, this tribe, this city, this nation, this kingdom. There
> is no 'I' apart from these.[81]

The contrast with the situation in modernity is very stark. Here
the modern social world is, as partly constituted by the liberal
state, an arena in which the individual pursues his or her own
private good. This is not to be understood as suggesting that the
importance of the social role in modern societies has been
diminished, but rather that the concept of the social role has
been redefined in such a way as to sharply demarcate the
societies of liberal modernity from virtually all others. I say
virtually because it is possible for those anxious about the
question of origin to find intimations of the modern conception in the work of some of the philosophers of classical
Greece, as Nietzsche was to find in the Sophists. However, for
MacIntyre the issue consists of the generalising and opera-
tionalising of a distinctive redefinition of the role of social
actor, as 'the individual':

> For 'the individual' in modern society is the name of a status
> and a role. 'The individual' is the name of a piece of social
> fabrication, of a social role created in the sixteenth and

seventeenth centuries in order to abstract human beings from certain aspects of their beliefs and circumstances. So it is not human individuals as such, bearing with them the complexities of belief and circumstance, including their allegiance to some theory of the good and their membership of social groups espousing such a theory, who are the agents who appear in modern practical reasoning. It is the individuals qua individuals of whom I am speaking, individuals viewed by themselves and by others as inhabiting the role of 'the individual'.[82]

Enough has been said to show I believe that MacIntyre's relationship to the classical dichotomies of sociology is, to say the least, complex, considerably more complex than in conventional sociological accounts of him. Only those who wish to uncritically endorse liberal modernity can resent the use of such historical materials to explore the specificity of modernity.

RATIONALITY, POLITICS AND THEOLOGY IN THE PRESENT

By the end of the 1960s MacIntyre clearly had grave doubts about the viability of any morally binding and overarching theory, religious or political, in a modern liberal society. His sense of the steady privatisation of belief and the subjectivist and emotivist nature of all arguments about ultimate values in such societies made him subversive of most of the fashionable intellectual positions of the period. In 1963 he produced a devastating critique of John Robinson's liberal theological work *Honest To God*, anticipating the arguments of the later essays like *The Religious Significance of Atheism*. A theology, MacIntyre suggests, that speaks of unspecified notions of love and God being whatever our deepest concerns are, must, in our type of society, lack any means of differentiating itself from a generous-minded secular liberalism and so becomes 'a form of practical atheism, for it clothes ordinary liberal forms of life with the romantic unreality of a catacombic vocabulary'.[83] At this stage then obviously MacIntyre was not any sort of orthodox Christian believer. For him the changing nature of the social context of belief brought about, in part, by certain understandings of science, and by the pluralisation of the social world, but also by the changes in theology, that were responses to this new situation, had robbed Christianity of content. It was not a matter of belief being impossible, but rather that the excessively personalised invulnerability of claims to faith point towards a loss of shared social context that once made belief comprehensible. This view he sums up in the sentence: 'It is now too late to be medieval and it is too empty and too easy to be Kierkegaardian.'[84]

Why by the middle of the 1980s has this sympathetic yet sceptical relationship to belief changed to that of an acceptance of Catholic Christianity? It is, of course, quite possible that there are deep-seated personal motives for this move as there no doubt are for most people's beliefs and unbeliefs. But only an arrogant secularism would assume that religious belief requires special personalised explanations not applied to run-of-the-mill agnosticism and atheism. However, some day a full intellectual and personal biography will be essential for a proper estimate of MacIntyre's development. But the short answer to the question of his change of position lies in his acceptance of the full-blooded Aristotelianism already referred to. In the context of theism it is perhaps inevitable that this Aristotelianism takes a Thomist form, Aquinas having been, as well as the greatest theologian of the Catholic Church, quite possibly the greatest Aristotelian since Aristotle.

Not much can be said about MacIntyre's theism, for he has written very little in his newer persona about it, at least in a direct form. His most recent books have been written from within the tradition of Thomism and therefore presuppose a particular version of Christian theism. But from within this context it is clear that MacIntyre's theism does not take the form of the kind of leap of faith he had earlier condemned. What he seems to like most about Thomism, is its ability to hold in creative tension the requirements of reason with those of revelation. In his most sustained recent treatment of these issues, the paper 'Which Gods Ought We To Obey And Why?',[85] MacIntyre argues that given the number of supposed deities who might make claims on our allegiance we need to use standards of justice and truth independently of, and prior, to an acceptance of divine claims. It seems that we are judging God by criteria external to the deity and in some way diminishing such a God in ways that may well pose the same kind of issues of plausibility that MacIntyre had criticised liberal Protestants for. However, MacIntyre suggests that this only appears to be the case at an early stage of the argument; he says that,

> if we progress beyond it, something we are able to do rationally only because and insofar as we first assented to the divine claims because we judged them to be just (and also, of course, true), then we discover, as our analogically and historically ordered concept of justice develops, that the standard by which we judged God is itself a work of God, and that the judgements which we made earlier were made in obedience to the divine commands, even although we did not and could not have recognized this at that earlier stage.[86]

It follows from this that faith and reason are not in some fundamental conflict that can only be resolved by abandoning one or the other. Instead this perspective sees natural justice and natural reason as divinely inspired. It would seem therefore that MacIntyre no longer believes it is not yet too late to be medieval.

It is, of course, unfair to characterise MacIntyre's position as simply medieval, for this presupposes the validity of certain modernist philosophical positions and social attitudes, a validity MacIntyre puts in doubt. He seems to have been impressed by the survival of a vigorous Aristotelianism in philosophy, both Catholic (e.g. Peter Geach) and otherwise (e.g. Martha Nussbaum), and challenges not only the dominant moral thought and assumptions of modernity but as he notes 'underlying this Aristotelian thesis is of course an essentialism governing modes of classification which is not only morally, but metaphysically and epistemologically at odds with any Humean view',[87] we could add, any Kantian or Wittgensteinian view. A great many questions and issues could arise from this position; for my purposes the question must be asked as to what are the consequences of this move for MacIntyre's attitude to political issues. For it would seem that MacIntyre has found it intellectually feasible to return to his Christian roots via Aristotelianism, but what now is his attitude to Marxism?

In the first place it is important to recall the social implications of MacIntyre's adoption of an Aristotelian morality. The crucial issue is that Aristotelian and, of course, Thomist[88] conceptions of justice are basically a matter of desert and merit, 'desert and merit in respect of contributions to or failures to contribute to the common life of a *polis*, of that type of political community in which alone human beings can achieve their good through that cooperative friendship which is itself a central virtue'.[89] It is quite clear that this pits the Aristotelian against the dominant forms of economic life in modernity. This is especially so if we recall as was mentioned previously that the vice of pleonexia (acquisitiveness) is viewed by Aristotle as a major source of injustice. MacIntyre unhesitatingly draws some very radical implications from this position, for as he says

> justice in exchange requires that conceptions such as those of a fair wage and a just price should have application. But to hold both those theses is to set oneself in radical opposition to any economy dominated by markets and requiring the accumulation of capital.[90]

It seems therefore unmistakably the case that MacIntyre believes that Aristotelianism is incompatible with capitalism. The reader might think at this point that not only has the mature MacIntyre moved back to Christianity but also to some version, at least at the level of social theory, of Marxism. But, despite the importance he attaches to Marxism as an intellectual tool, this seems not to be the case. At the end of *After Virtue* MacIntyre suggests that Marxism is flawed by the same commitment to liberal individualism that lies behind much other modern thought. He makes the same point as he made in *Marxism and Christianity* that when put to the test of complex practical situations as in the case of the revisionism debate of Kautsky and Bernstein or the post-Khruschev Eastern European debates, Marxists tend to fall back on a version of Kantianism or utilitarianism. The exception to this general condemnation is Trotsky, the seriousness and pessimism of whose last writings MacIntyre sees as marking the end of the Marxist tradition.[91] The principal reason for this lies in Marxism's apparently rather contradictory optimism about the future, for despite its criticisms of capitalist society it is committed to the view that within such a society all the moral and material conditions for a better future are being accumulated. But as he notes 'if the moral impoverishment of advanced capitalism is what so many Marxists agree that it is, whence are these resources for the future to be derived?'[92] MacIntyre sees many versions of twentieth-century Marxism as retreating into fantasy when confronted with this question, the Leninist Party being the most dangerous of these fantasies especially when underpinned theoretically by Lukács's messianic theory of proletarian consciousness. MacIntyre sees contemporary options as stark and unappealing, for 'when Marxism does not become Weberian social democracy or crude tyranny, it tends to become Nietzschean fantasy'.[93] MacIntyre then argues that the honest Marxist, of whom Trotsky is the key example, would have to concede at the end of this century, there is 'no tolerable alternative set of political economic structures which could be brought into place to replace the structures of advanced capitalism'.[94] This was the position he held in 1981 and yet, in later writings that we have referred to above, we have seen how MacIntyre has unreservedly condemned capitalism from the point of view of Aristotelian morality. This raises an important question: if Christian theism can be re-established, after years of MacIntyre's scepticism, as a coherent intellectual position via a proper understanding of the Aristotelian/Thomist tradition, why is not a parallel process available for Marxism? The question is not so strange as it may at first appear, for there is little doubt that Marxism is deeply rooted in the classical tradition, so, given MacIntyre's early commitment to Marxism, it is not surprising that Marxist commentators on *After Virtue*, such as Walter Adamson, find the brief dismissal in this work of Marxism 'breezy and glib', and that he, Adamson, finds it possible to argue that 'Hegel and Marx might well be seen as the modern – and therefore more up-to-date and politically realistic – representatives of precisely that Aristotelian tradition which MacIntyre wants to champion'.[95] The commonly accepted Aristotelian root of Marx's work does seem to raise some important questions for MacIntyre's present position and so I have decided to deal with the issue in a separate excursus below which will suggest some reasons why MacIntyre may be unhappy with a revived Aristotelian-cum-Hegelian Marx.

Chapter 2

An excursus on the possibility of an Aristotelian Marxism

True genesis is not at the beginning but at the end, and it starts to begin only when society and existence become radical, i.e. grasp their roots. But the root of history is the working creating human being who reshapes and overhauls the given facts. Once he has grasped himself and established what is his, without expropriation and alienation, in real democracy, there arises in the world something which shines into the childhood of all and in which no-one has yet been: homeland.

Ernst Bloch, *The Principle of Hope*

She had envisaged the iron necessity of history as something forceful and passionate and heroic; that in a General Strike . . . there should be crowds charging with banners; men with pince-nez urging them on from makeshift platforms on street corners. But now, in the actual General Strike, it was just nothing that seemed to be happening. Soldiers lounged here and there with their bedrolls and mobile kitchens. There was not even the impression of an enormous event just round the corner.

Nicholas Mosely, *Hopeful Monsters*

THE INTELLECTUAL 'CRISIS'

To understand how potentially radical and, perhaps, seemingly anachronistic an Aristotelian dimension to Marxism can seem, it is first necessary to understand the cultural and intellectual context of modern Marxism. In so doing we will be able to see more clearly how distinctive both the Marxist MacIntyre, and the post-Marxist Aristotelian MacIntyre, really are. Even if we grant the priority of sociological factors in deciding the fate of Marxism, we cannot neglect the role of intellectuals and ideas. For we know that intellectuals, at least in the west, have been crucial to the development of the Marxist tradition.[1] We should note, therefore, that long before political developments seemed to question Marxism, there was, by the end of the nineteenth century, a powerful weight of pessimism in European culture concerning the emancipatory potential of the application of human thought to the world. As H. Stuart Hughes has shown, this pessimism took the form of a critique of the Enlightenment in general, and of Marxism in particular, focusing positively on concepts like the Freudian unconscious and Nietzsche's 'will to power'. As Stuart Hughes puts it:

> psychological process had replaced external reality as the most pressing topic of investigation. It was no longer what actually existed that seemed most important: it was what men thought existed. And what they felt on the unconscious level had become rather more interesting than what they had consciously rationalised.[2]

Why this occurred is a large and complex question. It has been plausibly suggested by Stuart Hughes and others that it should be seen as part of the same process that produced various strands of Elite theory as an alternative to Marxism; in other words part of those intellectual currents, strong in countries that still contained large hierarchically based landed classes, who feared both democracy and Socialism.[3] But underlying much of this seems to be a highly variegated resentment, hostility or mere irritation, with features of capitalist industrial society. This could take many forms, from Weber's pessimistic but nationalistic liberalism, to Lukács's romantic Leninism and even Sorel's social poetry. We have in Thomas Mann's novel *The Magic Mountain* a powerful evocation of this atmosphere, and in the character Zaphta, based on Lukács, an unforgettable portrait of a radical romantic rejecting capitalist modernity; a type that could move to either left or right. Naturally such rejection of capitalism frequently meant the rejection of a Marxism that seemed its mirror image, that of the Second International.

The intellectual atmosphere of pessimism did not dissipate

after World War I, but forms a crucial background for the formation of the next generation of Marxist intellectuals. With the relative decline of mass Marxist parties and the Stalinisation of the remainder, Marxism after 1945 was to be increasingly the property of intellectuals. As Perry Anderson notes, the political experiences of these intellectuals did not encourage a more optimistic outlook: Adorno and Horkheimer politically formed by Fascism, Sartre and Althusser radicalised by the Spanish civil war, Della Volpe and Colletti coming to Marxism in the late forties and early fifties, respectively; all in a period of working-class defeat or under the influence of Stalinised communist parties.[4] These figures all turned to the most abstract questions of culture or philosophy and method. Their influence on the more empirically minded Marxists of the past twenty years has been considerable, with most Marxist scholars acknowledging one or more theorist as their guide.[5] But more generally most Marxist researchers have, in recent years, started out in the social sciences, which are both directly and indirectly shaped by elements of the broader philosophical culture. What are the currents here that oppose the hope of what might be termed the nineteenth-century Marx?

Firstly, we should note Anderson's observation that virtually all the western Marxists he surveys, 'resort to earlier philosophical authority within European thought'[6] to supplement Marx's work – Engel's work being generally considered unusable. Lukács and Marcuse turned to Hegel; Sartre to Kierkegaardian existentialism (even after his turn to Marxism); Della Volpe and Colletti to Kant and, in political theory, Rousseau; Althusser to Spinoza and the Freudianism of Lacan; and finally Gramsci, who turned to Machiavelli.[7]

If this need to turn behind Marx was felt by this virtually complete range of western Marxist theorists, then it seems likely that the same need would reassert itself with the younger and more numerous generation of Marxists schooled in the social sciences. They too had to locate themselves within specific traditions, that of Marx but also that of their own subjects and their theoretical and philosophical underpinnings. This has proved to be a problem. These theoretical assumptions are, for reasons we will examine, often profoundly, although perhaps obliquely, hostile to Marxism as a whole.

To illustrate why this is so, I intend to draw on a review essay by Richard Rorty – a review of a work by Saul Kripke whose importance will emerge later – which is valuable for the clarity with which it delineates the assumptions of modern philosophy. Rorty's point is that since Kant, the majority of philosophers have operated with certain central Kantian assumptions. Basic among these is the belief of philosophers that they have gone beyond the so-called naive realism of Aristotle and common sense. The old view involved the correspondence theory of truth, i.e. that there is a correct way to describe things that corresponds to how they actually are. Philosophers believed this common-sense view to be inaccurate; in reality what people did, e.g. whether they were natural or social scientists would, in some way, constitute the objects via concepts or intuition or whatever.

So Rorty states: 'This "condescending" view has been shared by people as far apart as Russell and Bergson, Whitehead and Husserl, James and Nietzsche, Carnap and Cassirer'. The basically Kantian view, is that we decide what will count as an 'object' by putting ideas together, 'we build a world, a world inside our minds, by tying concepts together so as to package sensations more conveniently'. Russell and Frege develop this further. For Russell names are really just 'lists of the qualities which we have decided to use to identify occasions on which we shall use a name'.[8] In other words, they are a kind of shorthand. This is based on Frege's claim that meaning determines reference, a view which is uncontroversial, if you believe that the universe is undifferentiated and merely requires conceptual structuring.

> But as Marxists and Neo-Thomists insist . . . such a view smacks of idealism. It leads fairly quickly to the pragmatist view that science and human inquiry generally makes truth rather than finds it – that we did not discover sub-atomic particles, but rather discovered that it was helpful to package the flux under such labels as 'position'.[9]

Rorty's reference to neo-Thomists and Marxists is significant because at least until the second Vatican Council and the liberalisation of Western European communist parties, referred to as Euro-Communism, both these philosophical positions had institutional bases in the Catholic Church and the Party, which explicitly – both in ideology and in institutional practice – stood outside the consensus of western liberalism. It seems likely that the survival of these positions in the twentieth century, is connected with this institutional protection. Indeed it is probable that the shift in Marxism's base, from party to university in the post-war period, is part indicator, part cause, of its intellectual 'crisis'.

Rorty's inclusion of Marxists as critics of Kantianism is also significant; because Marxism is clearly the heir to the immediate post-Kantian philosophy of early nineteenth-century Germany and, most particularly, Hegelianism. This grouping of philosophers stands out remarkably from the bulk of Kantian-influenced nineteenth-century and twentieth-century philosophers, for as Merquior has noted: 'the majority of post-Kantians had no qualms about reasserting speculative metaphysics'. Fichte, Schelling and, above all, Hegel sought to respond to the severe Kantian limitations on knowledge, which was seen as capable of forming only strictly empirically based concepts. They believed that 'to hold no adequate grasp of ultimate being (the famous thing-in-itself) can be rationally warranted, came as an intellectual attitude, "lacking the courage of truth, the belief in the power of spirit"'[10] – Hegel's words. Marx rejects Hegel's idealist metaphysics – to anticipate a little – but maintains the ambition of Hegel to grasp the *real natures* of things, in order to understand their developmental tendencies. As we will see in more detail later, the most obvious point to be made is that, this view implies, things have necessary properties attaching to them as real objects, which give them their character, and that these properties are knowable by the human mind.

From the middle of the nineteenth century in Germany, significantly after the failure of the 1848 revolution, the whole speculative tradition of philosophy – Hegel being its towering representative – became more and more suspect. A whole phalanx of anti-Hegelians emerged: Kierkegaard, Nietzsche, Wilhelm Windelbrand, Heinrich Rickert, Ferdinand Tönnies, George Simmel and Weber; out of this group emerged the philosophical basis of modern social science. As Jeffrey Bergner has shown, Kant was a fundamental influence on the founding of the social sciences.

For it was Kant's general understanding that scientific (theoretical) knowledge cannot provide a natural, unified view of the world which has general validity. Kant proclaims the independence of moral and aesthetic judgements from the canons of scientific knowledge . . . and it is philosophy's task to investigate and uncover them and their presuppositions.[11]

In this revival, that went a good deal further than the ranks of the official Neo-Kantians,[12] we see not only a scepticism about history as unfolding progress (stable nation-states, powerful bureaucracy, bureaucratical labour movements, etc.), but also a growing doubt about what Bergner calls 'the very possibility of an adequate comprehension of the whole'.[13] Neo-Kantianism is sure that it is quite impossible to get at the essential nature of a thing, and was able to offer this as the central plank of its attack on philosophical history. Figures like Simmel, Weber and Tönnies all make use of history in their work in the social sciences, but they were all quite certain that they were not revealing in theory the process that lies behind historical transformation. Rather they were abstracting from historical reality, classically in Weber's notion of ideal types but also in Tönnies' own ideal type conceptions of Gemeinschaft and Gesellschaft. There is no intrinsic meaning or purpose here, merely forms imposed upon history by the human mind.

Such a view is the necessary correlative of a philosophical culture that denied any necessary connections between the names of things and the things themselves. In this context it is hardly surprising that Marxism, when it aspires to be more than a social scientific description of reality, i.e. when it claims both authoritative knowledge of what will change, and how to change, runs up against acknowledged, or unacknowledged, scepticism amongst even its supporters in the social sciences. Naturally many have been aware of this problem of how to claim certain knowledge, alongside social scientific respectability. In the immediate post-1968 environment Althusser seemed to perform this function admirably with a clear argument for re-interpreting Marx along more congenial lines. Writers like E. P. Thompson and Simon Clarke have pointed to the role of a concept like theoretical practice as a perfect ideology for the academic seeking radical political respectability.[14]

Althusser fitted perfectly with both political needs and academic prejudices. In the first place no one could have been stronger in his denunciations of the apparently Hegelian metaphysical baggage in much of Marx's work; hence the need for the radical *epistemological break* between the pre-scientific Marx and the Marx of real science, for in the mature Marx

> There is no longer any original essence, only an ever pre-givenness, however far knowledge delves into its past. There is no longer any simple unity, only a structural complex unity ... If this is the case, it is clear that the 'womb' of the Hegelian dialectic has been proscribed and that its organic categories, in so far as they are specific and positively determined cannot survive it.[15]

In the second place, as is clear in this quotation, Althusser makes the move familiar to Neo-Kantians and positivists, of making a sharp divide – ultimately unbridgeable – between the real and the process by which we appropriate the real, for as Callinicos has put it:

> what he wants to do is to distinguish between reality and the process by which we come to know reality. The thought object is, if you like, the precondition of the latter process. It consists in the pre-existing concepts and theories which science sets about to transform in order to provide a more rigorous knowledge of the real.[16]

This provided the basis for Althusser's famous epistemological machinery of Generalities I, II and III. Generality I being not empirical reality, but the body of concepts which were to be transformed by Generality II, which was the body of concepts that constituted the theory or problematic which in turn produced the result of the so-called concrete-in-thought, i.e. Generality III.[17] All this must have seemed very sophisticated and up-to-date, avoiding any of the dangers of a naive realism, which as anybody with any philosophic sophistication knew was untenable. However, as is well known, the great emphasis on Althusserian theory as theory, led to an acute paralysis in intellectual work. The self-appointed guardians of this theory[18] led much of the young left through agonised considerations as to whether this new pristine theory could have an authentic relationship with the extra-discursive reality. The upshot of all this was a journey within a few short years from high theory to a pragmatically orientated empiricism.[19]

It did not, of course, escape the attention of Marxist social scientists that the dominant Althusserian trend of the late 1970s ultimately took an idealist path out of Marxism in the 1980s. This seems to have generated an interest in realist philosophies of science,[20] which are principally concerned with attempting to understand the mode of operation of unobservable entities that sustain the regularities of observable phenomena. In other words, it is concerned with fundamental or essential processes that underlie phenomena. Even a relatively cursory acquaintance with Marx's work would be enough to show the affinity of this approach with that of Marx. To take a most basic example, Marx's famous assertion in the Preface to *A Critique of Political Economy*: 'It is not the consciousness of men that determines their being, but, on the contrary, their social being that determines their consciousness.'[21]

However, such work, itself, has suffered from the pressure of the prevailing philosophic climate, as, for example, we can see in the work of two authors who are sympathetic to Marxism, R. Keat and J. Urry's *Social Theory as Science*. To escape Kantian criticism of the possibility of 'ultimate explanations' they argue that realism is agnostic 'as we have already suggested, this turns on the finitude of nature, and there is nothing in the realist position which counts for or against finitude' (on the implication of this question see Gillian Rose's comments, note 12 above). In dealing with the difficult question of essentialism, they begin with a definition of it being the 'essential properties, of things' so that 'Scientific explanation requires the discovery of such essences and thus of correct definitions'.

They ascribe these views to Aristotle and further add that this assumes a world 'that is objectively divided into "natural kinds" to which correct definitions must correspond'. This is, of course, precisely that view that Rorty has noted the philosophy consensus as being so opposed to. Unsurprisingly then, Keat and Urry argue that 'the realist is not committed to this theory of definition, to the view that explanations can be discovered by definitions, or to a belief in natural kinds'.[22]

More recently Urry has expressed the fear that the realist view (he has clearly been influenced by Althusser), 'may lead to viewing such societies as characterised by an "expressive totality", that all aspects or elements of it are merely the phenomenal form of the inner essence'.[23]

Slightly later and, in the Anglo-Saxon world, probably the most academically respectable versions of Marxism, are associated with the names of Gerry Cohen, Jon Elster and John Roemer. They are even more hostile than the descendants of French Marxism to essentialism. They are deeply rooted in the tradition of analytic philosophy. They can be seen as part of a wider process in academic Marxism and in the social sciences that is moving away from structure towards the question of agency,[24] in this case, most strongly connected with the work of Jon Elster, on the question of collective 'class' action.[25] However, it is fair to say that the foundation of this analytic Marxism was laid by Gerry Cohen in his book on Marx.[26] This book, appearing in 1978, was greeted with almost audible relief in many parts of the intellectual left. It could be said that this is when Anglo-Marxism came into its own in terms of a theoretical rigor, equal to the continentals. At this stage it was clear Althusserian Marxism was collapsing from within; in Britain many seemed to be deserting Marxism for more apparently radical French theorists like Foucault, Lacan and Derrida. Stuart Hall could write a year later, rather fearfully, of the 'Foucauldian deluges' about to be translated:[27] a prediction that was to prove prescient throughout the 1980s and into the 1990s. Cohen's book seemed like the answer to a failing Marxism and French domination of radical culture. Written in the cool clarity of the English philosophic idiom, this in itself was a relief for those to whom Althusserianism had become synonymous with pompous obfuscation, and intellectual and political arrogance. Cohen's book seemed to offer a good defence of Marx to both older and younger generations of Marxists.[28]

True to its roots in the Anglo-Saxon analytic tradition of philosophy, Cohen's reconstruction and defence of Marxism systematically stripped the theory of those phrases and assumptions that might be thought to link it to the speculative metaphysical and essentialist tradition. Cohen begins his book significantly with the major section of the 1859 Preface to *A Critique of Political Economy*, it is on this that he bases his conception of Marx's theory of history. Thus, in effect, Cohen is able to define Marxism in clear propositional form, partly by reducing it to two central points, easily derivable from the 1859 Preface. These points are:

1 that there is a tendency for the productive forces to expand; and
2 that there is a tendency for the productive forces to determine the production relations, so that whatever institutions and relations the expanding productive forces require, do in fact 'correspond' to them in reality.

Absent from the account is any notion of dialectics, nor is the account held to be dependent on the labour theory of value. Clearly this work is a strong form of technological determinism and is based, as Cohen makes explicit, on a form of functionalist explanation.[29]

My concern, however, is not with the particular validity or coherence of this approach,[30] but rather with its revelation of underlying assumptions. It would seem that Cohen's use of the 1859 Preface as the touchstone of orthodoxy reveals (in addition to whatever Stalinist connotations it may have) itself as a particularly crude form of Kantianism, with the sharp distinction between an abstractly presented method to be followed by application to its object. As the Hegelian Rose puts it: 'for all "method", by definition, imposes a schema on its object, by making the assumptions that it is external to its object and not defining it'.[31]

This is why a Hegelian Marxist like Scott Meikle is surely right in saying that:

Cohen has taken Marx's programmatic remarks and summaries of how he sees things, and reconstructs Marx on that basis alone. The only intelligent thing to do is to study the finished form, Capital; if done properly, that should show what the outline and summary really mean. To treat a finished form merely as a source of illustration of summary obiter dicta is a preposterous procedure.[32]

In addition to this procedure there is also the way Cohen presents Marx's theory in terms of what he calls: 'those standards of clarity and rigour which distinguish 20th century analytical philosophy'.[33] It is, of course, a moot point as to whether the analytical tradition really is clearer and more rigorous than (the obviously implied point) 'those waffling unsystematic types on the continent'; one can imagine responses from that quarter, about it being easy to be clear about banalities. However, name calling about style and exposition, only goes to mask rather deeper points about what it means to use analytical procedures on Marx's work. For, as Sean Sayers has ably pointed out, Cohen's work is in fact analytical in a very traditional way:

> like the philosophers of the 17th and 18th centuries, Cohen relies on the method of analysis. He insists upon analysing the whole that he is considering into its component parts. He insists upon separating and isolating the different elements and aspects of the given concrete totality, and considering and defining these in isolation. The effect of this method is to produce a fragmented and atomised picture of reality.[34]

In addition these elements are understood as quite distinct entities, and what these entities are, in themselves, is not defined or changed by the context, or the set of relationships, within which they are placed. Sayers characterises these relations as external; in other words external to what constitutes the entities in themselves. It would seem that this approach underpins Cohen's anxiety to make sharp and clear distinctions between the different elements that make up the basis of the explanation, as in, say, his concern, derived it is true from the 1859 Preface, that the forces of protection are to be sharply distinguished from the relations of production.[35]

> The economic structure (or 'real basis') is here said to be composed of production relations. Nothing else is said to participate in its composition [but] productive forces strongly determine the character of the economic structure, while forming no part of it.[36]

In other words Cohen seeks to discover causal functional relationships between distinct entities.

Cohen has quite self-consciously turned his back on what we can call the dialectical tradition of explanation. No doubt he feels that the tradition has so blackened the name of dialectics that professional seriousness demands establishing Marxism on analytical principles. However, there is no doubt also that Marx was not an analytical philosopher, but an applier of dialectics, as he was able to write as late as 1873 in a post-face to *Capital*: 'The mystification which the dialectic suffers in Hegel's hands by no means prevents him from being the first to present its general forms of motion in a comprehensive and conscious manner';[37] in the same place he applauds a reviewer's description of his approach and says, 'But what else is he depicting but the dialectical method?'

DIALECTICAL METHOD OR ESSENTIALISM REVIVED?

What is the 'dialectical method' that Cohen is rejecting, as are the others of his group such as Roemer and Elster (one obvious example of this being the stated methodological individualism of Elster's recent work)[38]? Following Sayers, we can immediately see that:

> For dialectics, concrete and particular things are always and essentially related, connected to and interacting with other things within a larger totality. This context of relations is internal and essential to the nature of things not external and accidental.[39]

However valuable Sayers' critique of Cohen is, in pointing out in considerable detail the disconnected and atomistic quality that Cohen's reconstruction of Marxist theory has, compared with the internally related accounts of an entity to be found in both Hegel and Marx, he never seems to take us to the heart of the question of dialectics, the question of internal contradictions and the process of change. By briefly touching on these questions we will be able to see more clearly the centrality of the problem of essentialism, and the way in which a variety of positions taken up on this matter illustrate the conditions for and against, a successfully reconstructed, nineteenth-century Marxism.

The whole question of dialectics and contradiction has proved very difficult for Marxists, especially for those with philosophical training, to the degree that many have abandoned the ground of real contradictions entirely.[40] The matter is most complex and cannot be adequately broached here, but the difficulties are not hard to see. The 1970s saw a lively debate in Marxist circles over the nature and viability of dialectics, sparked off by the work of Lucio Colletti. In the debate over Colletti's work it quite clearly emerges that the central aim of his work is to produce a positivistic Marxism based on Kant, with a strong rejection of Hegel.[41] Following from this he takes the view that dialectical contradictions must be logical contradictions because non-logical contradictions, i.e. those that might exist in reality, are impossible. He takes this position for reasons Peter Dews explains:

> Established science . . . pays no attention whatever to dialectics. Indeed, science as we know it, or in any sense we could understand could not exist at all if the principle of non-contradiction were flouted, since this principle merely expresses a condition of the continued existence of any object.

Once more the villain of the piece is Hegel, for as Dews goes on: 'Colletti has made clear that Hegel's suspension of this principle was intended precisely to dissolve the reality of the finite and the material'.[42] So Colletti, to defend what he sees as the programme of science, denies the validity of real contradiction and so must fall back on logical contradictions, but these breach the rules of formal logic so must be rejected, and so he famously embraces the notion of unreal contradiction in an unreal capitalist reality! This need not detain us, but is his opponent, Roy Edgley, more persuasive? Edgley attempts to get round the non-contradiction rule in formal logic by more or less inventing a logic of his own:

> if we are to make acceptable sense of the dialectic and its chief category, dialectical contradiction, we must shape a conception of logic different from that of formal logic . . . Basically what we need to do, following Hegel but without the idealising, is to break down the dichotomy between logic and reality and thus between logical and real opposition, which generates the bourgeois critique of dialectic as logic. Logic must become ontologic.[43]

However, a powerful paper by Meikle has argued that Edgley has conceded too much to Colletti and left himself vulnerable over the matter of fusing ontology and logic. Edgley agrees with Colletti that dialectical contradictions must be logical contradictions, but Meikle suggests it is foolish to deny the power of formal logic, or the notion that Marx somehow did not believe in it, or sought to contradict it: 'one is stuck with formal logic and dialectics', he suggests.[44]

Now, if formal logic implies, 'logical necessity' in its operation, and, as Meikle asserts, logical contradictions are not dialectical contradictions, it seems that dialectical contradictions must, for him, have the character of 'real oppositions', in other words they follow the line of 'natural necessity'. Dialectical contradictions are therefore real contradictions within reality. Meikle illustrates this via the contradiction most extensively analysed by Marx, namely the contradiction in the commodity between use-value and exchange-value:

> The commodity is the unity of use-value and exchange-value, in precisely the same way that water is H_2O, that light is a stream of photons, or that gold is the element with the atomic number 79. All these statements are necessarily true. They state truths that are true of necessity, not in virtue of any logical or 'conceptual' connections, but in virtue of the essences or real natures of the entities in question.[45]

Meikle goes on to show how Marx analyses the development of the commodity form; however, for our purposes it is crucial to point out how his starting point is possible. It is clear that the position is an elaboration of the 'notion of necessary truth' and based upon that 'given by its modern expositer S. Kripke'.[46]

We are now in a position to see the potential import of Kripke's work, as well as the motives for opposition to it. Basically, as Rorty has put it, Kripke has shown, 'that Aristotle as well as Kant can be successfully updated'.[47] In the first place in regard to Marxism, it has legitimated Meikle's move back to Aristotle as a grounding for his reading of both Hegel and Marx, in terms of the realisation of potentialities present within real essences; once Aristotle's metaphysics no longer seemed completely anachronistic it was possible to build upon them again, but more on this later. We need first to think about the significance the moves in fairly arcane levels of philosophy have in the wider context.

We are given some clues as to the potential significance of Kripke's work if we think of it in relation to competing approaches. We have noticed already the basic relationship of continuity between Kantian and Neo-Kantian philosophy and the project of Anglo-American analytic philosophy. Kant attempted to analyse how perceptual order was attained by human beings out of the profusion of impressions that are given to us in perception. It was achieved, he argued, by the imposition of a priori categories rooted in the subject, whilst in the post-Fregian analytic philosophy, the process of knowledge and perception is held to be structured by certain forms of linguistic prediction which are the fundamental guides to reference. Now the project of analytic linguistic philosophy parallels another, namely that of structuralism, because for Saussure and his followers, language was a complete system that structured our relationship with reality, access to which was only available through the structure of linguistic conventions.

No one has brought out more clearly the relationship between these two traditions of thought than Christopher Norris:

> there is a good deal in common between the structuralist and the logic – linguistic traditions. For Saussure as for Frege, 'meaning determines reference' in the sense that there exists no self-sufficient act of naming outside the criteria which language provides for deciding how – or on what specific terms – such an act achieves its designated object.[48]

Once this connection is established, then potentially much flows from it, for it seems likely that the analytic tradition will in turn be susceptible to the same fate as structuralism, i.e. of a post-structuralist deconstruction. Analytic philosophy attempts to cope with radical doubt by preserving some connection between meaning and logical necessity, but follows the Kantian tradition by ignoring the referential function of language, and using instead the structures of logic and semantics. This is why meaning precedes reference, to try and prevent a mass of variation. But to do this you have to be confident you have a way of distinguishing between necessary (or analytic) structures of meaning that give accurate delineation, and those that do not. But this is a distinction that Norris claims cannot hold; following Quine he says:

> supposedly a priori truths are themselves so linked to the total structure of knowledge that they may at any time be subject to revision, the field as a whole being 'undetermined' by its boundary conditions. This is effectively to collapse the distinction between synthetic and analytic judgments.[49]

Norris in effect suggests that scepticism has a logic of its own, and shows this with some telling and, for our purposes, highly relevant historical examples. Clearly Derrida did this with Saussure's structuralism by exploiting the arbitrary nature of the sign with its denial of a referential appeal to that which is signified. Derrida in effect deconstructs the notion of structure in Saussure's system; seeing it as a metaphor that had been passed off as a scientific concept, he overcomes it and realises what Derrida sees as the endless disseminating power of language,[50] i.e. the generation of new meaning. But perhaps an even more pertinent example for us occurs at the end of the nineteenth century with the Neo-Kantians, who attempting to stabilise knowledge in the face of Cartesian doubt, came up against Nietzsche. Nietzsche asked the question, why should we accept the Kantian a priori structures of knowledge as the final limit? Was this not, as Nietzsche saw it, one more attempt by reason – logocentricism – to repress the irrational and continue its centuries-long domination.

It seems that Norris is suggesting that the apparently moderate moves made by the conventional thinkers of the modern age, from Kant to the Neo-Kantians, to Anglo-American linguistic philosophy, and structuralism, have a radical instability about them. This is rooted in their common rejection of the directly referential function of language; this makes them prey to the radically sceptical and relativist moves of a Nietzsche and a Derrida.

Perhaps unsurprisingly Norris suggests an alternative, based on the work of someone who reasserts the referential function of language: Saul Kripke. Kripke crucially asserts, against all the conventional wisdom, the priority of reference over meaning. Naming is for Kripke a matter of 'rigid designation', that is of using such terms as can properly be used, to pick out the referent in question. As Norris notes: 'the paradigm case is that of "fixing a reference" rather than (as Frege or Russell would argue) applying a set of descriptive attributes which enable one to verify the object referred to.'[51]

The Frege–Russell position runs into many difficulties, exploitable by radical relativisers, as in the classic Fregian example, of who is Aristotle: many statements can be made of Aristotle that are also true of others and this leads to numerous ambiguities in trying to fix him in space and time. But Kripkean 'rigid designations' only use description to fix on to a referent, which, even when new descriptions appear or old ones are proved false, still leave the referent intact. As Rorty puts it, it all boils down to 'we'll call that "X" rather than saying we'll call something "X" if it meets the following criteria'.[52]

Clearly in natural science there are all sorts of technical

redescriptions of entities; to use Norris's example, light can be for some purposes a particle, for others a wave but as he states, 'There has to subsist a certain referential grounding without which no such refinement of theory could retain its grasp on the phenomena concerned'.[53]

The implications of such a move are really quite enormous, indeed absolutely staggering for anyone educated within the dominant philosophic tradition. Rorty has been eloquent on the shock that his colleagues felt or perhaps more accurately he felt, given his role as chief deconstructor of the western philosophic tradition. He claims:

> the whole idea of what it was to be an analytic philosopher, what it was to be sophisticated about the elation of thought to the world, began to totter. For a moment nobody could quite believe that a leading modal logician should seriously commend the Aristotelian way of looking at things. Perhaps it was merely affected Gothicising.[54]

But Kripke was doing nothing of the kind. Rather he was showing it was possible to see things as possessing properties that were absolutely necessary to them to be those things, and, most explosive of all, that essentialism and necessity would no longer be attributes relative to concepts. What is the relationship between this kind of philosophical thought and Marxism? Clearly Kripkean essentialism does not automatically lead to Marxism or the dialectical method. However, it does suggest a greater confidence in gaining a real understanding of things, natural and social, unmediated by a priori categories. Kripke-type approaches seem to shift the ground to arguments to escape the depths of radical doubt, and away from a pre-occupation with the methods of gaining knowledge. Such a move would be necessary to see any collective purpose in a human enterprise going beyond mutual tolerance and self-interest. It should therefore come as no surprise that it is by no means just Marxism and left social science that has made use of the revival of 'naive realism'; some Christian theologians have been quick to see its potential in reviving metaphysics.[55] This aside from reinforcing the view (held by the early MacIntyre) that at a deep theoretical level there are connections between speculative theology and Marxism. (We should recall that almost all the early nineteenth-century German post-Kantians,

Fichte, Schiller and Hegel, etc., had theological backgrounds.)
This would also appear to hint at the possibility that there is a
connection between relativistic forms of thought and capitalism.

BACK TO ARISTOTLE?

We have seen therefore something of the social and intellectual
context that Marxism finds itself in: fifty years of political
defeat, a century of much intellectual opposition and erosion
by a mainstream intellectual culture that is most inhospitable to
it. But, none the less, we have noted that even at the height of a
fashionable radical idealism – post-structuralism – some elements of an intellectual shift have occurred, that are more
propitious for what I have called the nineteenth-century Marx.
I now want to look at what I take to be the boldest attempt to
build upon these moves, Scott Meikle's defence of Marxist
essentialism[56], and then suggest some reasons why MacIntyre
has not embraced so seemingly natural an ally.

For Meikle, Marx's theory has three elements: his theory of
history, his theory of value and his dialectical form of analysis
and presentation; these together form a single unified theory.
To understand his analysis we must see how these elements
connect up together. As we have already touched upon the way
Meikle builds upon Kripkean essentialism to understand Marx's
dialectical approach, we will begin with this element of the
theory.

As we have seen, Meikle begins from the position that entities
in the world, both natural and social, are 'real referents', entities
with real natures that are susceptible, with due care, to human
understanding. Now from this Meikle makes his most fundamental move which is to argue that: 'the most fundamental
choice that has to be made in thought and method is between
atomism and essentialism.' This applies in all philosophy and
science, including of course the social sciences, it just cannot be
avoided because even those unaware of the explicit choice 'are
none the less committed in their intellectual operations to one
or other . . . since every method is a variety of one or other of
this exhaustive and mutually exclusive pair'.[57]

The basic difference between these two approaches lies in
their respective ontologies, 'between those on the one hand,
who think that there are organic wholes with real natures and

necessities (the essentialists and organists), and those . . . who think there are no (knowable?) essences (the atomists, empiricists, anti-essentialists)'.[58] Atomists work with simple ontologies, i.e. basic building blocks, complexities are reduced to simpler more basic elements, science consisting of understanding the combination and relationship of these simple elements. On the other hand essentialism:

> admits into its ontology entities or organic wholes with identity, complexity, and form. These are not considered reducible but irreducible to their parts. There are levels of complexity among entities from atom to nebula and from human individual to society.[59]

From this fundamental opposition flow, according to Meikle, quite distinct philosophies of science which affect all the categories of explanation such as, for example, the concept of law. This means that for the atomists events are primary, normally based upon the regularity of events taking place (the Humean constant conjunction of events). The basic problem of constructing laws on this basis is the necessity of placing exclusion clauses to explain why sometimes, something does not happen, hence the prominent role of statistics and probability theory in such accounts. But:

> for the essentialist a law is not epistemic but either a statement of the real ontological line of development of an entity, specifying some necessary change or changes which things of the kind typically undergo or else a statement of some piece of characteristic activity or ergon.[60]

Meikle claims that Marx's notion of law is of the essentialist kind, most centrally the law of value. One central advantage of Meikle's approach is that it places Marx's in an explicable philosophical tradition. It makes no claim that Marx produced a theory that was absolutely new; on the contrary the conflict between essentialism and atomism goes back to Greek thought, i.e. the conflict between the atomists and Aristotle, that Marx analysed in his doctoral dissertation. In the medieval world essentialism was dominant but atomism became dominant in the modern period with Descartes, Hume, etc., with essentialism appearing again with Hegel and his followers, including Marx. We note here that this history is important, for as we will see in a later chapter that deals with MacIntyre's account of the failure of the Enlightenment project, the fact that the modern period was born out of an attack by atomism on essentialist forms of thought, does not augur well for the reception of Marxism or a morality of virtues in the modern world.

However, by placing Marx in this essentialist lineage Meikle is able to provide us with a relatively clear account of what Marx meant by dialectics:

> the dialectical method is the seeking out of laws of the movement of society considered as a process of naturalistic history, and that the most important among these are laws of development, that is, of transition in the entity (human society) from one form to another.[61]

Marx comes by his categories in a study of principally Hegel and Aristotle, drawing on both and transforming both these essentialist thinkers' concepts in the process.

Although not so well known as Marx's connection with Hegel, Meikle is by no means the first to see Marx as at least related to Aristotelianism in his essentialist categories, for example the philosopher Allen Wood, whose work is a valuable complement to Meikle's has written that Marx in

> both his dialectical method and his concept of humanity [is] based more or less openly on the Aristotelian notion that things have essences and that the task of science is to understand the properties and behaviour of things in terms of these essences. Marx's concept of alienation involves the further Aristotelian notion that a fulfilling life for men and women is one in which they exercise their distinctively human capacities. Marx's historical materialism employs teleological explanations apparently presupposing that such explanations are legitimate . . . and applicable to social organisation. The dialectical method, by its intention to penetrate beneath the surface appearance of things and mirror their inner developmental structure, pretty clearly commits Marx to some form of scientific realism in opposition to most familiar forms of empiricism.[62]

However, this comment is tucked away at the end of his book, in the respectable 'The Arguments of the Philosophers' series. No one to my knowledge has foregrounded Marx's Aristotelian-

Hegelian essentialism in quite Meikle's way, i.e. to drive home
its theoretical and implicitly political conclusions, or challenged so openly the dominant anti-essentialist and anti-
teleological consensus.

In examining how Marx comes to dialectics, Meikle is able to
point to the degree of Aristotelianism there is in Hegel. He
locates three key Aristotelian moves; firstly starting from the
position that entities have real natures and essences, he excludes chance as the basis for phenomena; this is to be found in
Hegel's introduction to *The Philosophy of History*. The second
Aristotelian move, 'is that he conceives the form of law in terms
of the realisation of potentialities in a whole which has an
essence in which those potentialities inhere'.[63] Whilst the third
feature is that

> history arise[s] from a whole with an essence which under-
> goes transformation of form and has an end or telos. The
> essence of history for Hegel is that 'freedom of spirit (which)
> is the very essence of man's nature' and that the telos of world
> history is 'the actualisation of this freedom' which Hegel
> identified as 'the final purpose of the world'.[64]

On Meikle's reading these basic Aristotelian categories are
taken over by Marx, even though the content, 'spirit' etc. is
changed. But for Marx the most important advance Hegel
makes on Aristotle is the contrast he makes between natural
change and historical change, that is 'the manner in which
organic categories apply in the history of human society and in
organic nature'.[65] The difference for Hegel lies in the differences in the natures of the two processes, the organic one being
simpler, at least in the sense that its line of necessary development can be more easily traced. But in the process of
history, development is internally more complex. This is because
the relationship between its components can hinder development in unforeseen ways which are not the product of 'ex-
traneous accidents' (as in nature):

> this is an aspect of its nature as a dialectical process, the line
> of necessity in the development is not *immediate* and frustrat-
> able only by external, material accident. It is mediated: 'The
> transition of its potentiality into actuality is mediated through
> consciousness and will'.[66]

The crucial difference between the natural and the historical is that in the first you have the development of an unchanging essence or nature via e.g. biological evolution, i.e. random genetic mutation and selective environmental pressure. Whereas in history we do not have the development of the same nature, but quite new forms of nature so there is, in effect, space for conflict in the essence of history which accounts for the apparent regressions in human development. 'The historical process . . . does not *preserve* a nature through successive generations; it *develops* a nature through successive forms.'[67]

Stripped of Hegel's difficult language and his emphasis on spirit, Hegel argues that there are conflicts within the form or essence; as Meikle puts it: 'The basis of the instability here, *the contradiction, is between what exists and what is in the process of coming-to-be.*'[68]

There are many difficulties with Hegel's account, including his use of almost wilfully obscure language, and we have no need to pursue him further. The key to Meikle's account is what he believes Marx does with the form of the Hegelianism he inherits. Basically, his claim is the rather startling one that he, Marx, keeps the general theoretical structure but rejigs the whole system at the level of ontology, by making *real natures* the starting point. In other words, for Marx, the real problem with Hegel's system is that he ignores the real natures of the parts that make up the whole, so fails to examine their specific line of development, but instead, imposes an external system derived from a system of logic (this is his idealism) on the real pattern of development which had to be studied to be understood. This is what Marx is getting at in *Critique of Hegel's Doctrine of State* when he says: 'The crux of the matter is that Hegel everywhere makes the idea into the subject while the genuine real subject . . . is turned into the predicate.'[69] This is what is meant by Marx putting Hegel on his feet, i.e. he bases Hegel's categories on Aristotelian 'real natures' in which the real developments take place.

Having thus traced Marx's relation with Hegel, Meikle then sets out to define what exactly Marx's essentialist materialism is. He does this by explaining what Marx means by the very Hegelian-sounding expression that 'the universal is the real essence of the finite real'. This means:

a) that there are real natures or essences which are not reducible to 'simples'; b) that coming to identify them and know them involves tracking down what is general, universal or essential in the phenomena or 'finite realm'; and c) that that has to begin with an investigation of the facts of the finite real itself in order to discover (it cannot be known a priori) what is truly the general within it, so that d) the finite real, the reality itself, can then finally be comprehended in the light of the general, the universal or the essence, that the empirical investigation turned up.[70]

From this starting point Marx's clear objective must be to track down what the 'concrete universal' or essence of human society and history is. In *The Critique of Hegel's Doctrine of State* he speaks of 'socialised man', but by the *Economic and Philosophic Manuscripts* this has been identified as human labour:

which passes through a series of specific forms (which he comes to identify as organic social wholes in which a particular form of supply of human labour is predominant) each having specific laws or realisable potentially of development, and culminating in the attainment of socialism where the fullest potential of the essence is realised in a form of society adapted by man to himself.[71]

Clearly then, it follows that the Labour Theory of Value flows naturally from this conceptual framework, for if there are only social forms that have people's labour as their essence, the real content of value, whether in the money-form, price-form or capital-form, must be labour. On Meikle's terms, only atomistic Marxists could want a technical problem to solve, rather than the deeper question of the essence/appearance distinction, which underlies all debate over value.

It is important to draw out from this framework what Meikle believes Marx regarded as the historical basis of communism. Given the above, it is obviously rooted in the teleologically governed realisation of a real essence – a realisation that is, as in all essential development, potentially frustratable. In regard to communism, however, it consists of: 'the identity between the twin teleologies of the historical process of the coming-to-be of human society itself and the realisation of man's nature in it'.[72] What this means is that, for Marx, history is the way human society develops through particular forms to realise its fullest potential, i.e. a teleological process leading towards communism, the content of which is largely unknowable. But in addition to this, Marx also views man as *a natural kind*, i.e. a 'species of mammalian order, whose essence is differentiated from others of that and other orders by the essential properties of being conscious and social' (a highly Aristotelian view).[73] These two elements are only analytically distinct, because the individual is a social being, and 'the realised human society is a society of realised humans'.[74]

The detailed use of Marx's applied philosophical categories is, of course, in *Capital*, and a full understanding of the content of Meikle's rescuing of the dialectical method can only come from seeing it in its full application; this takes up the greater part of his book. None the less I have presented enough of his groundwork to see what can be built from essentialist foundations, i.e. once an ontology and epistemology of real natures and real reference is accepted. But what can we today make of it, if not only Aristotle but Hegel and Marx can be successfully updated; is our reaction bound to be 'this is all metaphysical madness', given the history of our century? The problem is basically that which Rorty locates with Kripke: 'the Russell–Kripke issue is probably a stand-off. One can play it either way, and develop a system from either starting point with equal completeness and elegance.' If this is true, then our choice will not be commanded by logic but by preference, and this strengthens a wider point of Rorty's when he says: 'it is very doubtful indeed that the Kantian ideas which are taken for granted in our culture are going to be refuted by anything that philosophy professors do'.[75] A teleological Marxism of real natures will be judged not by standards of internal logic or rigor, but by the sense it makes to people of real histories and experience.[76]

The question remains, however, after our move through Marxism's crisis and an attempted philosophic restatement of its traditional form, why does MacIntyre not seek his resolution of modernity here? Why does he seek in *After Virtue*, to restore teleological conceptions to our culture via the narrative features of human life,[77] rather than through the development of real natures or essences? At one level the answer is clear enough, he simply does not believe in Aristotle's naturalistic teleology or what he calls Aristotle's 'metaphysical biology.[78] He gives no argument in *After Virtue*, as to why he does not accept these concepts. In terms of the arguments presented in *After Virtue* the issue is by no means clear, but MacIntyre's later writing reveals a clearer philosophical commitment to some form of Aristotelian essentialism. However, MacIntyre has not repudiated his critical remarks concerning 'metaphysical biology' and I feel they must stand.[79] It seems very likely that he chooses a narrative, rather than a naturalistic version of Aristotelian teleology, for ultimately, political reasons. For possible clues to why this may be so, it is to an essay, by Cornelius Castoriadis that we must turn to furnish the grounds for understanding why such philosophical forms may have political connections.

Castoriadis in his essay 'From Marx to Aristotle, from Aristotle to Us', has, like Meikle, noted the importance of Aristotle as well as Hegel for Marx, but with very different conclusions. The basis of his argument is this: Marx's concepts and categories are at heart Aristotelian as, for example, in the case of the concept of labour:

> in a formula of the purest Aristotelian casting, materialises 'the faculties that originally lie sleeping in productive man' and only the through and through transformation of man into 'producer' completely awakens the dormant faculties, actualizes the telos of man.[80]

This is basically Meikle's point; but he claims at the heart of Aristotle's work is a tension which is not resolved and reproduces itself in Marx's work.

Castoriadis argues that the question raised at the start of the *Nicomachean Ethics* as to whether the supreme human good is either nature (*physis*) or law (*nomos*) is not finally resolved by Aristotle, in any of his work. Castoriadis argues that it is this ambiguity that also ultimately haunts Marx's work. As he puts it in relation to Marx:

> do the 'equality' of human beings and the commensurability of their labours depend on the physics of man ('natural' or 'social') or on *nomos*, the law, the social-historical institution of a particular society, capitalist society – in other words, is there a *physis* of history that requires that a particular *nomos* must be realised at a particular moment?[81]

Here is the tension within Aristotle, for Castoriadis, *physis* and *nomos*, nature and law. This is the tension between man as a natural kind species and man as socially constituted being. As Castoriadis puts it: 'Every being is in as much a being it actualises *what it was to be* [*to ti en einai*] in as much as it accomplishes its destination'.[82] But in human beings this is in some sense broken. But why? Because:

> virtue is the telos of man, his 'natural ends' but it is not 'natural' in the sense that men arrive there 'more often than not' and spontaneously. Almost all horses . . . accomplish the end of a horse; almost no man really accomplishes virtue, and strictly no city accomplishes its telos. And of course, virtue has not this 'power' to be accomplished in the case of man, because virtue ought to be created by paideia, that is to say, by the fundamental institutions of the city.[83]

This then is the problem, how can the *physis* and *telos* of man, i.e. the natural kind purpose of being human, be fulfilled, except by the *nomos* or law and institutions of the city. But since Aristotle knows most people do not become completely virtuous and most cities do not inculcate virtue in their inhabitants, how is this gap between the natural end and the social form to be overcome?

For Castoriadis, Aristotle's greatness lies in the fact that he does not simply collapse the one into the other,[84] he does not produce a false resolution, as does Plato, who 'presupposes that virtue is already effectively created as the goal of total justice capable of realising itself in the form of an instance that institutes – whether "the legislation or the people"'.[85]

Here then, is the basis for Castoriadis's condemnation of the Aristotelian Marx, for he does collapse *nomos* into *physis*, the social into a natural kind teleology, as he puts it:

> Does not Marx want to show that a certain physis of man and of history must lead them to their 'goal' to their predetermined telos communism? Does he not try to find in the proletariat the legislation, which by its own proper historical nature as a universal class does not have particular interests and would therefore vindicate the human essence/nature of man, such as will be undoubtedly manifested when 'labour will become the prime need of life'?[86]

Is this the real political problem that lies behind a move back to an essentialist teleology, Aristotelian or Marxist? Whether this is so, or not, it is likely to be a powerful consideration for theorists immersed in a liberal culture, and perhaps provide them with strong motives to resist a fully updated Aristotelian-Hegelian Marx.

MacIntyre has shown himself aware of this problem and the likely consequences these cultural resistances would have for Marxism. In the 1968 book, *Marxism and Christianity*, he registers the following picture of Marxism's fate, when he states, 'Marxism was overcome by and assimilated itself to the modes of thought of the very society of which it sought to be a critique.'[87] This happens he argues because implicitly, Marxism's chief representatives shed those elements that made it more than a set of private opinions, i.e. 'Marxism's Hegelian inheritance and with it the loss of that particular view of human nature upon which Marx's own moral critique had depended'.[88] This is the dissipation of a view of human nature and process, which as we have seen, had made theory an explicit political and moral view, that would guide social transformation.

MacIntyre argues that by the end of the nineteenth century, as is clear from the Bernstein controversy, most European Marxists accepted bourgeois moral formalism – Bernstein falling back on to Kantian moral imperatives and Kautsky, 'nothing other than one more version of "utilitarianism"'.[89] In effect MacIntyre argues that the same privatisation process that has happened to religion in the nineteenth and twentieth centuries has happened to Marxism. He writes:

> secularisation has not resulted . . . [in us] . . . acquiring a new and more rational set of beliefs about the nature of man and the world. Rather, men have been deprived of any overall view and to this extent have been deprived of one possible source of understanding and of action . . . the conditions which are inimical to religion seem to be inimical to Marxism too.[90]

In these conditions Marxism all too easily becomes a matter of personal intellectual conviction; if that is so, as MacIntyre is clearly painfully aware, it becomes trivial and in a sense not Marxism at all.

MacIntyre's critical resolution of liberalism is to start where the culture actually is. He, in Castoriadis's terms, is firmly in the camp of *nomos*. His narrative conception of human life and community focuses on the quest of defining the good life, as being the good life itself: there are no claims to any definitive end to history. Intellectual and moral traditions encounter one another in a Socratic rather than a Marxist dialectic, but always in substantive, indeed often quite local, contexts. Narratives are constructed from human lives, as they exist; purposes are the product of human interpretation, but with the need for such interpretation a permanent part of being human. Teleology reconnects morality with the realm of facts, but in a form that refuses a grounding in the politics of the ontology of labour. However, the 'moral critic' is placed back in history, the history of a particular life, with an inherited identity and into an inherited community. I shall explore some consequences of this in the conclusion.

Part II

Markets, managers and the virtues

Chapter 3

MacIntyre's evaluative history and Polanyi's historical sociology

There are few ways in which a man can be more innocently employed than in getting money.

Dr Johnson

Where the market is allowed to follow its own autonomous tendencies, its participants do not look towards the person, or each other, but only towards the commodity; there are no obligations of brotherliness or reverence, and none of those spontaneous human relations that are sustained by personal unions.

Max Weber

In this part I shall look at the relationship of MacIntyre's recent work to a particular sociologically informed historical narrative. I shall do this by supplementing and expanding the account that is partly assumed and partly present in MacIntyre's analysis in both *After Virtue* and *Whose Justice? Which Rationality?* What follows will, in an inevitably sketched form, try to examine some of the connections and determinations involved, between the account of the economic and social 'Great Transformation', narrated principally, but not solely, by Karl Polanyi, and the philosophic and cultural transformation, presented by Mac-Intyre – stressing the congruence of their approaches.

The process of the social transformation in its ideological and cultural forms will be clarified by the use of certain characters, but in this instance drawn from real life, who seem to me to represent the contradictions and complexities of MacIntyre's account of the rise of modernity. These figures are two conservative theorists, Edmund Burke the Tory philosopher and George Fitzhugh the defender of the slave plantation system in the American South. These figures help us think through, if only by example, the vexed question of the effects of social relations upon intellectual thought and culture.

Once having established the underlying similarities of method and objectives between MacIntyre and Polanyi, their approaches will be supplemented by philosophical and sociological considerations concerning notions of the self and the individual, in relation to the actual workings of a market economy. Here I draw especially on the work of Georg Simmel.

Finally in this section the importance and potential of MacIntyre's understanding of the role of the manager as a central character of modernity will be explored.

WAS THERE A 'GREAT TRANSFORMATION'? POLANYI VERSUS MACFARLANE

MacIntyre's philosophical and sociological theory presupposes a particular history. It is rooted in a sense of the development of a capitalist market order out of a feudal society. In this context this means being rooted in a sense of the possibilities of life being lived in very different ways; with purposes and meanings attached to practices and institutions that order life quite differently from the way we live now. For MacIntyre feudal society, whatever its distinctive features, shared enough in common with other non-capitalist, pre-industrial cultures (e.g. the classical world or the Arab Empire) to make the emergence of a capitalist market society a quite qualitatively distinct type of social order. In other words, MacIntyre's entire account is based upon the idea that some version of this radical transition or what, following Polanyi, we might call 'The Great Transformation'[1] thesis, has been vindicated. Recently, however, the reality of this Great Transformation has been challenged, most notably in Alan MacFarlane's *The Origins of English Individualism.*[2]

MacFarlane makes large claims for his work. He states that:

What is absolutely clear is that one of the major theories of economic anthropology is incorrect, namely the idea that we witness in England between the sixteenth century and nineteenth century the 'Great Transformation' from a non-market peasant society where economics is 'embedded' in social relations, to a modern market, capitalist, system where economy and society have been split apart. This view is most clearly expressed in the work of Karl Polanyi.[3]

MacFarlane is quite clear about the sociological and cultural consequences of his work. He suggests:

> Yet if the present thesis is correct, individualism in economic and social life is much older than this in England (post 1500). In fact, within the recorded period covered by our documents, it is not possible to find a time when an Englishman did not stand alone, symbolised and shaped by his ego-centred kinship system, he stood in the centre of his world.[4]

In certain respects it would not be unfair to say that Mac-Farlane's work could seem to be part of a sophisticated liberal/conservative intellectual move to eternalise the market, or at least push its origins so far back in history that it can appear a relatively permanent feature of the social landscape. This view would see the market as an 'institution' compatible with a variety of political, cultural and religious arrangements, the origins and specific character of which would have to be looked for elsewhere. In effect, he defends Adam Smith as he says:

> Adam Smith founded classical economics on the premise of the rational 'economic' man believing he was describing a universal and long evident type ... According to Polanyi, such a man had only just emerged, stripped of his ritual, political and social needs. The implication of the present arguments, however, is that it was Smith who was right and Polanyi who was wrong, at least in relation to England. Homo economicus and the market society had been present in England for centuries before Smith wrote.[5]

Whatever MacFarlane's political intentions, others were not slow to pick up the implications of his point. The popular British Conservative journalist Ferdinand Mount has used MacFarlane's book as if it presented an historical basis for saying that collective control is profoundly unEnglish. He wrote in a review shortly after first publication:

> If MacFarlane is right – and the battle is still raging – the English were always individualists and never enmeshed in, or aspiring towards tribal collective ways of life. In that case, why

should we not be allowed to cultivate our heritage? Is it not our destiny to be home-owning, self-employed, capital-acquiring, two-car nuclear families?[6]

But whatever the ideological uses of this work, it is clear that if MacFarlane's view were to be accepted, it would seriously undermine the necessarily totalistic element in MacIntyre's account. For this is in part dependent upon connecting, in a relatively loose non-deterministic manner, economic, political and cultural changes. MacIntyre makes the whole issue clear when he states:

> my preference for Polanyi's type of narrative is that it avoids the methodological mistakes which all three make (Marxist, Neo Marxist, Weberian), most notably the error of supposing that we can identify economic or social factors independently from ideological or theoretical factors in such a way as to produce causal explanations of a cogent kind. My thesis is not that we cannot distinguish economic or social items from ideological or theoretical items; there is indeed more than one way of making such a distinction. But when we try to understand the narratives of historical change in terms of any one of these sets of distinctions, the causal explanations which they yield are generally implausible. It is only when we understand and categorise the social and economic phen-omena in such a way as to recognise that agents' and participants' understanding of social and economic activity is integral to and partially constitutive of the characteristics of such activities that we provide characterisations which enable us to write rationally defensible explanatory narratives. Karl Polanyi's was just such a narration.[7]

It is open to question as to how fair this characterisation of Marxist explanation is, but it can leave us in no doubt as to the integral connectedness of economic and social, cultural and theoretical phenomena in MacIntyre's thought.[8] It follows therefore that the presence of widespread economically indi-vidualistic attitudes in thirteenth-century England would be very damaging to his conception of the transformation of social and moral thought and practice occurring at a later stage. For MacIntyre's account is built around a notion of the triumph or at least predominance, both intellectually and materially, of versions of liberal individualism, which became established in the period from the sixteenth century to the nineteenth century. He is quite clear that his account depends on there being:

> a sharp contrast between the self-aggrandising drive for power and money in the European communities of the 12th century and even 13th century and that drive in the 16th and 17th century, a contrast signalled by the different ways in which the relationship of the self to what it possesses is conceptualised.[9]

To understand if MacFarlane is correct in his claim that the forms of life that Polanyi and numerous other historians and social scientists believed to have emerged in the sixteenth century, were in fact present from at least the thirteenth century, we must examine his account with some care.

The core of MacFarlane's argument is as follows: the claim that medieval England was a peasant society is wrong because truly peasant societies have very definite characteristics, the principal ones of which are missing from England in the period from 1250 to 1750. It follows from this that MacFarlane challenges the view that England was radically transformed between the fifteenth century and the eighteenth century, as it made a move from a medieval peasant society to an agrarian capitalist society, with a corresponding development of ideas of autonomy and individual political rights. He claims that as early as the thirteenth century, the basic marks of a capitalist economy can be seen to have been present within the country.

MacFarlane is attacking the view, widely accepted, that England came to differ from the rest of Europe because its capitalist transformation occurred between the fifteenth century and the eighteenth century. Instead he claims that this change lay in a much earlier development of capitalism in England in the thirteenth century, while the rest of Europe remained largely peasant societies, for many more centuries. So, for MacFarlane the origins of English individualism are pushed right back, possibly, before we have adequate records and documents, to the early Anglo-Saxon Germanic settlements.

MacFarlane's thesis depends upon him making a key conceptual move in order to challenge the claim, of most medieval historians, that England at the dawn of the sixteenth century was a peasant society. This involves him in constructing a model of a 'peasant society', and arguing that certain key features of such a society are missing from England, in the three centuries leading up to 1500.[10]

So what is MacFarlane's definition of a peasant society? He has five criteria. The first two are taken from Daniel Thorner and are that 'half the population must be agricultural' and 'more than half the working population must be engaged in agriculture'.[11] The next two criteria are:

> that a peasantry can exist only where there is a state, in other words, a ruling hierarchy, an external political power sovereign over the particular community of 'peasants'. The second is that there are almost inevitably towns with markets the culture of which is quite different from that of the countryside.[12]

The final criterion is that 'the family farm is the basic unit of peasant ownership, production consumption and social life. The individual, the family and the farm, appears as an indivisible whole'.[13]

From this MacFarlane proceeds to point out that there is a very rich literature on the peasantry from almost all over the world. He suggests that to put together a general picture from all these sources would 'produce an unsatisfactory rag bag'[14] and instead he decides to concentrate on just one area for his model. This area is Eastern Europe. He does this because it has been subject to so much scholarly attention and also because it is just about the right distance from England, not part of the general area of Western Europe (the area that MacFarlane is trying to distinguish England from), but part of general European culture and permeated by Christianity. His final reason is that such important English medieval historians as E. A. Kosminsky, Sir Paul Vinogradoff and M. M. Poston, were themselves Eastern Europeans, and as such, he claims that: 'It is clear from their writings that they were consciously comparing medieval England with traditional Russia.'[15]

Hilton provides a compendious summary of what, for MacFarlane, a peasant society would really look like, allowing for the fact that MacFarlane astonishingly has almost nothing to say about the concentration of land ownership among landlords and the nobility:

the family, not the individual, owns the holding, the family on the holding is multi-generational; its emotions are identified with specific pieces of land; women had few, if any, rights; there is no wage labour; there is no social differentiation; there is hardly any production for the market; therefore there are virtually no markets; also, consequentially, there is no market for land.[16]

We can see now that the chief problem with MacFarlane's work lies in his construction of a model of what a medieval non-capitalist peasantry should look like. In the first place this allows him to ignore or disguise the fact that many of his supposed opponents amongst medieval historians, e.g. Rodney Hilton, have a quite significantly different notion of what a peasant society is, which allows them to deal with much of what MacFarlane sees as hostile evidence in a different way.[17] The second fundamental feature of his model is the family household, which is the basic unit of ownership, production and consumption. From this it follows that individual ownership cannot exist. White and Vann point out that many historians and anthropologists do not adopt this criterion. They note that: 'even anthropologists who stress that the peasant household is the main unit of production and consumption do not necessarily insist that it is always the primary unit of ownership'.[18] In part this emphasis seems to derive from the work of Teodor Shanin and as Keith Tribe – a noted critic of Shanin – has argued: 'MacFarlane's use of Shanin's work produces an extreme "peasantist" version of the Russian peasantry against which the alleged English peasantry are measured'.[19]

The question of ownership is central. It allows MacFarlane to move to the question of a market in both land and labour, the existence of which is crucial to his claim that capitalism existed in England in the thirteenth century. It is, I believe, in this area that MacFarlane becomes most seriously unstuck – partly because of confusion over definition and partly because of the nature of the evidence on peasant society in Russia. To begin with, on page 13, MacFarlane concedes that to distinguish tribal society from peasant ones, there normally has to exist markets and a state, with the clear implication that there is peasant production for the market, yet on page 152 he points to the existence of markets in medieval England as providing positive evidence that England was a capitalist society and not a peasant one. However, as both Tribe and Hilton point out, markets existed in Russia in both medieval and modern (i.e. nineteenth-century) times. Hilton states: 'Peasants in medieval Russia produced for the market, bought and sold land (women as well as men), gave dowries to their daughters and redistributed their land through partible inheritance'.[20] He goes on to point out that there is no evidence that they lived in multi-generational rather than nuclear families.

Hilton feels that the real difference between the Russian peasantry and those of the west lay in the fact that there was a great deal of land available to be colonised in Russia, which made for the easy creation of new households. As for the significance of the existence of a land market in pre-Revolutionary Russia, Tribe makes the important point that: 'private and state serfs bought and sold land in early 19th century Russia and while the form of land transfer was nowhere as significant as that shown by Smith (in MacFarlane) this does not indicate that serfs were individualistic'. Tribe goes on to make the general point, certainly entirely compatible with MacIntyre's theoretical principles, that what MacFarlane neglects 'is the simple principle that "individuality" is divergently constituted in law, economy, politics and so forth'.[21]

We have noted that there is some confusion in MacFarlane's account of the role of markets in peasant societies and, as a result, his views as to what constitutes capitalism are also confused. At various points he refers to the existence of markets (e.g. pp. 173–4, p. 155), to the existence of cash or money and the existence of wage labour and servanthood (pp. 151–5), complex division of labour (pp. 78–9): all seen as clear signs of the presence of a capitalist economy. There are many problems with this: firstly if we take Marx as our theorist of capitalism, then Marx never took the simple existence of commodity production as definitive of capitalism; he recognised that probably for all but the most primitive social formations some form of commodity production would exist. It was rather the dominant form of surplus extraction that, for Marx, was definitive of the nature of a particular social formation.[22] However, even if we leave aside attempts at theoretically coherent definitions, as White and Vann point out, no historian has ever imagined that an entirely 'natural economy' existed in England in the thirteenth century.[23] But as they argue 'markets', 'money', 'local exchange', 'production for market', 'hired labour', etc. can 'individually and in various combinations ... be found in unambiguously pre-capitalist societies. So can a variety of family and kinship relations ... there were nuclear families in Carolingian society and in many other parts of the pre- or non-capitalist world'.[24]

However, there is a deeper problem with MacFarlane's work, which makes him potentially far less damaging to MacIntyre than he otherwise might be. This lies in his refusal (a refusal which he seems to make a virtue of) to investigate the feeling, sentiments and mentalities of the people he is writing about. As White and Vann put it, he 'fails to pierce the veil of legal texts to see how villagers actually managed their lands and to identify the sentiments or attitudes that such practices may reflect'.[25]

This makes him critically vulnerable to MacIntyre's point quoted above concerning the difference between the drive for power and money in the twelfth and thirteenth centuries and the sixteenth and seventeenth centuries; the point being that if it is the case that economic relations are in fact embedded in social or customary relations, whatever the apparent 'letter of the law' may say, then the whole force of MacFarlane's polemic against Polanyi, and others who think like him, is lost.

MacFarlane argues that what matters is who owned the land. He claims to be going deeper than mere 'statistical tendencies'[26] of what was normally done, i.e. land normally being passed on through the family. MacFarlane is surely wrong in taking this strategy, for it can be misleading. For example, he relies a great deal on the official legal doctrines of the thirteenth century as presented in Bracton's *On the Laws and Customs of England*. It is by no means certain that they were even known to any of the villages that MacFarlane is concerned with, and the idea that they shared Bracton's assumptions is based on no evidence. His refusal to examine the social and moral context of inter-pretation and his narrow concentration on the family, leads him to miss the fact that these so-called English individualists were, in fact, members of village communities who often acted to-gether to restrict the way land might be used in particular cases, e.g. abuse of access to common land. We should also recall that all those peasants discussed by MacFarlane were either serfs or freeholders, both categories who would have had obligations, of various kinds, to their lords, which may well have severely limited what they could do with their property. MacFarlane's neglect of customs and sentiments prevents him from realising the problematic nature of the concept of property that he so freely uses. White and Vann point out:

> the tenements of villages were generally comprised partly of various use-rights in communal resources such as pasture, wastes, forests and water. He [MacFarlane] seems not to see how difficult it would have been for 'rampant individualists' to have carried on the complex system of village agriculture and husbandry which many medieval social and economic historians have described.[27]

It is clear, therefore, that MacFarlane's account of an essentially individualistic capitalist culture in medieval England, designed to vitiate the notion of a 'Great Transformation', is at the very least open to serious objection.

THE SELF AND HISTORY

MacIntyre makes clear that his historical narrative concerning the transformation of conceptions of self and human nature is critically determined by a particular kind of social context. He points out that we tend to think of the Enlightenment as being French, i.e. 'the *Philosophe*', but in reality they looked to England as an example of a just and 'modern' society. But England, in turn, was overshadowed culturally by the achievements of the German (Kant, Mozart) and Scottish Enlightenment (Hume, Smith, Ferguson).[28]

MacIntyre suggests that what the French lacked was a secularised Protestant background with an educated reading public; in effect although he does not greatly elaborate the point, MacIntyre seems to be laying emphasis on what Jürgen Habermas has described as the existence of a 'Public Sphere'.[29] This involved the disintegration of feudal authorities such as the Church, princes and nobility, which in the eighteenth century broke into private and public elements. The Church, of course, continued in existence although religion becomes increasingly a private matter,[30] with the Church becoming one public and legal body amongst others; whilst the emergence of public authority is marked by the separation of the private household expenses of a ruler from the public budget.

As the old feudal estates changed and the nobility's power shifted to bodies of public authority, merchants, traders and the professions, via their corporations and territorial bodies, there developed a sphere of society that stood apart from the state as a genuine sphere of private autonomy. MacIntyre places special emphasis on the existence of 'an educated class which linked the servants of government, the clergy and lay thinkers in a single reading public'.[31] This is the world of, in England, Dr Johnson and the coffee houses, in other countries a public linked with universities like Kant's Koenigsberg and, most especially for MacIntyre, Hume's Edinburgh.

This, very briefly, is the context in which a series of, by any standards, first-rate theorists, Hume, Kant, Smith, Diderot and later Kierkegaard, attempted to produce for this connected reading public valid arguments which moved from conceptions as to what human nature is, to conclusions about the authority of moral rules. In effect, MacIntyre claims that they failed, but interestingly he sees this as no simple intellectual failure, but rather as a failure inherent in the historical situation from which they emerged.

MacIntyre argues that these early modern philosophers inherited a moral schema from medieval Europe which contained both classical and Christian elements, but that its basic structure is to be found in Aristotle's *Nicomachean Ethics*.[32] Now this scheme is fundamentally teleological, involving a contrast between man-as-he-happens-to-be and man-as-he-could-be-if-he-realised-his-essential-nature (the very clumsiness of the language here is an accurate indication of our conceptual unfamiliarity with such concepts, as we have no precise terms for them). As he goes on to argue:

Ethics is the science which is to enable men to understand how they make the transition from the former state to the latter. Ethics therefore on this view presupposes some account of potentiality and act, some account of the essence of man as a rational animal and above all some account of the human telos. The precepts which enjoin the various virtues and prohibit the vices which are their counterparts, instruct us how to move from potentiality to act, how to realise our true nature and to reach our true end.[33]

This framework, then, contains three central components, all three of which only make sense in relationship to one another: a concept of a basic or 'untutored' human nature, a set of rationally groundable ethics and a notion of 'human-nature-as-it-could-be-if-it-realised-its-telos'. The ethical precepts are what allow you to pass from one state of human nature to the completed state, the final one being, of course, potentially present within the original. This meant that within medieval Europe and the classically influenced Islamic world, moral claims had something of the quality of facts (for us). For to say what someone should do, was to say as a matter of fact what would lead them to their true end, as ordained by God and comprehended by reason.

However, with the Protestant Reformation alongside the rise of Jansenist-influenced Catholic theology, and the scientific and philosophical rejections of Aristotelianism, the whole basis of this system was fragmented. The Protestants and Jansenists denied the power of human reason to understand man's true end, this being lost with the Fall (Aristotelianism was deeply suspect to the reformers, because of its association with the medieval Catholic Church, and Luther regarded *The Nicomachean Ethics* as the worst book ever written). Emerging seventeenth-century science was also hostile and here the crucial linking thinker between science and theology is Pascal. His role in developing the new science of probability meant that he carefully limited the role of reason in both theology and science.[34] As MacIntyre noted, for this view, 'Reason is calculative, it can assess truths of fact and mathematical relations but nothing more'.[35] No question here of understanding essences or potentials and transitions. The options then become faith or scepticism or, as in Pascal's case, a rather fraught mixture of both.

This process effectively eliminated the possibility of any concept of 'man-as-he-could-be-if-he-realised-his-telos'. What this left was an apparently unbridgeable gap between the two remaining elements in the moral scheme: on the one hand was a definite content of morality, which almost everyone in this period (atheists as well as theists) believed was important; on the other, a certain notion of human nature in its basic unreformed state. This was a major problem because the form of these ethical demands was designed to develop and educate the notion of human nature as it naturally existed, they were clearly not of a form that could be derived from an appeal to the reality of human nature:

> The injunctions of morality, thus understood, are likely to be ones that human nature, thus understood, has strong tendencies to disobey. Hence the 18th century moral philosophers engaged in what was an inevitably unsuccessful project; for they did indeed attempt to find a rational basis for their moral beliefs in a particular understanding of human nature, while inheriting a set of moral injunctions on one hand and a conception of human nature on the other which had been expressly designed to be discrepant with each other.[36]

The upshot of their efforts was that in their negative arguments with opponents they moved closer and closer to the view that no moral argument could move from factual premises to moral and evaluative conclusions. This is unsurprising since the intellectual material for such a move had been removed.

Now, we must bear in mind, that this picture, all too briefly sketched, is not an abstract intellectual history, but rather an element that partly presupposes and partly contributes to a change in social and political relations. But the question must be clearly posed as to why the fragmentation of this medieval moral framework is important for an analysis of the rise of a capitalist market culture. What is it that is implicit in MacIntyre's narrative that may cast new light on this process? Remember that it is not being suggested that philosophers and philosophies in any sense caused the rise of capitalism; no spirit of the age is being invoked as a causal factor. In some measures philosophers may be indicators of changes in social relations, although given their role at this time, normally dependent upon courts, patrons, universities and journals, they are most directly affected by institutional changes that would in turn have to be placed in a larger setting. But they are not just indicators of social change; they inherit forms of thought from the past, forms deeply implicated in prior social relations, in MacIntyre's sense of helping to constitute those relations.

These forms cannot be simply ignored; argument itself makes demands upon those who use it and live by it.

Ideas and values have a reality in quite another sense, in that they are produced and reproduced not merely by word of mouth or words on the page but via what has been termed the 'emotional economy of the family'. Psychoanalysis – whether fully accepted or not – points to the importance of family structures as productive of personalities, identities and ideals.[37] It is not insignificant then, that both Kant and Kierkegaard had Lutheran family backgrounds, David Hume, a Calvinist one, and John Locke a Puritan.

The case of Locke (although not discussed by MacIntyre) is most instructive for illustrating the methodological complexity MacIntyre wishes to sustain in understanding the relationship of ideas to large historical tranformations. There is no doubt that he was perhaps the greatest of the British liberal empiricists and that his theory of rights was a part of the underpinning of the capitalist market, and liberal individualism. But it is important to avoid economic reductionism. In the case of Locke, C. B. Macpherson's analysis in his book *The Political Theory of Possessive Individualism* [38] is a favourite target for this accusation. The distinguished Locke scholar John Dunn has been very critical of Macpherson; he has written:

> Living when he did and as he did, Locke was by necessity in part a bourgeois political theorist. But in so far as he was a Liberal, he was certainly not such because of his moral credulity in the market. Nor is there a shred of evidence that any of his major commitments – tolerance, rationality, individual rights and a modest degree of empiricism – had anything directly to do with the specific institution of capitalism at all . . . what Locke trusted in was the Christian God and his own intelligence and when it came to the crunch and the two parted company what he proved to trust in more deeply was the God and not the intelligence.[39]

But if we look at Dunn's further comments in another place on the motives for Locke's theory of property and Macpherson's argument:

> The boldest answer to this question, advanced most strongly by C. B. Macpherson is that Locke intended his theory as an

exploration of the moral legitimacy of capitalist production. There is little case for taking this seriously as an assessment of Locke's intention in building his theory. But it is a more interesting question how far this suggestion may capture if in mildly anachronistic terms, Locke's sense of his own achievement in having constructed his theory.[40]

The fact that many of his contemporaries and later liberals of the eighteenth and nineteenth centuries understood Locke in the light of this achievement, makes Macpherson's point rather more than anachronistic.

In any account of writers and thinkers we need to take full account of MacIntyre's argument concerning conceptual change:

> It was a matter of many different changes gradually acquiring a cumulative effect, so that the nature of those changes only became apparent retrospectively. Indeed, it is only because the outcome was what it was that those changes have the nature we now ascribe to them.[41]

Returning now to the issue of the fragmentation of a teleological moral framework, why was this so important for future developments? Here it is necessary to deepen and extend MacIntyre's narrative, in order to reveal its full implications. This can be done by drawing on Albert Hirschman's work, in particular his book, *The Passions and the Interests: Political Arguments for Capitalism before its Triumph*[42] (a work whose importance MacIntyre has acknowledged in *Whose Justice? Which Rationality?*). Hirschman's narrative is in effect one in which a whole intellectual and moral framework was fashioned in which reason, prudence and good sense all seemed to demand the construction of, or rather intellectual and moral support for, a social order based upon the pursuit of economic self-interest and individualism, rather than in buttressing values and institutions encouraging to communality, altruism and the pursuit of shared values and collective endeavours. In this process we will be able to grasp why it is implicit in MacIntyre's narrative that the capitalist market economy is perhaps the paradigm case of a system that favours what MacIntyre calls external over internal goods. As we shall see this is precisely what the early advocates of the capitalist system (before its triumph) believed it would achieve. This will therefore enable us to highlight precisely what it is about the market mechanism that makes it so inappropriate for the achievement of, as Paul Piccone has put it, 'a social individuality where ethics and politics are continuous with each other'.[43]

Hirschman's starting point is the emergence in the sixteenth century of a sense of crisis and disarray, the intellectual origins of which we have already referred to and can recognise in Hirschman's sense of:

> A feeling arose in the Renaissance and became a firm conviction during the 17th century that moralising philosophy and religious precept could no longer be trusted with restraining the destructive passions of men. New ways had to be found, which meant a detailed and candid dissection of human nature.[44]

This was the crisis of authority in late medieval and early modern Europe, as the old institutional forms and intellectual defences of medieval Europe were forced to come to terms with the new social forces: powerful independent states supported by new economic power.[45] But what possible response was there to this situation? Clearly the newly powerful rulers and states could themselves be appealed to to provide the necessary coercion and repression.[46] However, such an appeal lacked a certain intellectual coherence. Given the pessimistic views of human nature that were increasingly dominant, appeals to monarchs or rulers to act always wisely with reason and justice seemed to be asking of them what seemed to be impossible to ask of ordinary people.[47]

A second option that seemed to be rather more promising, lay in the notion of harnessing the potentially destructive passions of people, using the state and society as a transformer of 'human nature' for the greater good of all. This notion was clearly set out by Bernard Mandeville and followed later by Adam Smith.[48] In Mandeville's *The Fable of the Bees* skilful politicians were to manipulate the human vice or passion of luxury for the good of society. As is well known, Smith developed this notion in *The Wealth of Nations*, celebrating the 'invisible hand' operating through individual self-interest. But as Hirschman points out, Smith made an absolutely crucial semantic move: 'Smith was able to take a further giant step in

the direction of making the proposition palatable and persuasive: he blunted the edge of Mandeville's shocking paradox
by substituting for "passion" and "vice" such bland terms as
"advantage" or "interest".[49]

We must note a third option, really a subtle variant of
the second, but of great importance for understanding the
triumph of so-called external over internal goods (see below,
Chapter 6). This third option can be called, following Hirschman, 'the principle of the countervailing passion'. Here it was
suggested, assuming the awesome power of human passions,
why not use a relatively innocuous passion as a means of
limiting or restraining other more dangerous ones. But then
the question arises, what is to be thought relatively innocent
and what potentially politically destructive. The key to the
problem lies in the way in which certain passions or vices
become detached from others, and renamed under the label
'interest'. The passions all lumped together for condemnation
included ambition, lust for power, greed, sexual lust, avarice,
etc. Interestingly, Hirschman notes that in the many tracts on
the passions that appeared in the seventeenth century: 'no
change whatsoever can be found in the assessment of avarice as
the "foulest of them all"'.[50] This was the position it had
achieved towards the end of the Middle Ages.[51]

Given this position, it was ideologically necessary to enable
certain passions to triumph, for them to be redefined and in
effect renamed, under the rubric notion of 'interest'. In the
sixteenth century the term 'interest' began to be used in
common parlance in a way that shifted its meaning away from its
traditional legal sense[52] to become a notion expressing concerns and aspirations by no means limited to material aspects of
a person's welfare. But it always carried with it an element of
reflection and calculation on how this welfare was to be
achieved. In particular this was the sense others emphasised, in
relation to Machiavelli, in regard to statecraft, although he does
not use the term.[53]

However, by the middle of the seventeenth century we can
note the semantic drift in the meaning of interest towards
material and economic aspects. In this respect it parallels the
development of other words about this time, like 'corruption',
which Machiavelli had used to describe a decline in the quality
of government, but by the eighteenth century this word, especi-

ally in Britain, had become so tied to bribery that it drives out the other more inconclusive meaning. Much the same thing happened with the word fortune, with its older use again in Machiavelli (fortuna) covering most aspects of human endeavour,[54] but reduced gradually to the gaining of wealth in 'seek your fortune'.

Here the work of Benjamin Nelson is pertinent; obviously his well known work on changing attitudes to usury parallels our narrative,[55] but his lesser-known essay on the changing conceptions of friendship highlights changing notions of self and its relationship with money, which in turn parallels changing notions of friendship between states in international law, in the period from the sixteenth century to the eighteenth century. This reveals a similar drift from wider to more narrow notions of interest. Nelson argues that Antonio's surety for Bassanio in Shakespeare's *Merchant of Venice* represented medieval ideals:

> In the history of the ideal of Friendship, Shakespeare stands at the parting of the ways. The ancient and Renaissance ideals of friendship, as well as the medieval ideal of sworn brotherhood . . . was ambivalent and inviduous: friends and sworn brothers are supposed to share all goods, services and sentiments including hatred of one another's enemies. By Shakespeare's day the wordly-wise were already denying the usefulness of 'exaggerated' manifestations of friendship.[56]

Shakespeare seems to defend the friendship–surety motif in the play. Nelson argues that many Elizabethans shared Sir Walter Raleigh's views:

> suffer not thy self to be wounded for other men's faults, and scouraged for other men's offences, which is surety for another; for thereby millions of men have been beggared and destroyed paying the reckoning of other men's riot and the change of other men's folly and prodigality; if thou smart, smart for thine own sins.[57]

In the sphere of international relations, Nelson argues that from the sixteenth century onwards there is a systematic movement away from the 'utopian' ideal of the medieval and classical world. In accordance with the emergence of generally universalistic concepts of relations, which seem to parallel Kantian notions of personal morality, friendship between nations becomes more and more something to be defined negatively rather than positively, as Nelson says:

> All nations not formally allies or enemies seem to be reckoned as friends. It is held to be natural, desirable and mutually profitable for all men and all nations to be friends. However, little more seems to be meant by this proposition than that nations and individuals alike, are obliged to do their best – not to make others hostile to themselves.[58]

To sum up then, by the eighteenth century, one set of passions formally described as greed, avarice, etc. were seen as capable of being used to restrain other passions such as ambition, power lust, and sexual lust. In Hirschman's words:

> once money-making wore the label of 'interest' and re-entered in this disguise the competition with the other passions, it was suddenly acclaimed and even given the task of holding back those passions that had long been thought to be much less reprehensible.[59]

Hirschman's explanation of this takes us right back to the core of MacIntyre's argument, for he suggests that the term 'interests' actually carried – and therefore bestowed on money making – a positive and curative connotation deriving from its recent close association with the idea of a more enlightened way of conducting human affairs, private as well as public.[60]

Interest, as a concept, caused so much excitement because it seemed to provide a realistic basis upon which the social order could be founded, based upon the principles of 'predictability' and 'constancy' for as Sir James Stewart put it: 'were miracles wrought every day, the laws of nature would no longer be laws: and were everyone to act for the public, and neglect himself, the statesman would be bewildered'.[61]

The pursuit of economic self-interest could now be seen as a valuable instrument of social coordination as well as leading to national material prosperity. But most crucially for MacIntyre's account, the pursuit of economic interest with its 'predictability' and 'constancy' was a natural part of, and complement to, the new philosophies of the natural sciences and human nature, with their increasing emphasis on the Fact–Value distinction in morality. In a later chapter we see how MacIntyre argues that these intellectual moves foreshadow the way managerial power will operate with apparent value-neutrality and claim manipulative authority for itself, to an extent that MacIntyre will argue: 'twentieth century social life turns out in key part to be the concrete and dramatic re-enactment of 18th century philosophy'.[62]

It is with Adam Smith that Hirschman's account attains its apogee as 'interests' and 'passion' are seamlessly merged. In Smith's *The Theory of Moral Sentiments* he states:

> For what purpose is all the toil and bustle of this world? What is the end of avarice and ambition, of the pursuit of wealth, of power, and pre-eminence? . . . From whence . . . arises the emulation which runs through all the different ranks of men and what are the advantages which we propose by that great purpose of human life which we call bettering our condition? To be observed, to be attended to, to be taken notice of with sympathy, complacency and appreciation are all the advantages which we can propose to derive from it. It is the vanity, not the ease or the pleasure, which interests us.[63]

Here, as Hirschman notes, is the 'final reductionist step turning two into one'.[64] Here, economic interest is no longer separate from or restraining other desires, but rather seen as a means for their achievement. Non-economic desires are still seen as very powerful but they smoothly fit into and reinforce the drive for economic interest.

Adam Smith is describing and responding to a society in which the pursuit of external goods has triumphed over internal ones, in which the fateful transition to a capitalist market economy has been more or less accomplished. The pursuit of rational interests will be seen as a predominant dimension of social life. It becomes a key feature of social explanation from more positivistic Marxists, to the enormous literature on 'rational choice theory' and 'economic theories of democracy' and much else.[65] Most of these theories take rational, calculable and predictable aspects of human nature for granted, and like Smith, assume they can be used for the purposes of explaining human behaviour or as a means towards social and political integration. Claus Offe makes the point from within Marxism-cum-systems theory:

The ownership of the means of production, market competition and the private use of capital are institutional means that serve to separate the problem of system integration from the process of will formation, collective action and societal control. For an essential feature of markets is that they neutralise meaning as a criterion of production and distribution.[66]

This neutralising process reveals the deep connection between the triumph of bureaucratic managerialism and that of the market. For the role of the manager like the market is premised on the fact and value split. Just as the capitalist market cannot operate without the manager (for very specific reasons see Chapter 5) neither can the manager, as a pervasive authority figure, exist without the social and cultural triumph of particular conceptions of self and self-interest – over the older conception of both passions and virtues. It is in this context important that Adam Smith is the author of both *The Theory of Moral Sentiments* and *The Wealth of Nations*, for he along with his contemporary Scottish Enlightenment intellectuals, like Adam Ferguson and John Millar, marks the shift from a philosophical moral discourse to political economy and social science, a shift which is both partly constitutive, and partly a register, of the so-called 'Great Transformation'.

So far we have unravelled a little of the specific intellectual processes by which the market-dimension (implicit but underdeveloped in MacIntyre) of the culture of 'bureaucratic individualism' became triumphant. That is in short, how the intellectual and institutional fragmentation of the medieval synthesis created conditions which allowed key critical intellectuals to bestow upon the emerging capitalist market relationships a benign aura. At the very least this meant viewing them as innocent, clean, gentle, passions; at the strongest, seeing in them a new regulative principle of society that might preserve peace and harmony.

THE MARKET AND THE VIRTUES

Karl Polanyi in virtually all his writings sought to oppose ideas, popular with some economists and economic and historical anthropologists, that aimed at a unified economic theory which could cover all human societies past and present. Polanyi's contention is that those who have attempted to uncover an overall economic science, have imposed concepts derived from their understanding of market economies on to non-market ones. In this process, he maintains that they have done what we noted in the work of Alan MacFarlane; seeing past societies as filled with acquisitive individualists and thereby supporting the theory of human nature held by Adam Smith and his followers.

Polanyi sets out his basic theoretical orientation both in *The Great Transformation* and in a lengthy essay 'The Economy as Instituted Process'.[67] Here, he makes the very Weberian distinction between 'substantive' and 'formal' economies – a point, as we shall see, of considerable importance for his relationship with MacIntyre's work. Polanyi argues that:

> the substantive meaning of economic derives from man's dependence for his living, upon nature and his fellows. It refers to the interchange with his natural and social environment, in so far as this results in supplying him with the means of material want – satisfaction.

In essence this definition is alike to what Marx means by the concept of 'use value'. Whilst:

> the formal meaning of economic derives from the logical character of the means–ends relationship as apparent in such words as 'economical' or 'economising'. It refers to a definite situation of choice, namely that between the different uses of means induced by an insufficiency of those means.[68]

Clearly Polanyi's notion of formal economies also owes a great deal to Weber's notion of 'rationalisation', and we shall have cause to return to an analysis of the formal notion of the market economy later. For the moment it is enough to note that Polanyi believes the formal definition is readily applicable to the capitalist industrial societies of the west, and that to apply its terms of reference to earlier pre-market societies can only cause grave distortion. Indeed, he goes so far as to argue that:

> The two root meanings of economic, the substantive and the formal have nothing in common. The latter derives from logic, the former from fact. The formal meaning implies a set

of rules referring to choice between the alternative uses of insufficient means. The substantive meaning implies neither choice nor insufficiency of means: man's livelihood may or may not involve the necessity of choice and, if choice there be, it need not be induced by the limiting effect of a 'scarcity' of the means; indeed some of the most important physical and social conditions of livelihood such as the availability of air and water or a loving mother's devotion to her infant are not as a rule, so limiting.[69]

It is clear from Polanyi's comments that what he terms the empirical or substantive economy must in some sense exist everywhere. The crucial difference between market and non- or pre-market societies is that in these latter societies the economy is 'embedded' within the overall society, whilst in the former it is not. What does this embeddedness consist of? Principally Polanyi is referring to a wide range of non-economic institutions such as those of kinship, religion, political/state forms, that provide the context within which economic functions proper are performed. The consequence is that the goals or ends of economic activity are to a considerable degree shaped by these non-economic institutions and values, and it is almost never left simply to small groups or individuals to pursue their own material self-interest. This contradicts Adam Smith's move of subsuming a whole gamut of human desires and aspirations within the one moment of economic self-interest. Polanyi's view also has in its favour the fact that it is not based upon a static view of human nature. For Polanyi argues, in a whole variety of societies, tribal ones, small hunting or fishing communities, and even in great empires such as those societies at one time referred to as 'oriental despotisms':

> Neither the process of production nor that of distribution is linked to specific economic interests attached to the possession of goods, but every single step in that process is geared to a number of social interests which eventually ensure that the required step be taken.[70]

Is such a view based on romantic notions of primitivism and altruism? No. For, as Polanyi argues, in the case of a tribal society it is unlikely that most of the time an individual's absolute interest in survival will be put in question, because the community keeps all of its members from starving, unless there is a disaster that threatens all of them. However, for this support to operate, the maintenance of social ties is quite crucial:

> Firstly because by disregarding the accepted code of honour, or generosity, the individual cuts himself off from the community . . . second because in the long run, all social obligations are reciprocal, and their fulfilment serves also the individual's give-and-take interests best.

Polanyi goes on to suggest that the nature of these social relationships may be such that there is pressure

> on the individual to eliminate economic self-interest from his consciousness to the point of making him unable, in many cases (but by no means all), even to comprehend the implications of his own actions in terms of such an interest.[71]

So in non-market societies the human economy is enmeshed firmly in a variety of institutions both economic and non-economic, and this means that: 'religion and government may be as important for the structure and functioning of the economy as monetary institutions or the availability of tools and machines themselves that lighten the toil of labour'.[72] Crucially, therefore, an analysis of the changes in the role of the economy in society turns out to be: 'no other than the study of the manner in which the economic process is instituted at different times and places'.[73]

Clearly then, at the abstract level, the corollary of this notion of non-market societies being enmeshed economies within other dominating frameworks is that in market societies the economy with a capital 'E' is no longer so embedded. The market means that there is in some sense, a differentiation of economic activity into a separate institutional sphere, no longer regulated by norms that have their origin elsewhere. The individual economic agent is free then to pursue economic self-interest, without 'non-economic' hindrance.

One commentator on Polanyi, Joel Whitebrook, has argued that this concept of a disembeddedness of the economy requires modification; he states that:

> While it is true that economic activity becomes disembedded in market society in so far as economic activity is not

thoroughly merged with other activities and attains a realm of its own, none the less the economy, this independent realm as a whole, is itself embedded in an institutional and normative matrix without which it could not exist. The notion of the disembeddedness of the economy is therefore somewhat misleading. It would be less misleading to speak of the emancipation of economic activity ... what ought to be understood is that the denormatisation of economic activity does not preclude the existence of a new normative structure.[74]

Although the main drift of this point is largely correct and unexceptionable, it is rather unfair to Polanyi. The reference to 'denormatisation' is used by Whitebrook without citation or reference to Polanyi's works. Neither in *The Great Transformation* nor in Polanyi's essays is there an explicit or implicit argument claiming that market societies possess no norms, or that in some sense they have not generated a new normative structure. In fact, the very opposite view seems to be implied in the following: 'For once the economic system is organised in separate institutions, based on specific motives and conferring a special status, society must be shaped in such a manner as to allow that system to function according to its own laws.'[75]

However, having cleared Polanyi of the charge of theoretical naivety, it is important to add that the whole question of the relationship of the capitalist market and the strictly bourgeois realm of values and motivations is a complex one. Habermas, for example, has argued that capitalist societies have always been dependent on pre-capitalist norms and cultural traditions: 'Motivational structures necessary for bourgeois society are only incompletely reflected in bourgeois ideologies. Capitalist societies were always dependent on cultural boundary conditions that they could not themselves reproduce; they fed parasitically on the remains of tradition.' He goes on to point out, many of the traits we have rather unthinkingly associated with capitalist modernity are themselves based upon the past:

The 'Protestant ethic' with its emphasis on self-discipline, secularist vocational ethos, and renunciation of immediate gratification, is no less based upon tradition than its traditionalistic counterpart of uncoerced obedience, fatalism, and orientation to immediate gratification. These traditions cannot be renewed on the basis of bourgeois society alone.[76]

The issue of tradition is important for both Polanyi and MacIntyre (see final chapter), neither of whom believes that a pure capitalist market is possible. However, they both assert that there is a radically distinctive quality to bourgeois capitalist societies that mark them out from any other. Polanyi is at pains to stress the radical novelty of the market order of nineteenth-century capitalism compared with any other society from virtually any period:

> Whether we turn to ancient city-state, despotic empire, feudalism, thirteenth-century urban life, sixteenth-century mercantile regime or eighteenth-century regulationism – invariably the economic system is found to be merged in the social. Incentives spring from a large variety of sources, such as custom and tradition, public duty and private commitment, religious observance and political allegiance, judicial obligation and administrative regulation as established by prince, municipality or guild.[77]

It is worth noting that Polanyi does not deny that markets existed in many of these societies, rather his main contention is that isolated markets did not link up into an economy that made the rest of society a kind of appendage to it.

We are now in a position to understand MacIntyre's stated dependence on Polanyi's historical narrative in *The Great Transformation*.

In the first place as we have seen, MacIntyre believes this account is important for the narrative of *After Virtue* because it avoids common methodological errors, but yet treats the transformation as a total process. But MacIntyre's preference runs much deeper than this. In essence this is because Polanyi's account carries a moral charge, which emphasises the novelty and immorality of the transformation of human labour and the natural world into commodities. It is also characteristic of Polanyi's analysis that the similarities between pre-modern societies are emphasised, in contrast to that of the modern, as in the last quotation. We can compare this with the following, from MacIntyre:

> the modern world in everything that makes it peculiarly

modern is a society of strangers, that is, a society where the bonds of mutual utility and of appeals to rights have replaced older conceptions of friendship which pre-suppose an allegiance to the virtues.[78]

Both MacIntyre and Polanyi are involved in locating what is specifically new within modern western societies. In Polanyi's case he does not for a moment deny the enormous variety of institutional and economic forms present within the very different types of society that he lists, but he does insist that for all their differences there are some core elements of similarity, i.e. the embeddedness of the economic within the social. This is precisely the structure of argument employed by MacIntyre. In order to be able to locate and illustrate the unique aspects of the modern, MacIntyre must be able to extract, for purposes of comparison, elements of similarity from beneath the apparent diversity of moral concepts in pre-modern societies. His task is perhaps more difficult than Polanyi's, but they possess a unity of purpose none the less.

MacIntyre examines the role of the virtues in Homer, Aristotle, the New Testament and then for further comparison two more recent figures, Benjamin Franklin and Jane Austen. They would appear, at least at first, to have very different notions of the virtues, suggesting perhaps, that they differ as much amongst themselves as they do from our culture. The problem seems to become worse when one considers the enormous variety of social and cultural contexts that they inhabited. It is quite explicable in cultural terms that Homer saw the warrior as the model of human excellence and achievement, whilst Aristotle in the changed context of a fairly stable Athenian city-state, saw goodness and virtue embodied in the Athenian gentleman.

MacIntyre points out that in the case of Aristotle:

certain virtues are only available to those of great riches and high social status, there are virtues which are unavailable to the poor man, even if he is a free man. And those virtues are on Aristotle's view ones central to human life; magnanimity . . .[79]

No greater contrast could be found than in the New Testament, for here are virtues that find no place in Aristotle's thought such as faith and hope, but there is also praise for something

Aristotle would probably have seen as a vice, humility – the corresponding vice to his virtue of magnanimity, as he understood it. Aristotle's social priorities are reversed in the New Testament, as slaves seem to have more chance of achieving virtue than rich men.

The situation is no easier when we move to later figures like Jane Austen and Benjamin Franklin. For MacIntyre argues that in Austen we find an immediate contrast with Aristotle, for where he sees a virtue in 'agreeableness' she sees only the artificial simulation of a genuine virtue she calls 'amiability'. The difference lies in the latter's Christianity, as she attaches importance to the need for some real feeling to be involved. The case of Franklin is different again: 'Franklin includes virtues which are new to our consideration such as cleanliness, silence and industry; he clearly considers the drive to acquire, itself a part of virtue, whereas for most ancient Greeks this is the vice of pleonexia.'[80] Franklin is a complicating case for MacIntyre, as we'll see below, because of his relation with, and proximity to the modern market order. He is, none the less, important because there are few clearer examples, from his period, of the systematic redefining and reordering of older conceptions of the virtues.[81]

The differences, therefore, are numerous, and there seems little common ground. However, so far we've looked at particular virtues and changed definitions, but what of the underlying structure of argument in the placing of virtues in their various social contexts. We will see that at this deeper level similarities emerge.

To elucidate the underlying structure of virtues, we can follow MacIntyre's definitions of his five cases. In Homer, a virtue is a quality which enables someone to do exactly what it is that their social role requires of them; so that 'the concept of what anyone filling such-and-such a role ought to do is prior to the concept of a virtue; the latter concept has application only via the former'.[82]

In Aristotle, despite some virtues only being possible for certain kinds of people, his basic notion of human virtue follows his general understanding of metaphysics; virtue attaches to the nature of man's being as such. (Aristotle's metaphysics are briefly examined in the excursus on Marx.) It is the telos of humanity as a natural kind species which decides what behaviour counts as a virtue. But in the New Testament, although its virtues are different from Aristotle's, none the less, as MacIntyre argues: 'A virtue is, as with Aristotle a quality, the exercise of which leads to the achievement of the human telos. The good for man is, of course, a supernatural and not only a natural, but supernature redeems and completes nature.'[83]

We can add to this, that for MacIntyre's argument there is another extremely important similarity between the Christian and Aristotelian conception of the virtues; that is that for both, the relationship between means and ends is an internal one, and not external. What is meant by this, is that the means by which the end is achieved are inseparably connected, so that the very process of movement and development, partly constitutes what it is to achieve the end itself. It is, of course, precisely this internal relationship between means and ends, that Polanyi describes in his location of the role of the economy in pre-modern societies. Naturally, it is this deep parallel between the role of virtues in Aristotle and in the New Testament, that allows Aquinas to make his famous synthesis between the two. But MacIntyre argues for a deeper parallel between these two and the type of outlook represented by Homer. For both Aristotle and the New Testament, the concept of 'good life for man' comes prior to any particular virtue or hierarchy of virtues; so in Homer the concept of a person's social role was prior to any notion of a virtue.

In regard to Austen, MacIntyre (echoing C. S. Lewis and Gilbert Ryle) is able to subsume her also within the Christian and Aristotelian traditions; the latter she probably gained from reading Shaftsbury, he suggests.[84] The case of Franklin is more complex but interesting. MacIntyre's account is too brief here and requires supplementing. Franklin, in his understanding of the virtues, shares Aristotle's teleology, but his reasons are utilitarian ones. For MacIntyre this means that his conception of means–ends relationships are external rather than internal, i.e. governed by utility:

> The end to which the cultivation of the virtues ministers is happiness, but happiness understood as success, prosperity in Philadelphia and ultimately in Heaven. The virtues are to be useful and Franklin's account continuously stresses utility as

a criterion in individual cases: 'make no expense but to do good to others or yourself. Avoid trifling conversation'.[85]

These are typical of Franklin's ideas of the virtues, along with punctuality, industry, frugality plus many others, but always for utilitarian ends.

On the face of it, Franklin's utilitarianism may seem to pose problems for the argument so far developed. For utilitarianism features in *After Virtue*, and in much else of MacIntyre's work, as a paradigm viewpoint of modernity, which prioritises the pursuit of external goods and is, hence, ideally compatible with a rationalistic market order of society. For such a viewpoint the simulation of virtues would be quite sufficient to get what one wants, e.g. a hard-working reputation for credit-worthiness. But if this is true how can it be that Franklin has a teleological vision of the virtues?

The answer to this lies in Franklin's location as a transitional figure between two radically different cultures. His apparently pragmatic utilitarianism is in fact sustained by something far more fundamental, for as Weber puts it after noting the potential hypocrisy of Franklin's position:

> The circumstance that he ascribes his recognition of the utility of virtue to a divine revelation which was intended to lead him in the path of righteousness, shows that something more than mere garnishing for purely egocentric motives is involved.[86]

In effect, Franklin illustrates well the point we drew from Habermas concerning the dependence of capitalist societies on cultural boundary conditions that cannot be renewed by themselves. Franklin's teleological view of the virtues is therefore sustained by a key element in the tradition which saw the virtues as a system of internal goods leading to determinate ends, to which behaviour was subordinated. As is well known, later utilitarians such as Mill were to remove this underpinning from the theory.

In summary, MacIntyre argues that we have three conceptions of the virtues here: firstly, that a virtue is what enables an individual to carry out his/her role: this is the view present in Homer; secondly, a virtue is a human quality that allows an individual to move towards achieving a specific human telos, which can be supernatural or natural: the position of Aristotle, the New Testament authors, Aquinas and Jane Austen; thirdly, a virtue is a quality which has 'utility' in achieving earthly and heavenly success: held by Benjamin Franklin.

Is there, then, within these three forms, some core concept or shared conception of the virtues? There is enough here for a provisional judgement (we return to this in the final chapter). It should be noticed that one aspect of the virtues has emerged with some clarity. It seems to be the case that for the concept of virtues to operate at all in a society: 'it always requires for its application the acceptance of some prior account of certain features of social and moral life, in terms of which it (virtue) has to be defined and explained.'[87] This means that in Homer virtue is secondary to and dependent upon a clear concept of social role. In Aristotle and related accounts, it depends on what the 'good life for man as the telos of human action' is defined as. In Franklin it is dependent upon some specified notion of utility. For each of these writers prior agreement on crucial aspects of social and moral life cannot be merely theoretical, it must have some material embodiment for their conceptions to have any purchase at all. The obvious examples are the role of the Polis in Aristotle's thought – perhaps we should say more accurately that the Polis makes Aristotle's thought possible – the role of the Church for New Testament writers.

This is the heart of the matter. The very diversity of these writers and the cultures they in part represent, all, nevertheless, imply and demand some definite institutionalisation for their conception of the virtues to operate. Jane Austen requires a type of agrarian capitalism – a country house and a certain form of the institution of marriage – for her Christian Aristotelianism. This is the deep structure of similarity that unites these writers even in their diversity and most importantly what distinguishes them most profoundly from modern liberal individualistic thought. It can make no assumption about social context, except to say no way of life must have institutional precedence over others.

The parallel and connection with Polanyi is clear: for just as the wide diversity of pre-market economic forms all require embedding within some wider set of social relations to avoid economics being a narrow means–ends relationship of self-interest, so with MacIntyre's account. In order for virtue to be exercised, or even understood, there must be criteria embodied in some shared account of our own context. When that shared account collapses, then the moral self is as disembedded as economic relations are in the market place.

Chapter 4

The morality of markets and the 'crisis of authority'

Notes for a sociology in a world after virtue

In *Whose Justice? Which Rationality?*, MacIntyre sets up an opposition between two types of social order that existed in the eighteenth century, where passions and interests had become redefined (following broadly Hirschman) in such a manner as to constitute social relationships as market relationships. This, of course, is the social order of England. The second social order MacIntyre considers is Scotland and the contrast he draws could hardly be sharper. For Scotland in the eighteenth century was able to understand itself through a network of distinctive religious, educational and legal institutions which gave it a powerful Protestant public doctrine. These institutions were the precondition for the existence in Scotland of a:

> type of society which is understood by most of those who inhabit it as exemplifying in its social and political order principles independent of and antecedent to the passions and interests of the individuals and groups that compose that society . . . requires for its maintenance the generally shared possession – not necessarily universally shared – of some account of the knowledge and a set of institutionalized means for bringing those principles to bear on the issues of practical life.[1]

Much of the content of the second half of *Whose Justice? Which Rationality?* is devoted to outlining the contribution of this philosophical/theological tradition and to its intellectual subversion, as MacIntyre sees it, by David Hume (see especially Chapters 12, 13, 14 and 15). MacIntyre is in effect narrating the intellectual history of the social and economic defeat, albeit partial, of one social order by another, more economically powerful.

The England of the eighteenth century had a quite radically new culture, at least as compared with a society like Scotland, for England was by this stage the type of society in which appeals to moral standards:

> in such a type of social order will be such that to express them is to endorse the standpoint of mutual reciprocity in the exchange of benefits ... Thus the appeal to standards – moral, aesthetic, political standards of right judgement and action – will itself be a form of participation in the shared transactions of social exchange. The standards themselves will function within and as an expression of this form of political and social order ... They link, not individuals as such, but individuals identified in terms of the resources which they possess and upon which they can draw in contributing to the exchanges which constitute social life.[2]

This is essentially a society of property holders, in which status and power flowed from property, and to be without property invited the status of victim. Perhaps the most vital issue about this social order is that it prevents any appeal to any external or absolute standard of judgement:

> because all appeals to standards of right judgement and action are internal to that same system, functioning as expressions of attitude within it, there cannot be from the standpoint of this form of social and political order any well founded appeal against the property relations of the status quo to a standard of right external to that social order, to a standard expressed in principles whose truth would be independent of the attitudes and judgements of the participants in the order.[3]

Yet this powerful contrast between two very different social and cultural worlds, although very effective in revealing the crucial role of institutional life in preserving a coherent social and moral discourse, is not quite the whole story. It was possible to stand in England for an alternative vision, perhaps an England, as MacIntyre notes, with pre-Reformation roots. To do so might be deviant and hard to articulate in terms of the dominant discourse, but none the less the changes that had affected

English society were so great that they were bound to trouble those who inherited other traditions, other than that of the triumphant Whig modernity.

The process Polanyi commented upon, of turning nature into landed capital, was completely in place throughout the eighteenth century, although its consequences are only clear with hindsight. However, it is only in the latter part of the century that the other crucial component, the turning of human activity into labour as a market commodity, was achieved, as we shall see in a moment. By drawing on some of the conceptual resources of MacIntyre, we get a clearer picture of the contradictions at the heart of a market-based modernity and gain some sense of how his work helps us recast a sociology of the market. We can be assisted by firstly trying to understand the paradoxical position and attitudes of England's 'Old Society' to the market order they helped create. This issue is caught in a telling observation by MacIntyre:

> Burkeans, who, faithful to Burke's own allegiance tried to combine adherence in politics to a conception of tradition that would vindicate the oligarchical revolution of property of 1688 and adherence in economics to the doctrine and institutions of the free market. The theoretical incoherence of this mismatch did not deprive it of ideological usefulness. But the outcome has been that modern conservatives are for the most part engaged in conserving only older rather than later versions of liberal individualism. Their own core doctrine is as liberal and as individualist as that of self-avowed liberals.[4]

There is a great deal that can be unpacked from this quotation. The emphasis on tradition is important, for it marks a way of viewing oneself, one's class and one's nation's history, in a way that denies fundamental ruptures in life, even as, in this case, they had happened and were happening. It should perhaps be seen in the light of a probing remark by J. A. G. Pocock:

> Nothing could be more misleading than to picture the vehement assertion of the antiquity of English law and liberties as an inert acceptance of 'traditional society'. It was rather traditionalist than traditional . . . an assertion of conservatism; and conservation is a mode of action.[5]

The question of English 'traditionalism' is, of course, vast and too complex to really develop adequately here, but clearly the fact that in the eighteenth century the most advanced and successful European society could emphasise its continuity with its past is remarkable enough in itself. The assertion of the distinctiveness of England is present in both radical and conservative traditions with the concept of the Norman Yoke, on one side, and 'Great English Oaks' slowly maturing with the slowly evolving common law, on the other.[6] Clearly in Pocock's terms the powerful, innovative and successful landed class, towards the end of the eighteenth century, sought, through an ideologue like Burke, to stabilise its dominance via 'tradition' as a mode of action, to 'repair' the consequences of its own success.

Burke is a most interesting figure, for he attempted to provide some intellectual coherence for a landed class that was comfortable and prosperous, but still feeling its way to the liberal modernity of the cash nexus. Burke is widely known as the fierce opponent of the French Revolution, defender of rank, distrusting of reason, and as an icon of twentieth-century conservative European thought. His traditionalism is perhaps best caught in his definition of society - from his *Reflections on the Revolution in France* - as 'a partnership not only between those who are living but between those who are living, those who are dead and those who are to be born'.[7] However, the key issue from our point of view is that registered by MacIntyre, namely that Burke was also a staunch upholder and defender of the free market and capitalist property. He had long been interested in political economy and communicated with Adam Smith, who is reputed to have said of him 'that he was the only man who without communication, thought on those topics exactly as he did'.[8]

C. B. McPherson has been at some pains to defend the intellectual coherence of Burke, on the basis that capitalist property rights had been ratified in the 1689 settlement, to which Burke was loyal, so that capitalist relations had become the 'traditional society' of his time.[9] Such a view is highly questionable, not so much as a matter of intellectual coherence, but because Burke's commitment both to some paternalist relationships and to a free market political economy (he no doubt had a much firmer grip of this than most contemporaries) reflects a real tension in social relations and most particularly the mode of domination. These two commitments are in some part mutually exclusive, for paternalism, as historians as different as Perkin and Thompson insist, has to be something more than a show to disguise profit making. It demands not just subordination to rank, but some degree of reciprocity or mutual obligation for this 'field of force', as Thompson puts it, to exist.

In the end Burke could only come down on that side of paternalism that demanded subordination:

> the whole of agriculture is in a natural and just order; the beast is as an informing principle to the plough and cart; the labourer is as reason to the beast; and the farmer is as a thinking and presiding principle to the labourer. An attempt to break this chain of subordination in any part is equally absurd.[10]

He also realised that this would place great restraint upon, or demand great self-restraint by, the worker or labourer, seeing the apparent injustice in the relationship:

> They must labour to obtain what by labour can be obtained; and when they find as they commonly do, the success disproportioned to the endeavour, they must be taught their consolation in the final proportions of eternal justice. Of this consolation whoever deprived them deadens their industry, and strikes at the root of all acquisition and all conservation.[11]

He would not, however, take the final step which might make the paternalist hierarchy materially bearable; he would not allow interference with the labour market: he completely opposed the Speenhamland system.

The last five years of the eighteenth century saw very bad harvests and severe shortages and dislocation due to the French war; farm labourers' wages in several regions dropped beneath subsistence. Price rises in the period outstripped wages, but Burke's response was a product of his belief in the sanctity of the market: 'Patience, labour, sobriety, frugality and religion should be recommended to them: all the rest is downright fraud',[12] a response strongly reminiscent in our own day, for its implacable 'realism', of Enoch Powell on, say, Third World aid. However, across the low wage counties of southern England, JPs used a variety of measures such as subsidising food or topping up low wages; the alternative was hardship and even starvation. It is, of course, a moot point concerning who is being most faithful to the 'traditional order' (pace McPherson), triumphant property from the 'Old Wig' Burke or the Tory paternalism JPs of Speenhamland. But as the historian of social policy, Derek Fraser, has argued:

> social policy is an expression of social philosophy and a generation which resorted so quickly to allowances in aid of wages was clearly one which did not regard poverty or poor relief as degrading. Poor relief did not have the social stigma of debasement it was later to acquire.[13]

None the less, Burke's position confirms MacIntyre as to what notion of tradition Burke is defending, namely what we have termed the 'absolute rights of property'. The logic of this position for all its wrappings in rank, must pull it apart from the Tory paternalists with their real grasp of what the sociologist Zygmunt Bauman has called 'control-through-space' would mean as a system of hegemony.[14] It was significant that what became the Speenhamland system was really no more than a set of local initiatives; Parliament would do nothing. Pitt summed up the consensus in a debate on a Bill proposed to regulate wages in the dire and perhaps exceptional circumstances of the 1790s:

> It was indeed the most absurd bigotry, in asserting the general principle to exclude the exception, but trade, industry and barter would always find their own level, and be impeded by regulations which violated their natural operation, and deranged their proper effect.[15]

This was the wave of the future; it revealed that most 'advanced' opinion in the land-owning class accepted the logic of free market economics, although paternalism died hard at the local level, amongst Tory traditionalists. This now was the era of the Combinations Acts, the steady deregulation of labour and the freeing of the labour market which culminated in the Poor Law of 1834. This was what Carlyle referred to in his study of Chartism as the 'abdication on the part of the governors'. Perkin has summarised well the ultimate consequences of the contradictory social position that Burke so powerfully articulated:

Emancipation (from paternalism) was counterbalanced, and indeed provoked, by a rejection on the part of the higher ranks not of the whole relationship – for they insisted on paternal discipline and filial obedience, long after they were willing to pay the price for them – but of that part which alone justified it by the light and reason of the old society: paternal protection and responsibility.[16]

We can learn most about the ambiguities that the capitalist market generates in the position of the Burkean conservative, by contrasting it with the position of another conservative theorist, almost a contemporary but locked into a very different set of social relations: George Fitzhugh the defender of the slave-based society of the American South in the early nineteenth century.[17] Fitzhugh was probably the most sophisticated defender of slavery in the American South. Eugene Genovese has taken him as important because of this sophistication and self-consciousness, and sees in him more than an apologist for slavery but rather the emergence of a spokesman, and a relatively coherent theorist, for an entire class and social order. The Marxist Genovese pays Fitzhugh and his society a powerful tribute:

they did, none the less, stand for a world different from our own, that is worthy of our sympathetic attention. The questions they asked are still with us; the inhumanity they condemned must still be condemned; and the values for which they fought still have something to offer.[18]

Fitzhugh and his society cast an important light on MacIntyre's argument concerning the relatedness of the economic and moral forms of society, in that the Southern slave states of America had apparently a market economy, but they did not have what Polanyi or Genovese would describe as a market society. All George Fitzhugh's work was designed to make sure it did not get one. No market society existed for reasons that must now be fairly clear: there were areas of life in which markets could not form; principally there was no labour market. The relationship between master and slave is described by Genovese as 'organic', so although slave owners faced each other in the market place, labour existed in another realm.

The existence of exchange relations external to labour did not necessarily undermine the organic relationship between master and slave within. From 1808 onwards there were no new slaves coming from Africa, because of the British and later European ban. This meant that the Americans had to raise their own slaves, which inevitably required certain minimum standards of treatment. Genovese argues that any understanding of the Southern slave holders, 'must begin with an essential fact about their slaves: the slaves of the Old South constituted the only plantation slave class in the New World that successfully reproduced itself'.[19] This reveals more clearly than anything else could, the paternalist quality of the master, and the fairly good treatment of the slaves.

This material basis reveals a sustainable social order, at least in its internal relations. The plantation was the key institution, it was presided over by a resident planter who saw it as his home and the entire population of the plantation as a kind of extended family. Clearly the need to reproduce the absolutely crucial workforce provided a powerful motive for the paternalist ethos of the plantation to develop, but Genovese warns against any easy separation between economic interests and morals: 'once extended over a generation or two, the appropriate standards of treatment became internalised and part of the accepted standard of decency for the ruling class'.[20] The American War of Independence freed the South from British interference and allowed the slave owners to become a regional power. Given the social relations of production, Genovese argues that it is quite plausible to see the slave-owning class, taking its cultural model from the Old Virginian aristocracy, as on the way to becoming a landed aristocracy complete with an articulated set of anti-bourgeois values.[21]

George Fitzhugh was not in any sense typical of the South; no theorist is really typical since most people do not spend their time shaping their beliefs into a coherent logical form, but this is what he set out to do. He saw that the immanent logic of the plantation ideology led ultimately to a rejection of almost all bourgeois liberalism. He took the logical step of moving from the common belief amongst whites in the South, that Negro slaves were often better off than many 'free' workers and peasants in the western world, to arguing that slavery was the best system for every society and that ultimately capitalism was incompatible with Christian morality. Property was no absolute right; for him, it existed for the public good; he claimed: 'Slave property, like all other carries with it the duty of public leadership and a sense of responsibility towards the property-less. Society ultimately retains control of property; individual property owners are the trusted agents of society.'[22]

Fitzhugh acknowledged sympathy for socialism's arguments in his critique of capitalism. Indeed he saw the rise of socialism, in Europe, as a sign that capitalism there could not last. He accepted the need to overcome the alienation of capitalism, but did not believe equality was possible, and so was able to turn socialist arguments for the association of labour on their head, when he argued: 'The association of labour like all associations requires a head or ruler and that head or ruler will become a cheat and a tyrant unless his interests are identified with the interests of the labourer.'[23] Socialism was impossible, he believed, because it could lead only to the re-establishment of slavery. He was bitterly opposed to capitalism and the free market, for basically moral reasons; capitalism produced greed and ultimately destroyed all finer feeling and all bonds of domestic affection. His model of the relation between master and slave was familial, because the master is used to treating the slave as part of his family, so his sense of family is massively extended further than it ever could be under capitalism.

Therefore Fitzhugh's view, according to Genovese, is that: '"Capitalism" stands condemned as an enemy of the human race because it produces economic exploitation, degradation ... wherever capitalism has triumphed, the family has been undermined and all community has perished.'[24] It was above all the world market that carried the bourgeois to their position and it was the relentless external pressure of the forces of the market that Fitzhugh saw threatening the South. He knew slavery could only flourish free of the corrupting influence of the world market. He pinned his hopes on the collapse of European capitalism. He was no doubt foolish in his hope, but as Genovese says:

> What else could he have thought? His wisdom led him to see what few others could. Slavery could not exist much longer as a social system in contradistinction to and as an occasional or peripheral labour system, in a bourgeois world.[25]

Fitzhugh has never been taken up by modern Conservatism and we hardly need Genovese to tell us why, for the answer is clear from MacIntyre's account. Most modern Conservatives are committed to capitalist property relations and older forms of liberal individualism that help constitute those relations. The archaic George Fitzhugh standing outside those relations could articulate a genuine alternative, free of the one-sided obfuscations of an Edmund Burke. Fitzhugh's message for us is clear, and is, to quoted Genovese one last time:

> If you will the world to be thus, then you must will the social relations that alone can make it thus . . . Fitzhugh's message came to one simple point that few if any conservatives still want to hear: To have a world without market-place values you must have a world without a market-place at its centre. Go backward or go forward, but if you are in earnest, then go.[26]

THE SOCIOLOGY OF MARKET RELATIONS

If we view the onset of modern social relations as the onset of market relations then England's 'Great Transformation' was completed by the late eighteenth century. Economy was separated from society; the formation of markets was now a sacrosanct process, including the formation of labour markets. This process had hollowed out the substance of Burkean paternalism; morals and markets were separate. Burke's rhetoric stood to sanctify 'old' capitalist property relations as they followed into whatever profitable avenues were available. The market makes its own demands on the lives and minds of peoples, including theorists. The propertied class were to continue to insist upon moralising the economic behaviour of their subordinates and employees, but it was a moralising, as MacIntyre has seen so clearly, that took exchange relationships as normative. For this process to work, the 'character' and the 'passions' of the workers had also to be refashioned. But here a paradox should be noted that is not really grasped by MacIntyre's rather functionalised depiction of the English market order, quoted at the beginning of this chapter. For as Bauman has noted, the campaign for the creation of a work ethic amongst early industrial workers seems to be an attempt 'to exempt the workers from the rule of market rationality', i.e. greatest gain for least cost 'rather than, as common interpretations would like us to believe, to train the crude, preindustrial labour force in the art of life guided by commercial reason'.[27]

MacIntyre's rather ideal type contrast between England and Scotland is certainly useful for throwing light on some quite crucial cultural and institutional differences. However, MacIntyre's own analysis, especially *After Virtue*, reveals the difficulties and contradictions and, indeed perhaps, near impossibility of a society dispensing with all elements of the tradition of the Virtues. Once again we see capitalism's dependence on what we have seen Habermas refer to as pre-capitalist 'boundary conditions', for its continuation. Bauman argues that these English capitalists attempted to recreate 'the commitment to task performance which came to the craftsman naturally when he himself was in control of his time and work rhythm',[28] or in MacIntyre's terms, try to recreate the conditions in which craftmanship was still a set of distinctive social practices, that emerged from and extended a set of goods that were internal to those practices. Such attempts were, and are, constantly eroded by the workings of the market economy, as the 'rational' route to material well-being becomes quite clear to generations of workers.

It is now possible to see what at least the first stage of a MacIntyrian sociology of the market should look like. Clearly it must be a sociology that highlights the processes that undermine the practices that are the social embodiment of the tradition of the Virtues. As it happens we already have something of such a sociology, despite its apparently neutral tone, in the work of Georg Simmel. For the work of Simmel (to a lesser extent Weber)[29] reveals him as the sociologist of the triumph of 'external' over 'internal' goods as embodied in social practices.

Simmel's *Philosophy of Money* is preoccupied with the everlengthening 'teleological' chain of connections that spin out from the money economy, for the achievement of any given end. Money and the market principle, as we saw with Adam Smith's fateful reduction of human aims and aspirations to an economic drive, is the 'absolute means which is elevated to the psychological significance of an absolute purpose'. This as he goes on to acutely observe, is because there is no reason to, 'fear [it] being dissolved into something relative, a prospect that makes it impossible for many substantial values to maintain the claim to be absolute'.[30] In other words, as he puts it later:

As a tangible item, money is the most ephemeral thing in the external-practical world, yet in its content it is the most stable, since it stands at the point of indifference and balance between all other phenomena in the world.[31]

This seems very much what MacIntyre means by a society that can only recognise external goods (internal ones being goods that cannot be understood independently of the end, purpose or good of the practice of which they are part). External goods are those which can be most easily subsumed, in the manner of Adam Smith, within economic interest. McIntyre adds: 'And in any society which recognised only external goods competitiveness would be the dominant and exclusive feature.[32]

This would be so for the reasons Weber gives when he states that:

Within the market community every act of exchange . . . is not directed in isolation by the action of the individual partners in the transaction but the more rationally considered the more it is directed by the actions of all parties potentially interested in the exchange [a potentially almost infinite external series]. The market community as such is the most impersonal relationship of practical life into which a human being can enter.[33]

It is the centrepiece of Simmel's works to focus on the consequences for a society, of it being dominated by the impersonal nature of these exchange relationships and the connection between this and the subjective and objective aspects of contemporary human experience.

Simmel is certain that the dominance of the market principle makes for greater freedom for the individual in his or her relationship with others, but at the same time increases the subjection of people to the process of measurement and bureaucratic regulation. As Turner puts it in his paper on Simmel: 'Money is thus consistent both with individuality and individuation.'[34] Simmel, in effect, tells the story of 'The Great Transformation' principally from the subjective side. The consequences of the presence or absence of money relations in European history at its most abstract are put into three parts: the first stage is one in which:

the feudal lord's rights are extended to the whole of the

obligated person who had to forfeit his most fundamental possession or rather his being. This would have been the price at which the lord would have granted (for example) his female subjects the right to marry. The next stage is that he granted this right – which he can deny at any time – in exchange for a sum of money; the third stage is that the lord's veto as such is abolished and the subject is now free to marry if he or she pays the lord of the manor a fixed sum: bride-wealth, marriage money, bridal money, etc.

He goes on to point out that money is obviously connected with personal liberation but not completely at the second stage because the lord can reject payment: 'The relationship is completely depersonalised only when no factors other than money payment are involved in the decision.'[35]

What then is the relationship between this process of de-personalisation and 'freedom'? To understand this, Simmel attempts to examine the specifics that continuing relations of dependence possess. 'The money economy' he argues 'makes possible not only a solution (to dependence) but a specific kind of mutual dependence which, at the same time, affords for a maximum of liberty.'[36] In the first place this happens because a massive range of quite unknown obligations develop; for many reasons, including the diversified technical division of labour and the growth of banking and finance houses, which lend the funds of small and large savers and investors to anonymous others. Naturally these myriads of connections produce anonymous dependence: 'For these people gain their significance for the individual concerned solely as representatives of those functions such as owners of capital and suppliers of working materials. What kind of people they are in other respects plays no role here.'[37]

So money, when it achieves dominance, i.e. when a society is based on capital accumulation and commodity exchange, makes possible, because of its flexibility and divisibility, a great range of economic relations, whilst at the same time removing the personal element from them by its objective and com-pletely indifferent character: 'we are compensated for the great quantity of our dependencies by the indifference towards the respective persons and by our liberty to change them at will.'[38] Compared with all non-market societies with 'embedded' economies, we are extraordinarily independent of particular members of society because their relationship with us has been transformed into an objective quality, which can be effectively done by numerous others.

Simmel observes that: 'this is the most favourable situation for bringing about inner independence, the feeling of individual self sufficiency',[39] but this is by no means simply to be understood as an absence of relationships, because 'freedom' is not simply a state of inner being of an isolated subject, such a state exists rather when, 'extensive relations to others exist [but] all genuinely individual elements have been removed from them so that influences are anonymous':

> The cause as well as the effect of such objective dependencies, where the subject as such remains free rests upon the interchangeability of persons: the change of human subjects – voluntarily or effected by the structure of the relationships – discloses that indifference to subjective elements of dependence that characterises the experience of freedom.[40]

The narrative of the stripping away of the relations of personal dependence and authority, can as we have seen with George Fitzhugh, be viewed in a different light, which exposes the ambiguity of freedom. It can be seen as in MacIntyre's view, as 'having suffered a deprivation a stripping away of qualities that were once believed to belong to the self',[41] i.e. notions of personal identity founded upon sets of personal relations with others. Simmel, politically and ideologically a liberal, was well aware of the dark side of this, although clearly committed to the process. He saw in the situation of the industrial worker the problem clearly illustrated: compared with a slave, who could not change his master under any circumstances, a worker has a formal freedom to do so. Viewed in one light then the worker is on the way to personal freedom despite his present poor state: for here, as in other spheres, there is no necessary connection between liberty and increased well-being. This is because:

> the freedom of the worker is matched by the freedom of the employer which did not exist in a society of bonded labour. The slave owner as well as the lord of the manor had a personal interest in keeping his slaves and his serfs in a good and efficient condition.

He adds that freedom for the labourer is in effect paid for 'by the emancipation of the employer, that is by the loss of welfare that the bonded labourer enjoyed'.[42]

This takes us close to the heart of liberal market freedom and reveals more clearly the relationship between a particular sense of self and a particular economy, for freedom to engage in a market order means a change, 'from one of stability and invariability to one of liability and interchangeability', therefore, 'the relationship of individual persons to others simply duplicates the relationship that they have to objects as a result of money'.[43]

This, then, shows us the dilemma facing both Burkean conservatives and market socialists. For standing inside the pale of the market they must follow its logic and its cultural consequences. What then, happens to them? A leading liberal theorist, Ronald Dworkin, in a very public attack on the New Right in the 1980s, has provided some pointers. He argues that modern western politics is fundamentally about two issues: 'how to improve production and how to distribute it more fairly'.[44] He points out that 'arguments about privatisation for example, are not about the metaphysics of exploitation or the validity of Marx's labour theory of value, but about whether public or private ownership is *more efficient*' (my emphasis). He further claims that behind the old left–right divide, what we really have are two different and conflicting distributive theories, which both emerge from nineteenth-century liberalism not Marxian socialism.

The first of these theories is 'an informal, statistic-based version of utilitarianism. The present British government aims (successfully or not) at efficiency because it assumes government should make the community prosperous over all, for most people and in the long run'. The second theory is based on the notion that government should treat all individuals with equal concern. Rawls is its most sophisticated theorist: 'serious economic inequalities are justifiable only if they work for the benefit of those at the bottom', and this may lead to less than the overall maximum prosperity. Naturally this position has nothing to do with what he calls the 'ancestral' left of Marxism and class consciousness, rather he calls it 'Fabian'. And naturally this requires a degree of benign state intervention to carry out the redistribution of non-functional inequality and therefore to assess the position and needs of the individual.

Dworkin is an authentic voice of modernity, his views are the conventional wisdom of the age, and incidentally not just of the 1980s and 1990s, they were really the dominant assumptions of the whole period from 1945 in the west. The two versions of liberalism he outlines, fight it out under the rubric of individualism versus collectivism. The first version, to which Burkean conservatives are prone in practice, demands the classical bourgeois self of 'possessive individualism', the proprietor of his own person, the ability to enter contracts freely, contracts being the model of all human relationships. The second version of liberalism requires a self who also owes something to the Lockean 'possessive individual' tradition, but is also the ghostly inheritor of the moral philosophy and institutional changes that began in the eighteenth century, an abstract but unique self as moral agent, on a par with all other such agents.

This second version – it might be called social democratic liberalism – inheriting such a notion of self, must inevitably separate any notion of right from any particular conception of the human good, each individual must develop as they supposedly abstractly choose. No one can claim a privileged conception of the human good. No government, state, or historical community's views can be binding on the whole society. All that can be demanded of the state in terms of values, is its claim to protect freedom embodied in positive law.

Simmel in the course of his analysis of the multiple but anonymous dependencies generated by the proliferating possibilities of exchange in the market, examined this abstracting process at work. The particularity of real personalities was removed:

> such a personality is almost completely destroyed [by] . . . a money economy. The delivery man, the money lender, the worker . . . do not operate as personalities because they enter into a relationship only by virtue of a single activity . . . The general tendency . . . undoubtedly moves in the direction of making the individual more and more dependent upon the achievements of people, but less and less dependent upon the personalities that lie behind them.

Were this tendency to continue he argues, it would 'exhibit a profound affinity to socialism . . . for socialism is concerned primarily with transforming to an extreme degree every action of social importance into an objective function'. Interestingly he compares this with the role of the official whose position is objectively preformed so only limited aspects of his personality can emerge. So Simmel claims: 'fully fledged state socialism would erect above the world of personalities a world of objective forms', so eventually it could be that the official:

> no longer individually differentiated simply passes through the function without being able or allowed to put their whole personality into these rigidly circumscribed individual demands. The personality as a mere holder of a function or position is just as irrelevant as that of a guest in a hotel room.[45]

Simmel saw socialism as did the SPD as a rationalisation of capitalism, emerging from capitalism's own tendencies and ideologies.

This conception is that of abstract liberalism and has been well summed up by Brian Barry in his critique of Rawls:

> The essence of liberalism as I am defining it here is the vision of society as made up of independent autonomous units who co-operate only when the terms of co-operation are such as to make it further the ends of each of the parties. Market relations are the paradigm of such co-operation.[46]

Such a view may be a realistic vision of modern society as 'nothing but a collection of strangers each pursuing his or her own interests with minimal constraint'.[47] Can such a view of society and its concomitant concept of self be sustained, or are there elements in the cultural boundary conditions that capitalism is dependent upon, which provide a potential space from which a contrary view of self and society can be generated? These issues and some of the dimensions of MacIntyre's response to them are touched upon in the conclusion.

Chapter 5

Managerialism and the culture of bureaucratic individualism

The civil servant has as his nineteenth-century counterpart and opposite the social reformer: Saint Simonians, Comtians, utilitarians, English ameliorists such as Charles Booth, the early Fabian socialist. Their characteristic lament is: if only government could learn to be scientific! And the long-term response of government is to claim that it has indeed become scientific in just the sense that the reformers required.

Alasdair MacIntyre, *After Virtue*, p. 82

MARKET RE-EMBEDDING?

Fred Hirsch in his important book *The Social Limits of Growth*, has pointed to the real purposes of the so-called 'mixed economy', and to its problems as a mechanism for overcoming the crisis of authority in the market order. He sees it thus:

The essence of this strategy is to impose the necessary minimum of central control and guidance on an economy whose operating units remain motivated by individualistic aims and horizons and are guided by these individualistic aims in everyday behaviour.[1]

Essentially Keynesianism is an economic strategy to correct the systematic dangers within laissez-faire for liberal culture. In this respect it becomes important to note, with MacIntyre, that it was Keynes who wrote, on reading G. E. Moore's presentation of emotivist ethics: 'it was exciting, exhilarating, the beginning of a renaissance, the opening of a new heaven on a new earth.'[2] For Keynes, as Hirsch has pointed out, the role of the state as a guide for the market economy, was really a culmination of secular liberalism. It attempts to provide economic prosperity, along with market preference and maximising individual freedom: Keynes was 'attempting the ultimate in privatization – the addition of morality to the sphere of individual choice'.[3] This reworked liberalism for the twentieth century, meant that the managed market was still to be the market, and as such did what liberals wanted of it, i.e. to be neutral, for morality was what individuals would choose.

Hirsch, therefore, is aware of the critical relationship between the capitalist market and liberalism, its connections and its difficulties. His arguments are in some respects similar to both Polanyi and Habermas[4] in that he argues for the dependence of capitalism on pre-market and non-market forms, such as welfare intervention to cope with market dis-welfare and the necessary regulatory supervision of markets, to see they maintain a rational basis. Most important for Hirsch, is the production of a moral or normative framework, providing the necessary self-controlled, truthful, agents for contractual relations.

Hirsch argues that this moral legacy, which he views principally as a kind of religious capital stock, has been steadily depleted. His framework for understanding this tends to be a rather simple version of the secularisation thesis[5] and an emphasis on the operations of the capitalist system itself. In the latter part of the argument he makes a valuable contribution, as we will see. Religion's role in relation to capitalism is, of course, complex. In contrast to Hirsch, and following MacIntyre's general thesis, we are concerned with the collapse in the connection between moral frameworks and the social order, not their disappearance altogether. It is rather this separation that produces a privatisation and subjectivising of belief which achieves its apotheosis in the concept of emotivism (see Chapter 1). In relation to religion as a form, this is well brought out by Turner:

> impersonal property in late capitalism no longer requires the discipline of bodies or the physiological regulation of populations with the separation of moral bodies and regulated property, religion no longer significantly contributes to the unity of social classes, the discipline of bodies or the reproduction of economic relations.[6]

This does not imply that capitalism does not require normative grounding, rather that it achieved its autonomy as an economic system by rejecting religious regulation, but by also being parasitic upon the social character forms constructed by the older systems. However, the long-run consequences of this separation has meant that religious and communal forms are less reliable in producing the necessary characters, because once less socially central these forms are more likely to change or decay.

This is especially true when considered in relation to the operations of the capitalist system itself. For, as MacIntyre notes, all social orders imply a moral sociology and a moral philosophy. The market's moral framework is not sufficient (indeed has never existed on its own) to sustain non-market elements. But Hirsch points to what he terms the 'commercialisation effect' carried through by a 'commodity bias' which 'implies that an excessive proportion of individual activity is channeled through the market so that the commercialised sector of our lives is unduly large'.[7] Because of the search for profit maximisation this commercialisation increases, and leads to substituting explicit exchange relations for what were once informal sectors. It favours the presence of those services and items which can be most easily commodified and to the likely absence of that which cannot easily be treated so. This inevitably means an increase in individualistic concepts of self-interest as the area of communal goods shrinks and conceptions of the common good become increasingly thin.[8]

The consequences of this for Keynesian and more generally other forms of corporatist social organisation are important. Firstly, the form that the state and other managing institutions took, and their emergence as a neutral bureaucratic body, is a central problem. Hirsch could clearly see the difficulty of maintaining the liberal division, so dear to Keynes, of individual motivation and wider social results. As he argues:

> It involved the progressive extension of explicit social organisation without the support of a matching social morality – more rules for the common good, having to be prescribed and adhered to in a culture orientated increasingly to the private good. The burden placed on individual morality has in this way been greatly increased.[9]

Within this framework, and as the market system makes no claim beyond itself for legitimacy, the response of an individual within a bureaucratically regulated market is likely to be in terms of its own criteria. This means the appeal for reward for risk and effort is generally applied. We noticed in the last chapter Bauman's contention that early capitalists fabricated the 'work ethic' to elude this process. But because of such processes as 'commodity bias', the market framework will bring to prominence questions of 'fairness', i.e. the conditions of the contract become problematic. Profit maximisation means most reward for least effort. On this perspective, the various 'corporatist' experiments that precede the collapse of the Keynesian consensus look like very weak attempts to reintegrate one aspect of the labour market, namely wage levels, within the state as nominal representative of society.

The partial nature of this process is clear to most workers, because most other aspects of the market, including prices and control over the labour supply, are not so integrated. This means that what Hirsch calls *acquisitive power*, the product of market opportunity due to 'physical productivity, scarce talents, good contacts, scarce information and good luck'[10] is not restrained. Whilst the organisational power of, say, trade unions is. In developing Hirsch's work John H. Goldsthorpe notes that: 'within a growing market economy, market relations and the principle of "equal exchange" tend to enter an ever-enlarged area of social life, as the dynamics of the "commercialisation effect" work themselves out' which tends to undermine a

> status order of a wide ranging structure of relationships that are formed not by the 'cash nexus' but by obligation . . . grounded in moral acceptance . . . the distribution of economic advantage and in authority in work relations, class inequalities come increasingly to be seen for what they are – the products of the market economy – without the benefit of the normative camouflage which the status order previously created.[11]

The corporatist strategies of the bureaucratic state to patch up the spontaneous workings of the market economy, appear almost pathetically weak, lacking any real normative power. As such they have been replaced in most western countries by the grim discipline of the market mechanism.

The capitalist market remains the fundamental reality of western, 'modern' societies. But if the market erodes those

forms upon which it has depended, what mechanisms of control
and power are available to these social orders? It is to the
analysis of the apparently neutral, managerial and bureaucratic
forms of power, that we now turn.

MANAGERIALISM, IDEOLOGY AND ARBITRARY WILL

How then are power, coordination and cohesion maintained,
within the context of western liberal individualist conceptions
of the self, but still potent market mechanisms? MacIntyre gives
us part of his answer in the emergence of bureaucracy and its
embodiment in the form of the manager. It is essential to grasp
the relationship between this particular notion of self, and the
form of bureaucratic state which is its necessary complement.
We will piece together this process throughout this chapter,
but for the moment we must note MacIntyre's understanding
of the emergence of bureaucracy. He argues: 'It is when
traditions begin to break down that modern bureaucratic
organizations characteristically arise. Traditional societies have
always had formal organizations, always had to justify themselves against appeals to the authority of the tradition which
the organization served.'[12]

These traditions can be various, from the Catholic Church to
the disciplines of the natural sciences. The autonomous self can
have no conscious tradition but it requires managing. The
manager is generally seen in our culture as morally neutral and
in virtue of the skills he possesses, can devise the most efficient
means of achieving whatever end is proposed. He or she is the
supreme example of the prioritising of external over internal
goods: in appropriately Weberian terms, the high priest of
formal as opposed to substantive rationality.[13] The upshot of
this is that concepts of efficiency and effectiveness become the
ultimate source of their own legitimacy and become inseparable
from a form of practice in which the achievement of ends
means, of necessity, the manipulation of human beings into
compliant patterns of behaviour.[14] But if the manager is neither
morally neutral nor possessing special expertise, then once
more in human history we are presented with ideology and
spectacle, masking the exercise of power and domination. But is
this, in reality, the case?

MacIntyre claims that managerialism is a moral fiction,

because the kind of knowledge required to maintain it, does not exist, and that the claims of modern social science to possess such knowledge, are largely false. Managers, he claims, require something like factual law-like generalisations which would enable them to predict that if an event occurred, then some other event, of a specific kind, would result. In other words managers need causal explanations to control the social environment. Now we can break the claims of bureaucratic managerialism down into two component parts.

1 That there exists a domain of morally neutral facts about which the manager is to be an expert.
2 That law-like generalisations and following applications to particular cases, can be derived from the study of the domain of facts.

It hardly needs pointing out that the great bulk of what we know as social science from the days of Comte, through Weber himself (though he sought probabilistic laws), to the managerial sciences and organisational studies of our own day, have been concerned with variants of these two related issues. If bureaucratic power is an ideology (in the sense we will discuss below) then social science is what Marxist social scientists and other radicals, like M. Foucault, have always said it was, a crucial accomplice in domination.

But the question is, are these two points true? The nub of MacIntyre's response is clear; it consists, as he puts it, in turning W. V. Quine's *Word and Object* on its head.[15] Quine argues that to provide a science of human behaviour precise enough to have a law-like character, then it must be formulated in such a way as to eliminate all references to reasons, intentions and purposes, on the part of the human subjects involved. This is because knowledge of the beliefs of the subjects, and the massive complexity this would then introduce, due to the inherent contestability of beliefs, would not produce the kind of evidence which could be used to confirm or contest a law. MacIntyre agrees, but, because of his teleological Aristotelianism, regards a science of human behaviour which made no reference to beliefs or to intentions to be not worth having. Here he is able to build upon his earlier work presented in such papers as 'The Essential Contestability of Some Social Concepts' and 'Is a Science of Comparative Politics Possible?'[16] in which the normative character of almost all the key concepts of social life makes the notion of a 'scientific' debate about, say, education or political parties, quite impossible. When we categorise educational institutions, as we must if we are to make generalisations about them, we make implicit judgements about the norms that define education. It is no response to such a view, to simply accept public or more commonly state definitions of such institutions, for these too are normative judgements. To accept such definitions as neutral is to covertly introduce normative judgements in the spurious disguise of science.

In essence MacIntyre is arguing that no science of human behaviour can have the mechanistic quality that *may* be possible in the natural sciences. The principal reason for this is that our human behaviour is above all else a matter of the intelligibility of action, to ourselves, in the first place, and, of course, to others. In a paper on this issue MacIntyre has argued that a human action

> is an intelligible sequel to the immediately prior action or actions and as such presupposes an interpretation of that behaviour to which it is a response as an action of such and such an intelligible kind. Were we unable to evoke such responses we would be unable to participate in those networks of transactions within which the actions of individual agents find their place.[17]

If understanding intentions is vital to understanding social action, then what are we to make of the well known attempts in the nineteenth century to produce a mechanistic science of human society. MacIntyre notes that 'prophecies in this area may be translated not into real achievement, but into a social performance which disguises itself as such achievement'.[18] MacIntyre then proceeds in *After Virtue* to examine the fallacious underpinnings of such a project.

The most important element is to remember that bureaucrats and managers want, above all else from social predictions, knowledge concerning the outcomes of alternative policies, and that social scientists are very poor at providing such knowledge. If we look at one of MacIntyre's examples: Smythe and Ash have shown that forecasts based on the most sophisticated economic theory for the OECD since 1967 have produced less successful predictions than would have been arrived at by common sense, or naive theories for forecasting rates of growth, such as extrapolating the average rate of growth for the past ten years.[19] MacIntyre puts forward four reasons for supposing that the predicative law-like generalisations that bureaucratic power requires are in fact impossible to achieve, now or ever in the future.[20]

1 Radical conceptual innovation in the natural sciences or other disciplines cannot be predicted (he is following Popper) because in certain important ways making a prediction about what will be invented, has in some part contributed to inventing it already, at least as a concept, e.g. it is suggested that at some point we will be able to grow back damaged limbs. This cannot claim the status of radical innovation, because it puts together two elements of existing knowledge. a) Certain reptiles grow back limbs and this is connected with their genetic code; b) The existence of genetic engineering, which may allow humans to do the same. It follows that any new discovery based on radically new concepts cannot be predicted, therefore neither can their consequences.
2 This concerns the unpredictability of individual agents' actions. Briefly put, this entails the simple notion that if I have not made up my mind between two different courses of action, I cannot predict which one I will take. Others will possibly be able to estimate what my action may be but will not be able to predict their own future choices, which will in consequence have their effects on other people's choices including my own, and so on ad infinitum. As MacIntyre points out, following Aquinas, omniscience excludes making decisions: 'If God knows everything that will occur, he confronts no as yet unmade decisions. He has a single will'[21] which, as MacIntyre also points out, may give us some idea of what those who want to get rid of unpredictability are trying to do.
3 A further source of unpredictability can be understood because of the efforts of game theorists, in the social sciences, to predict the future. All complex situations have an open and indeterminate character, e.g. a general strike or a war have no limited set of factors which can be said to comprise 'the situation', situations are never static and anything with an international dimension is probably unmappable. Furthermore game theory is endlessly reflexive, 'I predict your move,

you predict mine. I predict you predict mine', etc. etc.
4 Finally, we come to the role of pure contingency, also present in 3. A crucial agent dies before getting to a meeting, or someone is ill and can't concentrate; such events can make all the difference. Incidentally, anyone who believes that awareness of contingency is alien to Marxism should read Trotsky's *History of the Russian Revolution* on the crucial role of Lenin, in making the Revolution.

All this does not imply that generalisations about social life are impossible or that a measure of predictability about life is impossible or that social science is worthless. It does imply that a well founded and thoroughly researched generalisation about the social world, will have to live with counter-examples to it, as it does now. Also that social science should not treat all predictive errors as a failure. The absurdity of the grander claims of social sciences to be able to predict the world, are, I would suggest, one of the reasons for their recent experience of disillusionment amongst their potential client groups.

MacIntyre, in his paper 'Social Science Methodology as the Ideology of Bureaucratic Authority',[22] elaborates his argument concerning the legitimising role of the social sciences for the bureaucratic manager. He argues that conventional social science methodology incorporates a very particular and limited view of the social world in its methodology, which in turn dovetails with the concepts and needs of managers and bureaucrats. He denotes five corresponding elements between social scientists and bureaucrats. Firstly, he claims the world is seen as composed of discrete and identifiable variables. Secondly, that the researcher can label these in a neutral and non-contestible way. Thirdly, that the process of conceptualisation about the subject matter, is a matter of his scientific convenience rather than culturally determined by social factors outside the discipline, e.g. 'operational definitions'. Fourthly, the researcher constructs law-like or probabilistic generalisations from the data. And finally, fifthly, the kinds of generalisation sought, provide some lever for producing reasonably predictable events in society; in other words, it provides those with access to this knowledge and resources, with certain types of manipulative ability.

The response of many social scientists will be that this ideal type is really a straw man. Donald Levine, for example, protests that few sociologists now want to produce universal, law-like generalisations but now rather concentrate on probabilistic ones.[23] In fact MacIntyre is well aware of this, but argues that restriction to probabilistic conclusions would not alter the nature of the methodological enterprise.[24]

The key question is why do private and public bodies commission research? Certainly not principally out of intellectual interest. Is it really possible for a social scientist to honestly admit that none of their number have aspirations summarisable in MacIntyre's five points? What of those in organisational theory, or business studies, who, like Herbert Simon, the author of a classic text of that genre, *Administrative Behaviour*, could write in the 1960 edition: 'We can predict that in the world of 1985 we shall have psychological theories that are as successful as the theories we have in chemistry and biology.'[25] But the affinity of this conception of social science with bureaucracy only becomes apparent when we see MacIntyre's description of the bureaucrat.

> First the bureaucrat has to deal in discrete items which can be given an established and unique classification . . . secondly the classificatory scheme which it gives rise to, which in an important sense creates those (discrete) variables, must itself be treated as non-contestable. The scheme has to be accepted independently of the evaluative viewpoint of particular individuals or social groups. Thirdly it is the bureaucrat who is free to create the classificatory scheme; it is he, who, so to speak, operationalizes his concepts so that items will be handable by him in his way.[26]

Obviously these correspond precisely to the form of the ideal typical, methodological scheme he set out. In themselves, they embody the idealised self-picture of bureaucratic practice.[27] The same is true for the final two elements, because the bureaucrat must operate upon the classified materials, to produce desired consequences, so he or she must be equipped with sets of rules that correspond to causal generalisation. The operation of these rules then has definite effects, i.e. social manipulation.

It is crucial to understand that MacIntyre's argument is, in important ways, a culturalist one. He is not claiming that bureaucracy or social science directly correspond to these forms, but that it is significantly important that they both exist together, in our culture, as modes of legitimation. The claim is that when authority is challenged, or answers are demanded for a problem, it is to these cultural forms that appeal is made. In this process conflict is made both marginal and manageable; technique and modes of manipulation triumph over the claims of substantive value.

It seems, then, we may well be in the presence of ideology, dependent, like all ideology is, on partial truths. There are built-in features of uncertainty in human action, but can probabilistic approaches fill the expert gap? MacIntyre argues not, because statistical correlations cannot alone provide a definite causal link between factors and because the social sciences have inherent problems of repeatability of *sets* of events, not present in the natural sciences.[28]

It would seem that the law-like generalisations, the expert bureaucrat or manager requires, are not available. But what of the other prior condition, that is, that there exists a domain of morally neutral facts, about which he (expert or bureaucrat) discovers out there, and then confronts us with. For even if law-like generalisations are not possible, cannot, at least, a manager or bureaucrat claim to be a master of the 'facts', and hence, the unavoidable nature of reality with which we must live. This is a peculiarly important claim within our culture, which takes us to the very heart of the claims made for the liberal state, and those of citizenship, and sovereign subjectivity. For a crucial dimension of modern liberalism has been the gradual withdrawal of the state from judgement about values and beliefs. This was partly the product of, and partly reinforced by, intellectual and ideal tendencies, which moved in the direction of the separation of 'is' from 'ought', 'facts' from 'values' or formal from substantive rationality; crucially for MacIntyre, in the philosophical and scientific rejection of Aristotle and the consequent giving-up of any notion of 'man-as-he-could-be-if-he-realised-his-telos' in favour of something like 'untutored-human-nature-as-it-is'.[29] In the first context ethics allows a human being to pass from where they are, to where it is in their nature to go. In the second, one is left with basic human nature on one hand, and a system of ethics on the other, which seem radically incompatible with one another, with no linking concept of necessarily guided development to an end. With the consequence that, ever since, moral conservatives like Kant have advocated duty in ethics, whilst radicals have emphasised release.

So, in the social and political realm, it has been common now for several centuries to deny the possibility of deriving an 'ought' from an 'is'[30], hence the strong emphasis placed on purely negative liberties in that tradition. Also the strong imperative to distinguish a distinct domain of empirically know-able entities uncontaminated by 'spurious' metaphysical as-sumptions like teleology. The implications of this radical dis-tinction between the domains of values and facts are quite awesome when transferred onto the analysis of social relations. For once normative value judgements had been thoroughly severed (a process that historically has taken a good deal of time to work through, in western societies)[31] from the binding externalities of both nature and social relations, they became the property of the sovereign liberal subject's choice. Then liberal theory becomes false, even on its own terms; this is because sovereign subjects must be free to choose, which they cannot all be; society must cohere, social relations continue, cohesion be achieved. It therefore follows that those liberal subjects who manage or engineer social reality, have little choice but to treat others in the manner of a Quinian social science programme. This is because intentionality and sub-jectivity are far too complex and lack the durability to enable them to be specified in a manner that might allow, other things being equal, accurate prediction.

MacIntyre explains: 'the concept of a state of belief or enjoyment or fear involves too many contestable and doubtful cases to furnish the kind of evidence we need to confirm or disconfirm claims to have discovered a law.'[32] What seems to happen when this is tried, is that subjectivity is frozen into the tabulated forms of public opinion polls or market research findings, which transpose consciousness into one more set of objective disconnected social facts to be accounted for in the process of manipulation, in line with the manager's subjective valuation of necessity.

MacIntyre notes, utilising Marx's *Third Thesis on Feuerbach*:

What Marx understood was that such an agent (i.e. manager)

is forced to regard his own actions quite differently from the behaviour of those whom he is manipulating . . . he stands at least for the moment as a chemist does to samples of potassium chloride and sodium nitrate . . . but [in the process of the] . . . changes the technologist of human behaviour brings about, [he] must see exemplified not only laws which govern such changes, but the imprinting of his own will on nature or society.[33]

Nichols and Beynon found this approach permeating managers' thinking, in that most sophisticated of 'managerial' industries, chemicals:

One manager pointed to a maintenance market board. 'Pity we haven't got one for labour. You know, with a column here to tell you which ones are defective, one for those completely u/s, one for replacement' . . . for the most part this view of workers as things – as people – objects, to be worked on – takes more subtle forms. But that managers think like this is not surprising, in view of these men's technical training and the job they are paid to do, which involves thinking in terms of 'labour costs' and treating the labour-power of other men as a commodity.[34]

This seems to support the view that liberal capitalist societies are, as Marx noticed (above all in the *Grundrisse*), societies of personal independence based on objective dependence. In this way they are not 'societies' in a traditional sense at all. Social coordination must take the form of either 'legitimate' coercion in the name of rational necessity or the manipulation of other apparently 'independent' wills, in accordance with social 'need' or 'utility', as expertly as possible, by those with knowledge, competence, and above all else, power.

But as we have seen, such competence does not in any strong sense exist (i.e. in the degree necessary to legitimise the grand claims daily made). It therefore follows that much of what passes as objectively grounded claims by managers and experts, are unreal performances which legitimise the use of power. It is at this point that we must develop MacIntyre's account of bureaucratic power. This involves the question of the concept of ideology and of capitalism itself.

MacIntyre agrees that all his talk of masks and theoretical disguise is deeply connected with Marx's conception of ideology:[35]

> Yet of course part of the conception of ideology of which Marx is the ancestral begetter does indeed underlie my central thesis about morality. If moral utterance is put to the service of arbitrary will it is someone's arbitrary will, and the question of whose will it is, is obviously of both moral and political importance.[36]

He goes on to say, that it is not his task to answer this question. This seems to be rather disappointing, though clearly connected with his disavowal of politics especially Marxist politics, but also with his view that 'what we are oppressed by is not power, but impotence'[37] because no one has the knowledge of a law-like kind to confer that kind of real authority, claimed by managerialism. This is a more important point than it may at first appear, for it explains, in part, why totalitarian societies like Hitler's Germany and Stalin's Russia are so inefficient, as well as why anything like total control by management in a capitalist society, is impossible.[38] But MacIntyre does concede that he has no intention of denying that 'the activities of purported experts have real effects and that we do not suffer from those effects and suffer gravely'.[39] He is principally concerned to expose a masquerade of authority, but looking at the effects of that apparent authority is clearly of equal importance.

However, disappointment remains for several reasons. Firstly, the notion MacIntyre presents of the absence of any real control over capitalist society, including that of capitalists, is arguably central to Marxism. No one does, or can, control capitalism. The capital accumulation process controls capitalists, as well as workers, hence the understanding that they are alienated too. But secondly, and more importantly in this context, is the fact that the whole drift of his analysis points towards a view, as I have shown, that our current conceptions are partly due to our market-based capitalist culture. Indeed, Frederic Jameson has gone so far as to claim of *After Virtue*, 'that the first section of this book offers the most probing and devastating analysis of the reification of moral categories under capital, which we possess'.[40] And, of course, we have previously reviewed this relationship in connection with the narrative of 'The Great Transformation'.

The simple truth is that a crucial aspect of that transition is the rise of a managerial capitalism, with both ideational or ideological and material aspects. For on MacIntyre's own account, there seems no reason to deny that in large part, the interests that lie behind the exercise of 'arbitrary will' are those of capital. At least as conceptualised in a sophisticated manner as, say, for example, by Claus Offe.[41]

Whatever MacIntyre's doubts about some of the metaphysical and perhaps more importantly political dimensions of Marxism, it does seem sad that he, in his critique of managerialism has not chosen to deploy some of the important recent work, in this tradition, on the origins of bureaucratic managerial power by such writers as Marglin, Pollard, Braverman.[42] (This seems to rather strengthen some of the suspicions voiced by Peter Sedgwick concerning MacIntyre's self-imposed isolation from supporting intellectual positions in which he might find some degree of fellowship.)[43] For what these writers stress in a variety of ways, and with a variety of emphasis, is the emergence of a new type of control and authority, which is no longer decked out in the traditional forms and images of a hierarchical social order, and without the powers of compulsion that can be exercised over unfree labour.

The matter is complex, but it seems from work like Marglin's and Pollard's that the emergence of a generalised commodity-based economy posed specific problems for capitalists in relation to one special commodity, namely labour. The fluctuations of the market gave the commodity producers at certain phases of the economic cycle a degree of control and leverage, *vis-à-vis* the capitalist, especially over the rate and efficiency of production.[44] The factory emerges as a key institutional embodiment of what Giddens describes as the transformation of allocative (rights of ownership) into authority relations (rights of control) via what is in essence the dual nature of the worker as both a human being and a commodity.[45] The transformation is, of course, mediated via the labour contract, which makes a certain period of the workers' time the property of the employer, to be done with, more or less, as the employer thinks fit. The modern division of labour meant, however, more detailed control than ever before and it is this, of course, that provides the background to the question of scientific management. However, unlike either most Marxist writers on the labour process and radical analysts of the emergence of surveillance and the disciplinary society like Foucault, my concern is not to emphasise the potency and effectiveness of such things, but rather their role as an ideology and masquerade of power.

In this instance, it is interesting to parallel the above analysis by MacIntyre of the 'performance' of managerialism with a Marxist critic of Braverman. Michael Burawoy[46] argues that what is absolutely crucial about capitalism, at least at a higher industrial phase of technique where relative and absolute surplus value are equally co-present, is that the capital–labour relation obscures surplus value not only from the worker, but also from the manager.

Burawoy argues that, compared with feudalism, where the dues owed by peasants to their feudal lords made exploitation clear and open, capitalist relations allow no clear distinctions for either workers or capitalists, between the production of value and surplus-value. The struggle over the surplus between capital and labour is not over a tangible entity, visible to all. Profits are the product of complex procedures and are not normally constituted until well after the process of production has taken place. The workers' share of total value is the result of struggle, material, ideological and political. But capital's securing of the necessary surplus for capital accumulation to continue, is no clearer. This is because value depends not only on production, but also on realisation on the market – frequently an uncertain arena. Therefore how much capital can concede to labour is almost always a question that is genuinely uncertain; company 'figures', 'projected profits' are therefore part of the class struggle. This means that the coming to consciousness of the surplus is as much a function of ideological and political factors as of purely economic ones. It follows from this that scientific management had an extremely important ideological role, in that 'crucial aspect of domination under advanced capitalism, namely the appearance of ideology in the guise of science',[47] as a part of the process of obscuring and securing the surplus for capital.

How does this process work? Burawoy's major contention is that interests, i.e. class interests, are not given, they are shaped by ideological and political understandings. This means: 'that capitalist control, even under the most coercive technology still rests on its ideological structure that frames and organises "our lived relationship to the world" and thereby constitutes our interests'.[48] Drawing on William Baldamus's work *Efficiency and Effort*, Burawoy points to the way workers construct compensatory strategies as means of coming to terms with unpleasant or monotonous forms of work, or as he significantly puts it, 'work realities'.[49]

These strategies, as Burawoy points out, normally take the form of games, and are present in almost all work environments, as some element of psychological compensation, but also as a means of resisting management demands. However, Burawoy develops this point in important ways, he suggests: 'that participation in games has the effect of concealing relations of production, at the same time as co-ordinating the interests of workers and management'.[50] In this context a 'game' consists of a set of rules with a range of possible outcomes, and a preferential ordering of these outcomes. The appeal of the game is that it is both controlled, by the workers, yet uncertain in outcome. They provide the appearance of control and the exercise of reason and skill. In reality, of course, they have a marginal impact on the work environment, which generally sets severe limits on what can be done. But:

> the ideological effect of the game is to take 'extraneous' conditions (like having to come to work) as unchangeable and unchanging, together with a compensatory emphasis on the little choice and uncertainty offered in the work context. Thus the game becomes an ideological mechanism through which necessity is presented as freedom.[51]

Burawoy argues that, for the most part, shop managers aid and abet these games, especially those connected with output. The preservation of these work games is one of the ways the interests of workers and managers are coordinated; day to day adaptions of workers create their own ideological effects; it is this reality that managers help to shape and utilise, in moulding the opaque social relations of capitalism.

Managerial ideologies can also be part of the process of shaping the concepts of interest and coordination; it is in this light that Taylorism should be seen. In the US it may have had paradoxical effects, in making it more difficult to secure the surplus through intensifying control and sharpening class antagonism, rather than coordinating interest. However, it was, despite this, incorporated into the self-image of management.[52] Burawoy shows, by drawing on C. S. Maier's work,[53] that scientific management was taken up, and played a crucial role in the 1920s and 1930s, in those European countries facing political crisis. Both Right and Left took up the approach, Fascists in Italy, the new Soviet leadership, conservatives in Germany and even the IWW in the US. Although clearly all very different from one another, they all, as Burawoy puts it, 'shared in the attempt to transcend immediate political institutions by mobilising scientism in the projection of a utopian vision of a harmonious society where "politics" becomes superfluous'.[54]

This is the recurring theme of managerial ideologies, the offer of pure technique, neutral and value-free: the environment of MacIntyre's emotivist self, because of its obliteration of the distinction of power and authority, manipulation and non-manipulation. It is in some versions of the Human Relations school of management that this process reaches a peak, especially in the blurring of authority. James J. Cribbin of the American Management Association can write of what he calls the 'collaborator manager':

> He does not hesitate to be forceful when circumstances require, but he does not resort to directiveness as a matter of course. He prizes self discipline and constructive suggestion, over submissive conformity. Viewing authority as based on competence rather than position. This leader interacts with his followers in a process of mutual influence. As a team builder he realises that his objective is to help employees satisfy some of their needs, while achieving the goals of the group and the firm communication is free flowing, constructive and directed to the purposes for which the group exists. Finally, if possible, conflict is resolved by the synthesis of diverse views.[55]

Richard Sennett tells us that this is a common view, held by those involved in American management training. He points out that just because the language is vacuous, does not mean it does not have real effects. Like MacIntyre, he views these psychological concepts as 'means of human manipulation; the point is not simply for the employee to develop him or her self, but for the employee to become more loyal and productive in the process. And in practice the manipulation can be subtle'.[56]

Theo Nichols has shown how 'Human Relations' approaches, encouraging 'participation', can carry it through for complex reasons. It is partly done because of a feeling that workers are under-motivated. He reminds us that even F. W. Taylor thought a 'mental revolution' among workers a pre-condition for maximum efficiency in factory work.[57] But Nichols, like Sennett, sees little sign of this happening. Sennett claims: 'In the midst of tight economic periods as well as prosperous ones, what industrial sociologists call unmotivated resignations have been steadily on the rise.'[58] Nichols notes that ChemCo workers' expectations of work are low:

> Accepting they are workers they do not expect their work to be satisfying and they have entered into a grudging bargain with their employer. Part of just one more generation of working class men and women, well used to being denied meaning and control over their lives, like industrial whores, they do enough, to get enough. 'It's a job', they say. This, is the real problem ChemCo managers face.[59]

MacIntyre argues that the problem is located in the forging of concepts of work and interest, upon which bureaucratic capitalism depends, i.e. in the wider context of Burawoy's 'game' situation. Bureaucratic authority, as simple and effective power, is dependent on the apparent merging of interests, i.e. of a particular conception of work and the institutions within which it is carried out, both public and private. He claims that:

> the dominant way of understanding such work under capitalism – and not only in America – is that whereby workers, management and investors all share in the distribution of what is jointly earned. In order to get as much as possible, what matters is that as much as possible is produced.[60]

So this means all three groups have a common interest to which their particular interests ought to be subordinated. This is, of course, the dominant view within all major political parties in Britain and America. But the basis of it is the view, as MacIntyre notes, that 'men are primarily consumers and they work in order to consume'.[61] This can be seen as a quite rational and viable way of conceptualising interests in Burawoy's terms.

Central to MacIntyre's case, is the view that this way of

conceptualising work, is also much at home in public bureau-
cracies, inhabiting as they do a society where external goods
have triumphed over internal ones. Evidence for this view can
be found in the recent work of Beynon, Hudson and Sadler on
the rundown of two British nationalised industries. In examining the process by which the Horden Colliery in the North East
of England was closed, Beynon et al. discovered a quite distinctive quality to the managerial ideology of this publically
owned industry:

> This monopoly of coal production and of coal markets was
> mirrored in its claim to the monopoly of knowledge relating
> to coal-mining matters. This approach . . . was extended to
> the review procedure itself . . . British Coal took exception
> to the format of the review and to the idea that its repre-
> sentatives should be cross-examined by representatives of the
> trade unions . . . [It was clear] that in the company's view, the
> review should be conducted within narrow economic and
> geological parameters. It should not, for example, be ex-
> tended to consider indirect economic costs and certainly not
> the social consequences of mine closures. On these matters
> British Coal studiously folded its arms; it was not concerned
> to present or to attend to evidence which considered the
> wider implications of coal-mining redundancies upon the
> coal districts.[62]

Resisting mine closures has meant stepping outside the dominant forms of conceptualising economic interests in our society;
often by asserting the value of particular forms of locally based
communal life, as opposed to, on occasion, the acceptance of
large redundancy payments. But, MacIntyre insists that such
assertions are equally rational ways of viewing work, in terms of
seeing 'what is essentially human is rational activity and consumption exists to serve activity and not to be served by it'.[63]

When work serves consumption then it is bound in some
degree to be uninteresting and sapping of motivation, hence
the endemic problem of motivation in well ordered and successful areas of capitalism. On the first view my fundamental
interest as a member of one group, is how large a share of the
product I consume. But on the second view I can have no
fundamental stake in a social order based on such motivations.
If the first view prevails, then conflicts over interest will be local,

although sharp and real, but ultimately capable of containment by able management, mobilising common concepts of interest. These conflicts would be distributional or simply defensive in nature, whether over power, resources or money. But on the second view conflicts would be central and endemic. MacIntyre claims that the

> managing and owning class, do not have to fight this particular battle over interest and privileges, as fiercely as they might . . . because they have for the most part won the battle over how interest and privilege are to be conceptualised and understood.[64]

In this view MacIntyre is supported by comparative sociological studies by Duncan Gallie[65] and Scott Lash,[66] on British and French workers and American and French workers. These works reveal the importance of ideological concepts, and traditions embodied, of course, in organisational forms, in maintaining political radicalism and alternative conceptions of work. As Gallie puts it:

> the experience of work, even in an authoritarian setting, was not sufficient to account for the translation of class resentment into specifically political terms. Rather the extent to which workers believed that the existing structure of society could be remoulded through political action depended on their exposure over time to radical party ideologies.[67]

Similarly Lash claims 'that worker militancy is not primarily determined by objective variables, but by political parties and trade unions as agents of socialisation'.[68]

It would seem that the opaque quality of social relations under market capitalism, compared with feudalism, does indeed make for a culture in which emotivism is at home; in which power is legitimate, because of its effectiveness in achieving ends that are organisationally given. If values and ends are private judgements, then it is those values and ends implicitly institutionalised in the market that will command power and will be pursued. For without strongly institutionalised counter-tradition, the logic of the following sentence of Adorno becomes hard to resist: 'In the market economy the untruth of the class concept was latent; under monopoly, it has become visible as its truth – the survival of classes – has become invisible.'[69]

Chapter 6

Conclusion

Narrative and communities

> What 'ought to be' is therefore concrete; indeed, it is the only realistic and historicist interpretation of reality; it alone is history in the making; it alone is politics.
>
> Antonio Gramsci

In this conclusion I shall attempt to reveal what I take to be some of the potential for social scientists in MacIntyre's recent conceptual innovations around the issues of traditions, social practices and the idea of narrative, and will attempt to see what light his work casts on some fairly recent social and political conflicts. In general I will be drawing principally on MacIntyre's *After Virtue*. The reasons for doing this are largely practical and reflect something of the intellectual climate of the social sciences. In the first place, *After Virtue* was at least partly intended to directly address a social science audience, by dealing with some of the philosophical issues underpinning the debates about social science methodology. It is therefore hardly surprising that some of its conceptualisations are, perhaps, rather easier to 'operationalise', than the more historical and philosophical ideas of *Whose Justice? Which Rationality?* and *Three Rival Versions of Moral Enquiry*. Secondly it is, no doubt, true, that given the still strong Enlightenment prejudices of most western social scientists, the intellectual content of *After Virtue* is more acceptable to them than the arguments of the latter books, with their strong and open endorsement of Thomist philosophy.

It would be quite wrong, however, to give the impression that these later works contain nothing of interest for even the most resolutely sceptical and secularised social scientist. As I stressed at the beginning of this study there can be no substitute for reading MacIntyre's books, for they are in a very real sense, and especially latterly, historical and philosophical narratives in which it is quite literally true to say that the whole substance is in the detail. For it is in the detailed historical reconstruction, written inevitably from within some tradition, that apparently incommensurable conceptual schemes, and ways of life, might seriously engage with one another. In particular it is worth mentioning, very briefly, the arguments of MacIntyre's Gifford lectures presented in *Three Rival Versions of Moral Enquiry.* For here MacIntyre sets up three contrasting patterns of enquiry within modernity.

The first of these is the self-confident Victorian rationalism of Adam Gifford which culminated in the extraordinarily ambitious project of the ninth edition of the *Encyclopaedia Britannica* (1873), which aimed to provide a completely coherent account of all human knowledge within the framework of a completely universal and 'scientific' rationalism. Counterposed to this, and emerging at the end of the nineteenth century, was the Nietzschean genealogical critique of this kind of rationalism, which suggested not only that there was no gradually emerging and progressing universal rationalism, but also that any claim to such a process was in reality a mask worn by a particular 'will to power'.

Finally MacIntyre articulates his own preferred understanding, namely what he terms the traditionalist Thomist position. For MacIntyre, Aquinas' successful and open-ended synthesis of Aristotle and Augustine, rooted in a divinely ordained natural law, provides a model which is capable of absorbing the best answers provided so far to questions about the nature and purpose of human life. The balance between Aristotelian reason and revelation may well be too much for many modern social scientists, but they would be foolish to leave unexamined the potential of Aristotelian-derived concepts. It is to the final examination of some of these concepts, and of their contemporary relevance, that I now turn.

PRACTICES AND TRADITIONS

It is crucial at this point to recall the importance MacIntyre has placed on seeking to recover from a simple and damaging usage a distinct sense of the importance of tradition. However, for the central role of tradition to be understood, it is necessary, as promised earlier, to explain MacIntyre's use of two concepts which logically precede it, namely a practice and secondly the narrative order to a human life.

A practice is above all else for MacIntyre, the social background within which a coherent practice of the virtues is intelligible. It can be most easily understood where in fact MacIntyre agrees that it is at its most simple, i.e. in his discussion of heroic society, those societies that immediately precede, and in some senses, continued to morally inform, those of classical Greece (societies described or idealised in Homer) and early medieval Europe (societies described or idealised in Saxon and Norse sagas). MacIntyre has been criticised for this emphasis especially when he develops from his claim that human beings are 'essentially story telling animals', and that 'there is no way to give us an understanding of any society, including our own, except through the stock of stories which constitute its initial dramatic resources. Mythology, in its original sense, is at the heart of things'.[1] One critic clearly worried about the fate of Enlightenment rationalism has argued that mythology is never 'understood as aiming at single stable representation of reality, one that would deserve the name of "truth"'.[2] But this misses the point: for MacIntyre myth is but an inescapable starting point for an historically grounded yet rational enquiry. The inescapable nature of myth in much intellectual discussion has now been conceded, by a contemporary liberal, as even constituting the basis of liberalism. Margaret Canovan writes that 'the mythical element in liberalism lies in a set of assumptions about nature: about the nature of mankind and the nature of society. Originally . . . these claims took mythical form in the shape of descriptions of an original state of nature'.[3] This is important, for once so much is conceded for liberalism, the most rationalist of political philosophies, the crucial nature of MacIntyre's wider point concerning the importance of myths and stories must be granted.

However, one dimension of the narrative nature of the sagas is of primary importance for his account. This is that

every individual has a given role and status within a well defined and highly determinate system of roles and statuses, the key structures are those of kinship and of household. In such a society a man knows who he is by knowing his role in these structures; and in knowing this knows also what he owes and what is owed to him by the occupant of every other role and status. In Greek (dein) and in Anglo-Saxon (AHTE) alike, there is originally no clear distinction between 'ought' and 'owe', in Icelandic the word 'skyldr' ties together 'ought' and 'is kin to'.[4]

Here morality and social structure are one and the same: questions of evaluation are for the most part questions of social fact, morality is inseparable from context, morality is wholly internal to definite social practices.

It is important for MacIntyre's argument that these societies are in most respects polar opposites to our own in regard to the connection between 'is' and 'ought', but it is also crucial that they and the intervening social forms, are part of our own tradition. It is the intervening social forms, especially the ethics of Aristotle, that provide, in amended form, the resources for reconnecting, in a critical manner, morality and the social.

A practice then is defined by MacIntyre as a

coherent and complex form of socially established co-operative human activity through which goods internal to the form of activity are realised in the course of trying to achieve those standards of excellence which are appropriate to, and partially definitive of that form of activity, with the result that human powers to achieve excellence and human conceptions of ends and goods involved are systematically extended.[5]

Now it is clear from MacIntyre's account of the concept of a practice that, although such a conception is perhaps marginal to our political and social life today, it is at least recognisable in such activities as playing a game, writing serious poetry, engaging in academic research. It is also clear that it is not only in modern society, but also in ancient and medieval ones that practices may be complex and highly diverse in character. Heroic society provides a kind of ideal type, rather than ideal form; for these practices are integrated and virtually synonymous with social structure. Here the possibility of deep conflicts within and between practices is limited, but also the possibility of change and historical development is curtailed.

Let us now turn to see how a practice operates before

discussing its implications any further. What then is meant by goods internal to a practice? MacIntyre uses the example[6] of wishing to teach chess to a child who has no particular desire to learn. So you encourage the child, by telling him/her that although it will be difficult, with effort he/she can win a game for which he/she will get some sweets. However, so long as the child plays for sweets, he/she will have no reason not to cheat and indeed will have every reason to do so, if he/she can get away with it. But as MacIntyre argues,

> we may hope, there will come a time when the child will find in those goods specific to chess, in the achievements of a certain highly particular kind of analytical skill, strategic imagination and competitive intensity, a new set of reasons not just for winning on a particular occasion, but for trying to excel in whatever way the game of chess demands. Now if the child cheats, he or she will be defeating not you, but himself.[7]

MacIntyre finds himself forced into using examples from games or other highly specific practices, like portrait painting, in part because of the meagreness of our language for speaking of internal goods and because of the extremely subordinate place for such practices and goods in modern industrial capitalism. However, there remain even in these societies, partial elements of such practices sufficient for us to understand the difference between internal and external goods. The Thomist MacIntyre now sees such phenomena as 'evidence of the work of *synderesis*, of that fundamental initial grasp of the primary precepts of the natural law, to which cultural degeneration can partially or temporarily blind us but which can never be obliterated'.[8] We saw in previous chapters how the market functioned almost as a paradigm case of the dominance of external goods, and there can be little doubting that MacIntyre sees societies dominated by the market as quite extreme examples of degeneration. However, it is worth emphasising that almost any practice, including chess, can convey both internal and external goods, i.e. those goods that are contingently attached to chess-playing and other practices, by the accidents of social circumstances. What is crucial is which predominates in the actor's motivation. Now here we can begin to see important social differences between internal and external goods. It is a basic characteristic of external goods that when they are gained they are always some individual's property and possession. On top of this it is also true that the more someone has of them the less there is for others. This is true, both for tangible goods like money or property (in a market system) and intangibles like fame, or charisma which by their very nature can only be had by some. Therefore external goods are always the object of competition, in which there are going to be losers as well as winners. Now it is also true that internal goods will be gained by competition to excel, but it is also characteristic of them that their achievement is good for the whole community who participate in the practice. For example when the four-minute mile was run, or when Joyce's *Ulysses* was written, a practice was extended in a way that practitioners could in some sense share in, emulate and perhaps ultimately surpass in turn.

We can now see how virtues have a key role in sustaining these practices, for practices must generally have some kind of institutional setting, and are not maintained simply by the excelling in the goods of that practice. MacIntyre put it thus:

> Every practice requires a certain kind of relationship between those who participate in it. Now the virtues are those goods by reference to which, whether we like it or not, we define our relationship to those people with whom we share the kind of purposes and standards which inform practices.[9]

However, practices are not to be simply equated with institutions, because institutions are of necessity involved with the getting of resources, the distribution of power and status, and hence with external goods. But the relationship between an institution and a practice is generally intimate and quite crucial; the practice cannot be sustained without the institution, but is always vulnerable to the corrupting power of an unrestrained pursuit of external goods. Hence the making and sustaining of human communities, and hence of human institutions, has all the hallmarks of a practice, and an important one for it is upon this practice that the success of other human practices ultimately depends. It is this crucial question that inevitably raises issues concerning the political implications of this type of communitarian analysis. In its hostility to liberalism it must raise an alternative politics that is protective of institutional life within market-based modernity. I will touch on this later, when I suggest MacIntyre's work implies a politics of the common good.

So far we have seen how the concept of a practice, drawn in part from the past as well as limited areas of modernity, might connect up with the pursuit of non-market-based internal goods. However, the question arises, how is one to choose between the multiplicity of goods available from within the context of a variety of practices. MacIntyre refuses to place practices in any ad hoc hierarchical relationship, although he will allow a causal priority within his scheme to those practices which foster institutional forms which in turn provide the necessary social context, within which other practices can be sustained. This in itself, does not, however, settle the question that is Aristotle's, 'what is the good life for man?'. Even the causal priority of the sustaining of institutions may conflict with the manifest good of, say, being an artist or writer, they may even on occasion be incompatible, e.g. the poet Gerald Manley Hopkins' desire to write poetry, with his commitment to the Jesuit order.

In this context, has not the culture of 'bureaucratic individualism' reappeared, in which the goods internal to practices after all find their ultimate justification within the apparently arbitrary choice of the modern criteria-less self. Finally, the question of authority in our lives raises itself, i.e. that which binds us to the social, that which is threatened to be severed by much modern epistemology. For without some conception of a telos for human life viewed as a unity, an inevitable arbitrariness must enter, which leaves us trapped in a modern differentiated market order. As we saw in the chapter on Marxism, this was a major element in understanding its, i.e. Marxism's, appeal for MacIntyre. No sense (as Scott Meikle shows positively and Castoriadis negatively) can be made of Marx's concept of a fully communist society without the unifying concept of labour as the trans-historical essence of humanity, able to fully realise itself in a free social individuality.

The question remains, can some teleological unity be salvaged on some theoretical and social basis, other than that posed by Marx? As is no doubt clear, the central terrain for rescuing these conceptions lies in the formulation of human life in terms of narrative and tradition.

The key to MacIntyre's argument lies in the view that there is no such thing as 'behaviour', that can be identified independently of intentions, beliefs, and settings. We can understand a human action only by situating it in two kinds of context. Firstly by locating the action with reference to the person's own history and secondly by reference to the actor's role in the history of the setting or settings. The example he uses to illustrate these points seems banal enough, a man gardening and the possible reasons for doing so, but this example has deeper significance, as we will see. MacIntyre asks what is this man doing, 'digging', 'gardening', 'taking exercise', 'preparing for winter' or 'pleasing his wife'. Which of these descriptions is the more important for the man is clearly crucial for understanding the significance of the activity.[10]

Firstly, the action is placed in a cycle of domestic activity because the behaviour presupposes a household-cum-garden setting with its own particular narrative history of which this behaviour is part. Secondly, this behaviour is also situated in the narrative history of a marriage in a different but related social setting. So therefore the behaviour is part of two particular narrative histories which happen to meet. It follows, that as we cannot understand this behaviour without knowing the intentions, it is also true that we cannot understand the intentions independently of the setting or context which make the intentions understandable to the agents themselves. However, the setting of these two narrative histories may well have histories themselves, the household may have a history stretching back decades or centuries. The marriage itself clearly has a history which itself must presuppose the particular point that has been reached in the history of the institution of marriage.

The example focusing on a household activity does seem to contain for MacIntyre a prescriptive charge, for his work is itself dependent on the historical origins of our own concepts and our own institutions. He is at pains to tease out older elements in our culture of modernity that still exist in an incomplete form. The focus on the household seems opportune, as the household in pre-capitalist times was both the centre of economic production and the locus of moral and emotional life and ties. It is precisely the relatively marginal persistence of such forms in the modern world, that makes MacIntyre's work intelligible to us and upon which he hopes to build. For as he says in his preceding discussion of *self* as a narrative unity:

> Just because it has played a key part in the cultures which are historically the predecessors of our own, it would not be surprising if it turned out to be still an unacknowledged presence in many of our ways of thinking and acting. Hence it is not inappropriate to begin by scrutinising some of our most taken-for-granted . . . insights about human actions and selfhood in order to show how natural it is to think of the self in a narrative mode.[11]

The prescriptive implications of the household example can be clearly seen in the only vaguely political conclusion MacIntyre can allow himself to draw: 'what matters now at this stage is the construction of local forms of community within which civility and the intellectual and moral life can be sustained through the new dark ages which are already upon us.'[12] Unsurprisingly, forms of life that stretch back behind the emergence of our capitalist market culture, make a natural point of reference for MacIntyre. Through such examples he seeks to re-educate our intuitions, by reconnecting us to older patterns of human narrative so easily hidden within our culture. He is therefore bound to place some hope on the cultural and ideological impact of these examples, being able to contribute in whatever small measure, to a redirection of our conscious attention. How is this possible?

If there can be no pure science of behaviour, because beliefs and intentions are central, indeed constitutive, elements in human behaviour, then even the sociological pressure of modern industrial capitalism with its prioritising of external over internal goods and separation of public and private (work and leisure consumption, from production), cannot totally eliminate the elements of narrative-based understandings, from human life. Possibly much of our 'unhappy consciousness' stems from attempts to do so.

MacIntyre provides a particularly telling vindication of this in his paper 'Epistemological Crisis, Dramatic Narrative and the Philosophy of Science',[13] where he reveals the inability of Descartes' own radical doubt to disown the particular historic-ally conditioned tools of interpretation, particularly his knowledge of French and Latin. As he argues he does not put in doubt what he has inherited in and with these languages, namely, a way of ordering both thought and the world expressed in a set of meanings. These meanings have a history; seventeenth century Latin bears the marks of having been the language of scholasticism, just as scholasticism was itself marked by the influence of twelfth and thirteenth century Latin . . . he [Descartes] did not notice . . . how much of what he took to be spontaneous reflections of his own mind was in fact a repetition of sentences and phrases from his school text books. Even the cognito is to be found in Saint Augustine.[14]

MacIntyre goes on to point out that to have put these matters into doubt would have been to take the road to mental illness not philosophy.

It has been suggested, notably by Michael Bell in an interesting and instructive essay[15] that MacIntyre's emphasis on narrative, athough valuable as a device to overcome the abstract and reductionist accounts of moral life that emerged after the Enlightenment, is none the less used rather too literally. Bell suggests that in reality MacIntyre is using the concept of narrative in a manner which is essentially metaphorical, in other words it is 'as if' the life of virtues was governed by a teleological narrative. The problem with this for Bell is as follows:

MacIntyre's use of narrative as a model of the moral life seems to me to be justified for his purposes. But the need for this metaphor to be so deep and subliminal as not to appear metaphorical at all leaves it with a slippery and potentially misleading value when extrapolated from its context. The essential problem here is that narrative has to be a different kind of thing from lived temporality or there is no point in drawing the analogy between them.[16]

On the face of it this seems a powerful objection to the overextension of the concept of narrative. However, it seems to be based on an assumption, admittedly partly encouraged by MacIntyre, that equates rather too easily the process of narrative construction with historical analysis and above all with literary texts. My reading of MacIntyre seems to suggest that he is making a larger claim about the nature of human culture,

namely that human beings are for the most part engaged always
in the construction of narratives and that literary and historical
accounts are but special instances of a more general process.
This is not to conflate all 'lived temporality' with narrative, but
rather to suggest that purposeful human action is partly constituted through narrative. I take this to be, at least in part, what
MacIntyre is getting at in the distinction he makes between
intelligible and unintelligible actions:

> Intelligibility is a property of actions in their relationship to
> the sequences within which they occur. Sometimes this is a
> matter of an immediate temporal relationship . . . But some-
> times that to which an action is either an intelligible or
> unintelligible sequel may have occurred many years previously
> . . . An unintelligible piece of behaviour may none the less be
> an action. That is to say, it may be informed by intention and
> be performed deliberately and voluntarily. But it will be able
> to provoke in others only some kind of baffled response and
> the agent him-or-herself will only be able to give a very limited
> account of what he or she takes or took him or herself to be
> doing . . .[17]

Frequently acts of vandalism seem to others, and often to agents
themselves, to fall into the second category. It should also be
recalled that many events in a human life, like, for example, the
accidental spilling of a cup of coffee, are certainly part of the
'lived temporality' of human experience, whilst not forming
part of an intentional or narrative construction by human
beings.

We are fortunate enough to possess some sociological evidence, informed by an Aristotelian conception of narrative,
which supports the contention that narrative construction is
partly constitutive of human existence. In his paper 'The
Genesis of Chronic Illness: Narrative Reconstruction',[18] Gareth
Williams engages in the intriguing exercise of examining the
disruption chronic illness causes in the life narrative of a
number of patients. Amongst Williams' cases he presents us
with Bill a 58-year-old who has had eight years of rheumatoid
arthritis, who says in the course of an interview, 'and your
mind's going all the time, you' re reflecting . . . "how the *hell*
have I come to be like this?" . . . because it is't me'.[19] Williams
points out that what is most significant about Bill's questioning,

and what positivistic medical science offers so little in the way of understanding, is that 'it points to a concern with something more than the cause of his arthritis'.[20]

The crisis that chronic illness creates in people's lives seems to throw into relief the narrative reconstructions that seem to accompany everyday life. Williams' findings seem to suggest to him that 'the individual's narrative has to be reconstructed both in order to understand the illness in terms of past social experience and to reaffirm the impression that life has a course and the self has a purpose or *telos*'.[21]

If narrative, then, is crucial to being human, we can return to the process of spelling out what use the narrative ordering of a human life can have in overcoming market-modernity. How does MacIntyre specify narrative role? Firstly by posing the question 'In what does the unity of individual life consist?' and answering 'unity is the unity of a narrative embodied in a single life'.[22] The good is then defined by how best to live out that narrative and bring it to completion. Facts and values are reconnected in human praxis by the necessarily interpretative and connected nature of human action. To ask what is the good for man, is to find what all single life narratives have in common. Naturally, they have much in common because in a crucial sense, they are embedded in particular historically conditioned settings. However, at this point a further quality of a narrative must be noticed, namely that it is going somewhere, moving towards an end, not just any end, but towards some resolution or completion of the narrative itself.

Every human narrative must then embody some purpose, quest or telos, which it is constantly striving to move towards. As MacIntyre puts it: 'Some conception of the good life for man is required'[23] for the narrative to have any meaning at all. His own provisional answer at this point is the apparently circular one, that the good life for man is the search for the good life for man. But this is only so because the analysis lacks its final component, which could be called that of a corporate tradition. For no one can be a questing agent, as a pure individual; it is not simply that the conception of the good life varies, from one place and period to another place and period, but also that each individual enters their social circumstances as the bearer of a particular social identity whether they realise this, or *pace* Descartes, do not. The agent always belongs in a whole set of ways to a community, or set of interlocking communities; son or daughter of someone, citizen of some city or nation, member of some political, religious or intellectual tradition. All these elements are inherited in a way quite opposed to all liberal individualist thinking, that assumes we are always free to choose in the abstract about what one will choose to take responsibility for. This conception must not be taken as automatically or necessarily conservative; it is not an argument for accepting the limitations of a tradition as we found it. One can rebel against a tradition, by adopting another historically available tradition. Or on the other hand, one can also dissent within a tradition, for a tradition as MacIntyre defines it, is partly composed by the debate over what the tradition consists of, e.g. what it means to be English, Irish or a socialist.

The crucial point being made concerns the futility and danger of attempting to ignore or disregard the presence of the inherited practice or tradition itself:

> I am born with a past, and to try to cut myself off from the past, in the individualist mode, is to deform my present relationships. The possession of an historical identity and the possession of a social identity coincide.[24]

Without particularity to begin from, there could be no beginning and no movement towards culturally constituted goods and truths. To recognise this is to reconnect ourselves to our pasts; this can renew confidence and avoid the spurious arrogance of the detached observer, coming from nowhere and going nowhere.

We are writing of what is specific to being social products: something constitutive of being human, but which Enlightenment liberalism has hidden or refused to recognise for its own ideological reasons. Enlightenment liberalism could only use tradition as a negative; something to be abandoned. It left the concept to be taken over by conservatism, starting with Burke, who made a positive virtue of the implicit liberal contrast between reason and tradition. Modern conservatism (when it is not liberalism in another guise) is liberalism's alter ego, both failing to realise that all conflict and development take place within the context of some historically given traditional thought and action. For MacIntyre, Burkean tradition is always a tradition in decay. This is because a concept of tradition, that simply counterposes it to reason, means that a key element in the life of a tradition has been lost. For, as we have noticed, a tradition to be meaningful must involve debate about what constitutes itself as a tradition.

Clearly, therefore, the pursuit of the end or telos of a human narrative can neither be a one-sided celebration of the past, nor an individualistic practice. It is the fact that our market-based liberal culture is still marked by the inheritance of past non-individualistic communities, that makes possible the internal critique of these societies, from a perspective other than their own value system. In some respects, MacIntyre's work on a telos-governed human praxis, built from the forms of the past, recalls, despite differences, something of the form of the Hegelian Marxism we discussed in the first and second chapters. There is something of a developmental notion of human consciousness that in its movement from the Greeks to the present, recalls the structure of Hegel's *Phenomenology of Mind*.

REPUBLICS, COMMUNITIES AND POLITICS

I wish now to illustrate some connections between the kind of concepts employed by MacIntyre and some recent developments in communitarian thought. This means work that takes both narrative and community with great seriousness. The first of these tendencies renews emphasis on 'civic virtue' and is represented by writers like William Connolly and Michael Walzer and Christopher Lasch in the USA and to a lesser degree the final work of Raymond Williams in Britain.[25] These writers are, significantly, from the left and hence confront the problems facing Marxist socialism as it has been summarised by MacIntyre:

> Marxist socialism is at its core deeply optimistic. For, however thoroughgoing its criticisms of capitalism may be, it is committed to asserting that within the society constituted by those institutions all the human and material preconditions of a better future are being accumulated. Yet if the moral impoverishment of advanced capitalism is what so many Marxists agree that it is, whence are those resources for the future to be derived?[26]

This is a question that must haunt serious socialist and communitarian thought, if it is deprived of the developmental logic of essentialism. But even Hegelian essentialism which sees history mediated through consciousness, must be aware of the possibility of massive subjective blocks on communitarian or, socialist development. The tradition of civic virtue, therefore, self-consciously identifies itself with now older and historically marginal traditions. Connolly sees modern utopian socialism as the bearer and preserver of the republican tradition, with its desire to promote civic virtue among citizens who reflectively identify with a way of life shared with other citizens. And who adjust their political demands and behaviour to the norms embedded in that way of life.[27] In this sense this socialist tradition is very close to MacIntyre's own argument concerning the bearers of the tradition of the virtues for, as he says: 'Republicanism in the eighteenth century is the project of restoring a community of virtue.'[28]

MacIntyre sees something of the tradition of the virtues at work in the Jacobin republican clubs, inheriting from the medieval guilds and the renaissance republics, a desire for equality between members, with a strong corporate ethos; each member having equal rights and equal obligations, to the society and its members. It was also older traditions, handed down from pre-market societies that produced the new named virtue of fraternity, embodying something of the Aristotelian virtue of friendship and the Christian love of the neighbour.[29]

Andrew Fraser's work on American Republicanism and its complex and ambivalent relationship to American capitalism, is instructive at this point,[30] especially in the case of the rise of the modern business corporation. Fraser shows that despite the élitist nature and class bias, inscribed in Republicanism in the early nineteenth century, it represented an attempt to hold on to a political community facing destruction in the shape of a generalisation of capitalist social relations. As he put it: 'Under the impact of money and commerce the realm of the political as a distinct sphere of human experience dissolves.'[31]

In a fascinating reworking of the managerialist thesis of Berle and Means,[32] he shows how the separation of ownership and control was crucial in generating a purely capitalist market-orientated entity, the new corporation. Fraser argues that: 'Most leftist critiques of the managerialist thesis have failed to perceive that the fusion of ownership and control endowed the

traditional logic of property with a decidedly political significance.'[33] In essence he argues that:

> the common law doctrines governing the corporation
> assumed that even the private business corporation should be
> treated as a 'body politic', that is 'as an association of persons
> imbued with the civil ethos appropriate to a genuine repub-
> lican community'.[34]

What this means is that the separation of ownership and control
was a crucial step towards the elimination of the political
dimension that the common law had introduced into the
investment relationship. Now it was possible for stockholders to
relate to the new corporation as simply investors and not as
members of a legally constituted political community. Paradoxically this shift, in the USA at any rate, was no simple
working-out of bourgeois class interests. For the shift seems to
have been achieved in part, by an important element of American radicalism, i.e. individualistic and anti-institutional, evangelical Christianity – secularised versions of which are important elements in contemporary western radicalism. The reason
for this, Fraser argues, is that so long as the corporation stood as
a 'little republic' endowed with an identity and purpose of its
own (by act of the legislature) it remained open to radical
attack as a bastion of monopoly and special privilege. It was only
when general incorporation opened the corporation up to
anyone who had the means to utilise it for their own private
economic gain, that the spirit of radical individualism was
satisfied. It would be hard to find a clearer example of the
process of 'bureaucratic individualism' triumphant. In this
sense it sets for us one of the clearest historical examples of
the political problems MacIntyre's work depicts and the terrible
weakness of both Left and Right in grasping the real significance of the emergence of capitalist market societies.

In so far as the Left partakes of individualistically orientated
politics, it both celebrates and intensifies the conditions of its
own subordination. As Fraser points out in this context:

> Capitalism is a process of generalised abstraction which
> involves the ever deepening alienation of human beings from
> their own social being . . . Capitalism becomes a process of
> generalised social wealth that liquidates both private property

and the public realm, thereby undermining the necessary foundations of a genuine political community.[35]

If, as MacIntyre argues, the potency of bureaucratic forms in our culture, is in reality the other face of the individualisation of the human subject through a set of abstracted general principles, corresponding to the abstract nature of market relations, then what can an Aristotelian communitarian tradition do to oppose it? Fraser suggests in the American context – in his article on radical legal thought[36] – that:

> it is not inconceivable that the vision of a regenerated republican polity may yet turn out to be a more realistic solution to the 'fundamental contradictions' of our social being than a form of critical legal discourse that stands so much in fear of any stable or enduring source of authority . . . They [radical lawyers] may find they have much to learn from those who once championed a conservative republican ethos grounded in the 'traditional logic of property' against a socially corrosive . . . capitalist rationalisation.[37]

In the light of this line of thought it is surely important to register the emergence of a theorised populist politics in the United States, that parallels MacIntyre's own defence of local and traditional communities, based around some conception of the 'tradition of the virtues'. The new populist analysis calls for both local, decentralised community control and a strong federalism to protect these communities from the state and possibly from one another; but critically rejects, in the context of a discussion of the Lombard Leagues of Italy's dismissal of language and ethnicity as opposed to locality as a condition of membership, a reactionary politics of nostalgia. As Paul Piccone notes, 'living communities cannot be reorganized *permanently* on the basis of nostalgia, external threats or bureaucratically mandated ideological tenets'[38] The key point would seem to be close to MacIntyre's, the need for communities that can protect their existence and through argument and debate reconstitute and renew themselves. For as Piccone goes on to say, communities:

> must develop organically in face-to-face relations and within socio-economic networks characterized by participatory forms

of political institutions which can alone guarantee government accountability and responsiveness. Any concrete populist alternative to the de facto bureaucratic centralism of the
liberal-democratic state today must emphasize not only the
manageability (and therefore the relatively limited size) of
the various political units but also concrete sets of shared
values which, as all thriving traditions, remain open to
periodic reconstruction and modifications in the light of
changing social conditions.[39]

If elements of the American left seek to build upon the republican tradition to resist market rationalisation and liberal dissolution, is it possible to discern in Britain resistant social forms?

It is not very difficult to see the most severe socio-economic
conflict in post-war Britain, i.e. the 1984–5 miners' strike, within
a similar perspective. Here a determined workforce, located
within very specific communities, were fighting an equally
determined modernising right-wing government, prepared to
use force and the arguments of neo-liberalism to break both a
union, and forms of communally organised life.

The year-long strike astonished many observers, in revealing
the degree of communal self-organisation and the powerful
sense of purpose felt by the mining communities. It seems likely
that miners were sustained in their struggle by the manner in
which class, occupation and community frequently coincided,
and this, combined with the sheer desperation of their situation,
produced a level of communal mobilisation not seen since
1926. Initiated as an attempt to prevent pit closures, and the
massive reduction of coal-mining capacity, the miners' strike
has been the most important strike to protect employment for
decades. The desperation, and the way the strike was policed,
'produced' as Huw Beynon has written, 'an uncompromising
amalgam of solidarity and bitterness, emotions so intense that
"this will never be forgotten; not in my lifetime anyway"'.[40]

In some respects there are similarities in the nature of the
miners' radical opposition, with that of the radicalism in early
nineteenth-century England. As Craig Calhoun has emphasised,
this radicalism was greatly dependent upon the nature and
organisation of the community, which acted as a crucial material
and ideological resource.[41] Raphael Samuel has noted these
similarities:

in the first place a struggle for the survival of villages. Its heartland is in places knit together by an almost private sense of collective self. Like village radicalism in the 19th century it is animated at the local level by an exclusive sense of belonging, a republican spirit of independence; and an assertion of total and unilateral control over the conditions of the everyday environment . . . The ideology, as so often in the popular movements of the past, is that of radical conservatism, a fight to protect the known against the unknown, the familiar against the alien, the local and the human against the anonymous and the gigantic.[42]

Just as the early radicalism of the last century had been fought over the moral terrain of craft control and the 'moral economy', so the 1984–5 strike was fought largely in defence of crucial aspects of the 1945 Labourist settlement. This settlement had, in partial and, perhaps, contradictory but none the less important ways, reproduced elements of this village culture in the network of social arrangements within the mining industry in its nationalised form; especially in the central place of the union in the complex set of industrial committees that administer much of the industry.[43] The miners, indeed, have, more than any other group of workers in Britain, looked to the state for elements of industrial regulation, from the Mining Acts of the nineteenth century right through to state ownership in the twentieth century.[44] It is this phenomenon that explains the depth of the miners' political commitment to a form of state intervention. As McCormick puts it: 'The coal mines were nationalised because the miners were no longer prepared to work for the private coal owners.'[45] The miners undoubtedly fought the closure programme because they had no alternative, but there can be little doubt also, that much of the bitterness sprang from the feeling that a whole set of long-established political and moral obligations had been unilaterally severed.

The miners' experience has been remarkable and important. It illustrates two aspects of modern state power, on the one hand as an apparent bearer of communal purpose and identity, and on the other as managerial power acting 'efficiently' to impose the external pressures of the market.[46] The Thatcher government had come to power in 1979 with a clear commitment to the neo-liberal strategy of the imposition of market

discipline on British society as a whole. From the beginning this
government had wished to break the old consensus; doing away
with the class compromises and collective forms of life and
relationships. So the NCB was seen to be too 'cosy' in its
relationship with the unions and Ian MacGregor was put in to
restore discipline and market competitiveness. With all corporate forms apparently in crisis the powerful articulation of
individualism was made to seem both fresh and plausible.
During the strike the tension between the strands of com-
munalism and individualism in working-class culture surfaced
frequently, orchestrated and amplified by the aggressive neo-
liberal rhetoric of the government. The phrase 'right to work'
was deflected from its social-democratic meaning of a public
commitment to full employment, towards a citizen's right to sell
unhindered, one's labour, as an individual, in the market place.
The issue of the absence of a national strike ballot was connected
to this theme (and exploited by the government) as the democratic and the solidaristic traditions of trade unionism pulled in
different directions.

The long tradition of balloting in the NUM has strengthened
and deepened the democratic tradition, so that one miner
could describe feelings in the 1982 ballot: 'It's my vote, that's
the way they think.'[47] But, on the other hand, the pattern of
proposed closures meant some areas seemed safe and others
not, so that Peter Heathfield could argue: 'it cannot be right
that one man can vote another man out of a job.'[48]

The Thatcher government in Britain has raised in many
painful ways the question of individual self-interest versus a
collective tradition run into deep trouble. Such a tradition is
heavily dependent upon state-regulated forms of work to sustain
locality and community. In 1912 the pamphlet *The Miners' Next
Step*, published by the Unofficial Reform Committee in South
Wales, insisted that nationalisation was not the way forward and
would merely create a national trust backed by the state. In the
same year Noah Ablett, the Welsh Syndicalist leader argued that
nationalisation would 'simply place an important section of the
working class in the hands of a state servile to capitalists'
interests who would use their opportunity to increase the
servility we abhor':[49] a profound intuition of the immense
difficulties of constructing forms of communal living and self-
regulation that can eliminate or minimise the pressures of the

market.[50] It was perhaps inevitable that late nineteenth-century workers would begin to turn to the state to alleviate what Marx had called their subjection to the 'violence of things',[51] as this state claimed to be the collective 'we' of all citizens. But as we have noted this state could only provide a limited communal form whilst the capitalist market economy remained the dominant external reality. This state form would continually manoeuvre between the twin bases of legitimacy of democratic representation, and technocratic efficiency, corresponding to its twin roles as 'illusory community' and administrative power.

Both these themes were powerfully present throughout the strike. The miners were portrayed as anti-democratic and a threat to the rule of law. The government, most of the non-Labour opposition and most liberal commentators, were agreed that the miners must be beaten for this reason. But perhaps more fundamentally they were treated as deeply unrealistic in their objectives. Their heartfelt defence of their communities may have been applauded but 'hard-headed' realism had to prevail in the end.

This last point is quite crucial, for it would be difficult to find a clearer example of what MacIntyre has taken to be the spurious theatricality of managerial power (see Chapter 5). For during the strike, the deeply opaque and contentious social and economic relationships of advanced capitalism, were constructed as simple and clear-cut, by the state and the NCB. The NCB, it was claimed, was massively unprofitable, therefore uneconomic pits had to be closed. But we now know that this is a particular rendering of reality; an alternative set of 'experts' could construct the NCB accounts in quite another way. One leading accountant who has examined these accounts, has described them as 'a supreme masterpiece in the art of obfuscation' and that for the purpose of identifying uneconomic pits these accounts are virtually useless.[52] This authority turned, in his analysis, the NCB operational deficit of £358 million into a surplus of £17 million.

The correctness, or otherwise, of these figures is not our immediate concern; they do indicate, however, how the state reified a complex and shifting situation for political and coercive purposes. Public authority in effect used apparently formal and technical procedures to legitimate, as Raymond Williams has pointed out, a series of shifts of meaning, that as it were, constructed the meaning of the market place within the state sector. As Williams puts it:

> what 'management' says, is offered as a set of unchallengeable technical decisions, when the actual management – now very clearly the old master or employer – again and again arrives at these within a determining context of short-term political and commercial calculations.[53]

In this context, talk of restoring the 'right to manage', is clearly an excercise in the theatricality of power. It is a means of reasserting in an apparently modern and neutral guise the fundamental realities of power in a capitalist society. As Williams adds: 'It is in fact double-talk for the categorical and arbitrary rights of an employer.'[54]

The connections MacIntyre has laid out between individualistic conceptions of human association and bureaucratic power would seem to indicate that a communitarian challenge must attempt to transcend the limits of liberal radicalism, building on the core aspects of human sociality, and perhaps on older intellectual and political traditions. For the problem is, to quote Raymond Williams again, but in another context:

> what has really failed inside the movement and inside the whole society, is any valid concept of the general interest. That is why appeals to it are so often resisted or rejected. In the forms in which we have known it – the undifferentiated 'nation', the needs of the 'economy' – it has again and again been a false general interest . . . That is a sort of success, for these versions . . . are indeed in their usual form false. But it is a dangerous sort of success, if all that is left is the defence and advancement of particular interest.[55]

The question is, do we know any other? Is it possible to rescue elements of the older traditions of social and political community, both intellectual and material, to resist the worst consequences of our market-based culture on our lives? Some guidance may be given by William Connolly who has attempted to revive the anti-liberal concept of the common good. The concept deriving from eighteenth-century Rousseauist origins, was crucial for the formation of civic republicanism and in many ways anticipated the political content of Marx's socialism.[56] In anticipation of the kinds of criticism Williams referred to, Connolly is anxious to distinguish the common good from the politics of the public interest. The public interest, he argues, frequently amounts to no more than an aggregation of individual or group interests. The interests the majority of people have as private individuals, as workers, consumers or owners, may at any particular moment outweigh the interest they share as members of the public. When the public interest is conceived in this way then policies designed to further it tend to concentrate on policies giving incentives or imposing penalties designed to bring the individual interest of each person more closely in line with the public. This is the familiar picture of compromise, badgering and on occasion, coercion or exploitation, experienced by all who live in the capitalist democracies.

The common good takes us squarely back to the civic ethic and republican ethos, that was so clearly seen by MacIntyre as looking both back to organic societies of Europe's pre-modern past, whilst looking towards the future of a free equal citizenship. They had sought to preserve the ethic of a political community from the depredations of the capitalist market. Connolly attempts to articulate a concept of the common good that will yield to a communitarian resolution of our discontents. In language that is strikingly similar to MacIntyre's, he defines an appeal to the common good as an

> appeal to a set of shared purposes and standards which are fundamental to the way of life prized together by the participants. The participants have an obligation to respond to these appeals, even when the net interests of everyone, when each consults only his own interests moves in another direction ... The citizen with civic virtue is asked to give presumptive priority to those dimensions of his own good shared with others.[57]

Connolly quickly notes the obvious objections of liberals and radicals. The liberal must fear a rhetoric of the common good, which suppresses the autonomy of the individual; radicals will fear that in a stratified capitalist society such appeals will amount to no more than those at the bottom carrying the bulk of the sacrifices while the ones with money or power prosper. Connolly recognises the moments of truth within these criticisms but then points to the logic of failure inscribed within the concept of public interest minus civic virtue. Our context, he argues, is one of expanded self-consciousness among citizens via the mass media, literacy, visible interdependence between states which makes people realise they participate in an order resting on human convention, rather than nature. Without civic virtue the public interest policy will be a hollow sham, as atomised cynical individuals keep the letter of the law whilst evading the spirit, summed up by Rousseau's dictum, 'Laws are equally powerless against the treasures of the rich and the indigency of the poor; the first eludes them, the second escapes them, one breaks the net and the other slips through'.[58]

Are there resources for mobilising an authentic communitarian-orientated concept of the common good, amidst the exploitation and corruption that Connolly, like MacIntyre, sees all around him. Like MacIntyre, Connolly attempts to see amongst division, dissolution and heightened consciousness of self, those basic elements which are common to human beings: that to be an individual one must first be in society, and share a language which is acquired before our capacity to criticise. To share a language is to share criteria for making distinctions and making judgements. He says:

> to participate in life is to carry an enormous load of settled criteria of judgement standards of appraisal and beliefs. In sharing a language we share imperfectly these pre-understandings, and we bring them to bear on specific issues.[59]

The similarity of this formulation with Wittgenstein's appeal against radical Cartesian doubt, and clearly, the critique of the private language argument, underlies MacIntyre's own treatment of Descartes, noticed above. However, it does run in quite the opposite direction to another and very influential radical theory of the construction of a common interest, that of Jürgen Habermas. Habermas argues that the very existence of human language creates the possibility of a rationally arrived-at consensus between people. This is possible because:

> the 'rationality' of the discursively formed will consists in the fact that the reciprocal behavioural expectations raised to normative status afford validity to a common interest ascertained without deception. The interest is common because the constraint-free consensus permits only what all can want;

it is free of deception because even the interpretation of needs in which each individual must be able to recognise what he wants became the object of discursive will-formation.[60]

I will not enter into the full ramifications of Habermas's views here, except to point to the excessively formal rationalistic element in this approach. Compared with MacIntyre and Connolly, Habermas, as Anderson has noted, is a rationalistic intellectual. Within his work 'lies no fin-de-siècle Wagnerian overtones, but the earnest ideals and serious optimism of the German Enlightenment'.[61] In surveying Habermas's later work Jeffrey Alexander has revealed the sharp contrasts between mythical and rational thought, interpreted in a progressivist way, that creates problems for his handling of culture.[62] Alexander argues that this problem flows from Habermas's desire to argue for communication based on agreements that are completely unconstrained. This means that actors must not only be 'free from external material constraints; they are also free from internalised controls that would place the meaning and the origin of their behaviour out of their conscious reach'.[63]

It seems then, that Habermas is the latest social theorist seeking to ground what MacIntyre calls the Enlightenment Project, but now in the 'transcendental' guarantees of the rules of speech:[64] an assumed world of subjects without presupposition making their rational choice! But the problem for such theorists, as Alexander points out, and MacIntyre would concur, is that despite cultural differentiation and the real growth of rationality,

arbitrary, unconscious, fused and, yes, irrational elements of culture have not at the same time disappeared. Language and world view continue to predefine our understanding of the object world before we even begin to subject it to our conscious rationality. Nor can we regard our linguistically structured world views as simply humanly constructed interpretations, which are therefore completely open to criticism, since our 'regard' is, ineluctably, conditioned by the preconscious world itself. It follows, then, that there is an inevitable investment in the world of things and the world of ideas with some kind of dogmatic, uncritical status . . . there seems to be abundant evidence that moderns still seek to understand the contingency of everyday life in terms of narrative traditions whose simplicity and resistance to change makes them hard to distinguish from myths.[65]

It is clear that both MacIntyre and Connolly place a good deal of weight upon these rooted, pre-understandings and the elements of cultural particularity, as providing the basis of a shared life and, of course, forming the basis from which any rationally grounded understanding of the world must begin. The fragility and uncertainty of such an approach is clear, Connolly is painfully aware of it when he states somewhat hesitantly: 'Out of this background of imperfectly . . . shared distinctions, standards and purposes a sense of the common good, might crystallise, though there is no guarantee . . . that it will occur.'[66]

For both MacIntyre and Connolly, the institutional setting for pre-understandings is vitally important. But again such institutional settings must share collective values and purposes to orientate behaviour towards some desired good, whether it is scientific research or the production of an affluent society of free and equal citizens. This is why MacIntyre in the conclusion of his latest work feels it necessary to call for the existence of competing and conflicting university institutions each embodying distinctive modes of enquiry learning and teaching,

> each modelled upon, but improving upon, its own best predecessor, the Thomist perhaps upon Paris in 1272, the genealogist upon Vincennes in 1968. And thus the wider society would be confronted with claims of rival universities, each advancing its own enquiries in its own terms and each securing the type of agreement necessary to ensure the progress and the flourishing of its enquiries by its own set of exclusions and prohibitions, formal and informal.[67]

Such institutions might represent or articulate and above all rigorously develop the outlook of distinctive communities within society, and provide plans and criteria for those communities to realise their conception of the good life. Clearly the social sciences would have important roles within such universities. The roles would be different between these very different institutions, depending on the place of a social science in the tradition the institution set out to embody. An Aristotelian university, Thomist or otherwise, would have to share a common moral framework committed to constraining economic growth, and the unfettered use of the criteria of market efficiency as life's framework.

A progressive sociology after MacIntyre could contribute to this, as Donald Levine suggests, by being a discipline that

> seeks to identify the social and cultural functions proper to particular historical settings, to delineate the external resources and internal practices needed to realise them, and to show ways of establishing conditions that both sustain us in the quest for the good and furnish us increasing self-knowledge and increasing knowledge of the good.[68]

In arguing this he is only echoing MacIntyre's own call for a new sociology, which is in reality an old sociology, that of Adam Ferguson. 'It is Ferguson's type of sociology which is the empirical counterpart of the conceptual account of the virtues which I have given, a sociology which aspires to lay bare the empirical, causal connection between virtues, practices and institutions.'[69]

Notes

1 CHRISTIANITY AND MARXISM: ACCEPTANCE AND REJECTION

1 London, SCM Press, 1953. The book was completed at the University of Manchester when MacIntyre was only twenty-three years old.
2 Op. cit., pp. 9–10.
3 In his last two volumes, *Whose Justice? Which Rationality?*, London, Duckworth, 1988, and *Three Rival Versions of Moral Enquiry*, London, Duckworth, 1990, MacIntyre makes quite clear his commitment to being an Augustinian Christian and his general philosophic loyalty to Thomism and its institutionalisation in the Roman Catholic Church.
4 Alasdair MacIntyre, *Marxism: An Interpretation*, London, SCM Press, 1953, p. 10.
5 In itself, of course, this claim is by no means unique. Many have been ready to point to the apparently religious character of Marxism as a form of social theory and to the Church and sect-like quality of Communist and Trotskyist political movements. The Christian theological origins of the Marxian dialectic are stressed in the first volume of Leszek Kolakowski's now classic work on Marxism, *Main Currents of Marxism: 1: The Founders*, Oxford, Oxford University Press, 1978, Chapter 1. Some very sharp observations on the religious inheritance of Hegelian Marxism are to be found in J. G. Merquior, *Western Marxism*, London, Paladin Books, 1986, Part 1. Alvin Gouldner in his *The Two Marxisms: Contradictions and Anomalies in the Development of Theory*, London, Macmillan, 1980, makes a crucial point after first endorsing MacIntyre's view of Marxism as a secular version of the Christian religion (p. 122) when he says

> In having noted the religious elements in Marxism, I must repeat what I once said in making a similar analysis of sociological functionalism. I have always found it odd that people who profess to a respect for religion act so triumphantly when they find a religious side to Marxism, and that they should brandish

this as if it were a conclusive argument against it. It is of course no argument at all against Marxist ideas. Although not 'religiously musical', I experience such exercises in righteousness as repellent; I cannot share in the sport of baiting the 'false religion' because I have too keen a sense of the close connection between religion, any religion, and human suffering, and thus experience contempt for religion as callousness toward suffering (p. 123).

6 Op. cit., p. 12.
7 Ibid., p. 13.
8 Ibid., pp. 13–14.
9 Ibid., p. 17.
10 Ibid., p. 20.
11 See the essay by Alasdair MacIntyre, 'The Strange Death of Social Democratic England' which originally appeared in *The Listener* and is republished in D. Widgery (ed.) *The Left in Britain 1956–1968*, Harmondsworth, Penguin, 1976. MacIntyre writing in 1968 here produces a quite savage indictment of the Wilson Labour government at a time when unemployment had gone over half a million – the highest June figure since the war. He argued that this level had been deliberately created by government policy and he felt that

> We ought all surely to be a little more astonished and appalled than we are. Every previous Labour government regarded rising unemployment as a defeat, as a sign that its policy was not working or that it had chosen the wrong policy. This is the first Labour government that must regard rising unemployment as a victory for its policies, as a sign they are working.

He goes on to describe this process as the effective disenfranchisement of the working class from the political system. Whatever MacIntyre thought about the theoretical significance of Marxism in 1968 there is no doubt that he still stood firmly on the left of the political spectrum.

12 The classic statement of this position is Gustavo Gutierrez, *A Theology of Liberation*, London, SCM Press, 1983, alongside the writings of the great radical Brazilian Bishop Helder Camera, such as his *Church and Colonialism: The Betrayal of the Third World*, London, Sheed and Ward, 1969. See also the quite extraordinary work by a well-known liberation theologian, Jose P. Miranda, *Marx and the Bible: A Critique of the Philosophy of Oppression*, London, SCM Press, 1977. Also the same author's *Marx Against the Marxists: The Christian Humanism of Karl Marx*, London, SCM Press, 1980. This book is a very strange mixture of serious scholarship and complete wishful thinking especially when attempting to make the quite ludicrous claim that Marx in his maturity was a believing Christian theist. Liberation theology is and has been a largely Latin American phenomenon but there have been some attempts to apply its blend of Christian eschatology and Marxist theory to western countries;

for the British case see the collection by Rex Ambler and David
Haslam (eds) *Agenda For Prophets: Towards a Political Theology For
Britain*, London, Bowerdean Press, 1980. For an interesting over-
view written by a sympathetic outsider who can clearly see the
political naivety of many of the theologians, see Jose Casanova,
'The Politics of the Religious Revival', *Telos*, No. 59, Spring 1984.

13 Op. cit., p. 21.

14 J. G. Merquior in his study *Western Marxism*, London, Paladin
Books, has an interesting and useful discussion of the Hegelian
background to Marxism, and points to the distinctive character of
the philosophical generation that followed Kant. Kant seemingly
having cut the ground from under metaphysics the next generation
did their best to restore it; as Merquior puts it: 'Whereas Kant had
severed absolutes from knowledge, Fichte (1762–1814), Schelling
(1775–1854) and Georg Wilhelm Friedrich Hegel (1770–1831)
strove to make philosophy intimately acquainted with the absolute.
Kant's epistemological scruples were simply brushed aside. To hold
that no adequate of ultimate beings (the famous "thing-in-itself")
can be rationally warranted came to be seen as an intellectual
attitude lacking "the courage of truth, the belief in the power of the
spirit"', pp. 11–12.

15 The account of Hegel is to be found op. cit., pp. 21–9.

16 In MacIntyre's original account, ibid., p. 28, he is able to make the
Marxist materialist point conform to what he understands to be a
Christian position; he says 'Hegel seeks to deliver man by right
thinking. But he claims for an autonomy that the Bible never gives
to it. Man as a thinker is not autonomous: he belongs to a material
world, from which his thinking arises'. The reference to the Bible
is missing from the later revised edition, *Marxism and Christianity*,
London, Duckworth, 1968; the rest of the quotation can be found
on p. 16 of this edition. In case anyone should believe this
association of Christianity with such a materialist position is
entirely maverick, it is worth noting that this is precisely the
position adopted by the distinguished Roman Catholic theologian
and present Norris-Hulse Professor of Divinity at the University of
Cambridge, Nicholas Lash, in his work *A Matter of Hope: A
Theologian's Reflections on the Thought of Karl Marx*, London, Darton,
Longman and Todd, 1981. See especially Chapter 12 'Christian
Materialism'.

17 Karl Popper, *The Open Society and its Enemies*, Vol. 2, London,
Routledge & Kegan Paul, 1966 (originally published 1945).

18 Op. cit., p. 36. This is, of course, the issue of the materiality of the
Christian promise of redemption. The underlying contention in
most radical discussions of Christianity seems to rest with the
decidedly materialistic quality of the inheritance from the Judaic
tradition with clear and quite non-Platonic emphasis on salvation
involving a radical renewing of a fallen world including a resur-
rection of the body that is most definitely still a human body. There
is an interesting philosophical discussion of the possible com-

patibility of Christianity and Marxism as theoretical systems to be found in Denys Turner, *Marxism and Christianity*, Oxford, Blackwell, 1983. Turner's discussion focuses on the question of the Marxist claim to be able to expose the ideological nature of the social world of which Feuerbach's analysis of Christianity is a paradigm case. Turner is quite cleverly able to turn the tables on the leading modern Marxist philosopher Louis Althusser by suggesting that his account of the human subject is in fact idealist. Turner is able to suggest (building on Aquinas) that his

> minimal notion of the subject . . . has nothing in common with Althusser's subjects, which are Cartesian egos. Mine are language-bearing lumps of sensuous matter. As language-bearers they are capable of misdescribing their needs. As material social individuals (bodies) they necessarily construct their misdescriptions in the form of a social order – or more accurately their misdescriptions come in the form of a social order in the first place (p. 202).

In other words his account of the subject better fits Marxism than Althusser's. See also the same author's 'The "Subject" and the "Self": A Note on Barker's Cartesianism', *New Blackfriars*, March 1978. See note 16 above.
19 Op. cit., p. 39.
20 Ibid., p. 50.
21 Ibid., p. 56.
22 It is clear that MacIntyre is making use of many of Marx's early writings, including *The Economic and Philosophical Manuscripts*, at that time unavailable in English and by no means well known. The source that MacIntyre seems to be using is Karl Marx, *National Ökonomie und Philosophie*, ed. Erich Thier, Köln und Berlin, Verlag Gustav Kiepenheuer, (no date given). As far as I am aware the only sustained treatment of the early Marx in English was H. P. Adams, *Karl Marx in his Earlier Writings*, London, Frank Cass & Co, 1965, originally published by Allen and Unwin in 1940. The first full English edition of *The Economic and Philosophical Manuscripts*, did not appear until 1975 in the Pelican Marx Library, Harmondsworth, Penguin. It is interesting to note that not only do these themes of the early Marx appear in the latter works of humanistic Marxists like E. P. Thompson but also fed back towards the next generation of Christian radicals around the journal *Slant*, where all the themes of alienation and the capitalist destruction of community can be found; see Adrian Cunningham, Terry Eagleton et al., *Slant Manifesto: Catholics and the Left*, London, Sheed and Ward, 1966.
23 Op. cit., p. 57.
24 Nicholas Lash, op. cit., pp. 248–9. See note 16 above.
25 See for example, Andre Gorz, *Farewell to the Working Class: An Essay in Post-Industrial Socialism*, London, Pluto Press, 1982.
26 Op. cit., p. 58.

27 It is worth noting at this point that in the revised version of the book MacIntyre merges the two chapters entitled 'Marx's vision of History' 1 and 2 into one with the same title. In effect MacIntyre simply stitches together the two chapters with virtually no rewriting at all; what he does is simply remove some forty-five lines of text at the end of the first chapter and at the beginning of the second. The excised section begins with the sentence 'The essay is a watershed for Marx's thought' (p. 57) and ends with the sentence 'We have to learn to understand our views as symptoms of our condition, as expressions of our place in history, rather than as judgements of an impartial reason' (p. 59). The connected passage can be found in *Marxism and Christianity*, p. 57, op. cit. The relative smoothness of these excisions of Christian theological commentary from the text could raise doubts as to the fundamental seriousness of the original exercise, if it is viewed as an attempt to theologically appropriate Marx, rather than principally as an excercise in the exposition of his thought. However, I shall argue that what is crucial for MacIntyre is the types of moral claims both Marxism and Christianity make as compared with contemporary liberalism.

28 MacIntyre soon becomes very sceptical of such a positivistic notion of science as we note below. See the essay 'Breaking the Chains of Reason' in E. P. Thompson (ed.) *Out of Apathy*, London, Stevens and Sons, 1960.

29 It seems likely that MacIntyre felt rather exposed in the earlier version given his leftist political involvements of the fifties and sixties. Such a doyen of the New Left as Perry Anderson could still write in 1980, in his critique of Edward Thompson, 'Closer to Thompson's own circle, MacIntyre was fresh from providing books on Marxism for the Student Christian Movement, imbued with Anglican devotion. Was there no evidence of rightism in these currents?' (*Arguments within English Marxism*, London, Verso, 1980). Clearly for the likes of Anderson, religious commitments border on treason to the Left. Anderson goes on to mention in passing, as more damning evidence, MacIntyre's later political essays on Marxism published mainly in *Encounter* (the most important can be found in A. MacIntyre, *Against the Self-Images of the Age: Essays on Ideology and Philosophy*, London, Duckworth, 1971). Far from being simple rightist products they are critical appreciations of Marxists like Lenin and above all Trotsky, whose later writings MacIntyre vindicates as genuinely opposed to the tyranny of Soviet Communism. These he contrasts with the semi-apologetic attitude of orthodox Trotskyism (and indeed Perry Anderson) with its talk of Soviet type societies being deformed or degenerated workers' states, but workers' states none the less.

30 Op. cit., p. 69.

31 Op. cit., pp. 70–1.

32 See the work of Bryan S. Turner for some stimulating and theoretically informed analysis of the social importance of systematic attempts by most of the major world religions to construct

successful theodicies. *(For Weber: Essays in the Sociology of Fate*, London, Routledge & Kegan Paul, 1981); also the same author's *Religion and Social Theory: A Materialist Perspective*, London, Heinemann, 1983.

33 Op. cit., p. 71.

34 See especially MacIntyre's, *After Virtue: A Study in Moral Theory*, London, Duckworth, 1981. See Chapters 7 and 8.

35 It is not, of course, literally true that Marx has no account of the existence of revolutionary bourgeois intellectuals. Gouldner provides us with a number of careful accounts of the issue, which highlight the tensions in Marx's thought. In the first place Marx makes a claim that part of the intelligentsia became aware of the plight of capitalist societies and sided with the historically progressive forces. But why only some, why should not all of the old ruling class go over? On the face of it Marx's answer seems to involve a conception of education providing insight beyond class interest, an apparently rather idealist account of social change. In essence Gouldner argues that Marxism is not quite what it seems; he argues in his final book that

> Marxism was the product of an historically evolving social stratum, a secular intelligentsia which had been committed to a long-standing search for an historical agent, whom it wished to tutor, in whom it wished to develop a correct consciousness, and who it hoped would transform the world in desirable ways. Far from simply being passive recipients of ruling class initiatives – though it is that, too, frequently enough – the intelligentsia, secular or clerical, has often its own politics around its own special interests and it has actively taken initiatives on its own behalf.
>
> Alvin Gouldner, *Against Fragmentation: The Origins of Marxism and the Sociology of Intellectuals*, Oxford, Oxford University Press, 1985, p. 25.

This was published after Gouldner's untimely death and constituted the final part of his lengthy analysis of Marxism and its relationship to what he saw as the emergence of a 'New Class', that he undertook in the three volumes that collectively he entitled 'The Dark Side of the Dialectic', *The Dialectic of Ideology and Technology: The Origins, Grammar and Future of Ideology*, London, Macmillan, 1976; *The Future of Intellectuals and the Rise of the New Class*, London, Macmillan, 1979; *The Two Marxisms: Contradictions and Anomalies in the Development of Theory*, London, Macmillan, 1980. See also the same author's 'Prologue to a Theory of Revolutionary Intellectuals', *Telos*, No. 26, Winter 1975–6. Also very relevant to contemporary issues and developments is the attempt by one of Gouldner's students to apply his New Class theory to the nature of some of the latest developments in social theory: Cornelis Disco, 'Critical Theory as Ideology of the New Class: Rereading Jürgen Habermas', *Theory and Society*, Vol. 8, 1979.

36 Op. cit., p. 90.
37 'Notes From The Moral Wilderness I', *New Reasoner* 7, Winter 1958–9, p. 90.
38 Ibid., pp. 90–1.
39 Ibid., p. 91.
40 Ibid., pp. 91–2.
41 Ibid., p. 98.
42 Ibid., p. 100.
43 Ibid., p. 100.
44 'Notes from the Moral Wilderness II', *New Reasoner* 8, Spring 1959, p. 90.
45 Ibid., p. 91.
46 Ibid., p. 95.
47 *After Virtue*, op. cit., pp. vii, viii.
48 Ibid., p. vii.
49 These details are to be found in Alasdair MacIntyre, 'Moral Rationality, Tradition and Aristotle: a reply to Onora O'Neill, Raimond Gaita and Stephen R.L. Clark', *Inquiry*, Vol. 26, No. 4, December 1983, p. 447.
50 *After Virtue*, op. cit., pp. 11–12.
51 *A Short History of Ethics*, op. cit., p. 63.
52 *After Virtue*, op. cit., p. 22.
53 'Notes from the Moral Wilderness II', op. cit., p. 97.
54 *After Virtue*, op. cit., pp. 24–5.
55 Ibid., p. 31.
56 Ibid., p. 33.
57 Ibid., p. 52.
58 MacIntyre's formulation, ibid., p. 52.
59 Ibid., p. 152.
60 Ibid., p. 211.
61 Ibid., Chapter 15, especially p. 206.
62 Ibid., p. 203.
63 *Secularisation and Moral Change*, the Riddell Memorial Lectures, delivered at the University of Newcastle upon Tyne in November 1964, Oxford, Oxford University Press, 1967. *The Religious Significance of Atheism*, authored as two sets of essays with Paul Ricoeur, the Bampton Lectures delivered at Columbia University 1966, New York, Columbia University Press, 1969.
64 *The Religious Significance of Atheism*, op. cit., p. 8.
65 Ibid., p. 9.
66 On the whole issue of relativism and, perhaps, the inevitability of ethnocentrism in contemporary anthropology, see the stimulating analysis in Jonathan Friedman, 'Beyond Otherness or: The Spectacularization of Anthropology', *Telos*, No. 71, Spring 1987.
67 See MacIntyre's paper 'Relativism, Power, and Philosophy' in J. Baynes, H. Bohman, T. McCarthy (eds), *After Philosophy: End or Transformation?* Cambridge Mass., Harvard University Press, 1987.
68 Op. cit., p. 11.
69 Ibid., p. 14.

70 See MacIntyre's paper 'Is Understanding Religion Compatible With Believing?' in J. Hick, *Faith of the Philosophers*, London, Macmillan, 1964.

71 'Public Virtue', a review article, *London Review of Books*, 18th February – 3rd March, 1982, p. 14.

72 Ibid.

73 Op. cit., pp. 16–17.

74 'Moral Rationality, Tradition and Aristotle: a reply to Onora O'Neill, Raimond Gaita and Stephen R. L. Clark,' *Inquiry*, Vol. 26, No. 4, December 1983, pp. 465–6.

75 Op. cit., p. 24.

76 *Secularisation and Moral Change*, op. cit., p. 12.

77 See the claims made by Stauth and Turner that MacIntyre's account of morality and secularisation, 'has to assume the absence of significant cleavage in the social structure of feudalism of either class formation or status stratification' in G. Stauth and B.S. Turner, *Nietzsche's Dance: Resentment, Reciprocity and Resistance in Social Life*, Oxford, Blackwell, 1988, p. 47. See also the analysis of Ross Poole, *Morality and Modernity*, London, Routledge, 1991, pp. 146–50.

78 Op. cit., pp. 12–13.

79 *After Virtue*, op. cit., p. 155.

80 Op. cit., pp. 47–8.

81 Op. cit., pp. 160–1.

82 MacIntyre, 'Practical Rationalities as Forms of Social Structure', *Irish Philosophical Journal*, Vol. 4, 1987, p.13.

83 'God and the Theologians' in Alasdair MacIntyre, *Against the Self-Images of the Age*, London, Duckworth, 1971, p. 19.

84 'Is Understanding Religion Compatible With Believing?' op. cit., pp. 76–7.

85 MacIntyre, 'Which Gods Ought We To Obey And Why?', *Faith and Philosophy*, Vol. 3, No. 4, October 1986.

86 Ibid., p. 370.

87 MacIntyre, 'How To Seem Virtuous Without Actually Being So', Centre For The Study Of Cultural Values, Occasional Papers Series, No. 1, Lancaster University, 1991, p. 14.

88 For a most interesting and persuasive account of the potentially radical nature of St Thomas Aquinas' views on the limitations of private property in relation to natural law, see Joseph Ferraro, 'St Thomas Aquinas and Modern Catholic Doctrine' in *The Monthly Review*, June 1986.

89 Op. cit., p. 14.

90 Ibid., p. 15.

91 MacIntyre discusses Trotsky's life and work in more detail in his essay 'Trotsky in Exile' in *Against the Self-Images of the Age*, op. cit. In this essay MacIntyre stresses the political and intellectual honesty of Trotsky compared not only with the Stalinists but also western fellow-travellers and the debased Trotskyite sects. For MacIntyre Trotsky's greatness lay in his struggle to try to make sense of the Soviet regime under Stalin and his preparedness close to the end of

his life to examine the possibility that the Soviet Union might actually constitute a new form of collective exploitation that would establish beyond doubt the death of socialism there. See pp. 54–5, op. cit.
92 *After Virtue*, op. cit., p. 244.
93 Ibid., p. 244.
94 Ibid.
95 Walter L. Adamson, *Marx and the Disillusionment of Marxism*, Berkeley, University of California Press, 1985, p. 1.

2 AN EXCURSUS ON THE POSSIBILITY OF AN ARISTOTELIAN MARXISM

1 On this see Alvin W. Gouldner's work, especially his last book, *Against Fragmentation: The Origins of Marxism and the Sociology of Intellectuals*, Oxford, Oxford University Press, 1985.
2 H. Stuart Hughes, *Consciousness and Society: The Reorientation of European Social Thought 1890–1930*, London, MacGibbon & Kee Ltd, 1959, p. 66.
3 Ibid. On the question of these theories' relationship with social structure, see Chapters 4 and 5 of Arno J. Mayer, *The Persistence of the Old Regime: Europe to the Great War*, New York, Pantheon Books, 1981, and Tom Bottomore, *Elites and Society*, Harmondsworth, Penguin Books, 1966.
4 Perry Anderson, *Considerations on Western Marxism*, London, New Left Books, 1976, pp. 25–9.
5 Althusser is the classic example with numerous pieces of Marxist sociology in Britain referring to his work. Gramsci is a slightly different case; theorist and politician, his influence has been more subtle, especially on historical work by historians like E. P. Thompson and E. Genovese, with the Centre for Contemporary Cultural Studies reflecting both influences. Although it seems certain that of these two figures Gramsci's impact now seems to have been the more durable as the concept of civil society gained such prominence in the late 1980s and early 1990s.
6 Perry Anderson, op. cit., p. 60.
7 This return behind Marx is also an index, as Anderson has also noted, of the continuing pessimistic pressure upon twentieth-century Marxist thought, for these 'borrowings' greatly affect the structure of the theory,

> Gramsci's revolutionary temper was tersely expressed in the maxim, 'pessimism of the intellect, optimism of the will' . . . The pervasive melancholy of the work of the Frankfurt School lacked any comparable note of active fortitude. Adorno and Horkheimer called in question the very idea of man's ultimate mastery of nature, as a realm of deliverance beyond capitalism. Marcuse evoked the utopian potentiality of the liberation of nature in

man, only to deny it the more emphatically as the objective
tendency in reality, and to conclude that the industrial working
class was itself absorbed past recall within capitalism. The
pessimism of Althusser and Sartre had another but no less grave
horizon, the very structure of socialism itself. Althusser declared
that even communism would remain opaque as a social order to
the individuals living under it, deceiving them with the perpetual
illusion of their liberty as subjects, Sartre rejected the very idea of
a true dictatorship of the proletariat as an impossibility, and
interpreted the bureaucratisation of socialist revolutions as the
ineluctable product of a scarcity whose end remained incon-
ceivable in this century.

Perry Anderson, op. cit., p. 89.

8 Richard Rorty, 'Kripke versus Kant' (a review essay of Saul Kripke's
   Naming and Necessity, Oxford, Blackwell, 1980), *London Review of
   Books*, Vol. 2, 4th September–17th September 1980, all quotations
   from here unless otherwise stated.
9 Ibid.
10 J. G. Merquior, *Western Marxism*, London, Granada (Paladin), 1986,
    pp. 11–12. The Hegel quotation is on p. 12.
11 Jeffrey T. Bergner, *The Origins of Formalism in Social Science*, Chicago,
    University of Chicago Press, 1981, p. 67.
12 Gillian Rose, *Hegel Contra Sociology*, London, Athlone, 1981. In
    Chapter 1 of this powerful and difficult book, Rose lays bare the
    Neo-Kantian basis of both Weber and Durkheim and most of
    twentieth-century western Marxism. She says of Kant,

> The demarcation of legitimate theoretical and practical knowl-
> edge turns out to be the demarcation of new areas of ignorance
> ... In sum, the finite only is knowable, while the infinite
> transcends the realm of thought ... The unknowability of what
> Kant calls, among other names, the 'unconditioned' or the
> 'infinite', results in the unknowability of ourselves, both as
> subjects of experience, 'the transcendental unity of apper-
> ception', and as moral agents capable of freedom. Pari passu, the
> unknowability of ourselves means that the social, political and
> historical determinants of all knowledge and all action remain
> unknown and unknowable (p. 44).

In its place Rose presents what she calls a speculative reading of
Hegel, as opposed to reading his work as ordinary grammatical
propositions. To read 'speculatively' in this sense 'means that the
identity which is affirmed between subject and predicate is seen
equally to affirm a lack of identity between subject and predicate'
(pp. 48–9). The whole book should be taken as a critique of
formalism, so there can be no question of a distinction between
theory and method, nor can the subject be given a definition prior
to working through the text and its consequent experience. Hence
she seems to be suggesting a rooting of theory in a Hegelian re-
education of consciousness, i.e. a phenomenology.

This difficult nomic work seems to be an attempt to avoid what Adorno termed Identity logic (Rose is author of a study of Adorno) in which the irreducible particularity of existence is reduced to its formal-rational component. Her work may open the way to a proper Hegelian/Marxian theory of consciousness that would take Marxism away from the structure/action question, which is, on her terms, another version of Kantian formalism.

13 J. T. Bergner, op. cit., p. 64.

14 E. P. Thompson, *The Poverty of Theory and Other Essays*, London, Merlin, 1978, especially p. 376. See also Simon Clarke et al., *One Dimensional Marxism*, London, Allison and Busby, 1980. Also relevant in a wider context is Alvin Gouldner, *Against Fragmentation*, op. cit., and the same author's 'Prologue to a Theory of Revolutionary Intellectuals', *Telos*, No. 26, Winter 1975–6.

15 Louis Althusser, 'On the Materialist Dialectic' in *For Marx*, London, NLB, 1977, pp. 198–9.

16 Alex Callinicos, *Althusser's Marxism*, London, Pluto Press, 1976, p. 33.

17 For anyone who wants to, Althusser's thought on these matters can be followed in E. P. Thompson's *Poverty of Theory*, op. cit., pp. 202–5. Paul Piccone's 'Structuralist Marxism?' *Radical America* III, No. 5, September 1969, pp. 25–30 is probably the best short critique of Althusser's conception of science, written from a more or less Hegelian Marxist viewpoint.

18 Especially the group around the journals *Theoretical Practice* and then later *Economy and Society*; the most famous members of this group are Paul Q. Hirst and Barry Hindess.

19 The fate of the British Althusserians can be traced through Paul Hirst and Barry Hindess's, *Pre-Capitalist Modes of Production*, London, Routledge & Kegan Paul, 1975, to the same authors' *Mode of Production and Social Formation: An Autocritique of Pre-capitalist Modes of Production*, London, Macmillan, 1977, down to, co-authored with the above by Anthony Cutler and Athar Hussain (old hands from *Theoretical Practice*), *Marx's Capital and Capitalism Today*, two volumes, London, Routledge & Kegan Paul, 1977 and 1978. In the final works the authors de-construct most of the concepts of Althusserian Marxism, such as the mode of production, any version of the Labour Theory of Value, economic determination, etc. The result of all this was the reduction of Marxism to 'a medium of political calculation' (P. Hirst, *On Law and Ideology*, London, Macmillan, 1979, p. 3), the practical consequence of which seems to have been the foundation of the relatively short-lived bi-annual journal *Politics and Power*, vols 1–4, London, Routledge & Kegan Paul, 1980–2. For a valuable survey of the varieties of Althusserian and post-Althusserian work, see Ellen Meiksins Wood: *The Retreat from Class: A New True Socialism*, London, Verso, 1986.

20 Perhaps the most influential work has been that of Roy Bhasker: *A Realist Theory of Science*, Brighton, Harvester, 1978.

21 In David McLellan (ed.) *Karl Marx: Selected Writings*, Oxford, Oxford University Press, 1977, p. 389.

22 Russell Keat and John Urry, *Social Theory as Science*, London, Routledge & Kegan Paul, 1975, pp. 42–3 all quotes.

23 John Urry, *The Anatomy of Capitalist Societies: The Economy, Civil Society and the State*, London, Macmillan, 1981, p. 8.

24 This point is elaborated in a realist critique of so-called 'Game Theory Marxism', although sharing many of its anti-metaphysical premises; see Scott Lash and John Urry, 'The New Marxism of Collective Action: A Critical Analysis', *Sociology*, Vol. 18, No. 1, February 1984.

25 See Jon Elster's *Logic and Society*, Chichester, Wiley, 1976, and his most important statement of this 'New Marxism', *Making Sense of Marx*, Cambridge, Cambridge University Press, 1985.

26 G. A. Cohen, *Karl Marx's Theory of History: A Defence*, Oxford, Oxford University Press, 1978.

27 Stuart Hall uses the phrase at the end of a review article of Nicos Poulantzas's last book, *State, Power, Socialism* (London, NLB, 1978), in *New Left Review*, 119, January/February 1980, p. 69. This article captures well the tension between the structuralist Marxism of Althusser and looser action orientation, both competing for radical allegiance.

28 See, for example, Perry Anderson's praise in *Arguments within English Marxism*, London, Verso, 1980, where it is said of Cohen's discussion of the whole base/superstructure metaphor: 'It so happens, in fact, that we now possess a stringent and persuasive vindication of its role within Marxist theory, in Cohen's work whose intellectual force supersedes virtually all previous discussion' (p. 72). Note that Cohen is being deployed against Thompson who in the process of his critique of Althusser in *The Poverty of Theory* (op. cit.) was also making his break from orthodox Marxism although in a very different style and intention to Hindess and Hirst etc.

29 Cohen, op. cit., Chapters 9 and 10, pp. 269–89 defend functional explanations in general and their relevance, to Marxism in particular.

30 The debate over functionalism raged for a time, particularly between Elster and Cohen: see J. Elster, 'Cohen on Marx's Theory of History', *Political Studies*, Vol. 18, 1980, pp. 121–8 and the reply, G. A. Cohen, 'Functional Explanation, Reply to Elster', *Political Studies*, Vol. 18, 1980, p. 129–35 and also the subsequent discussion: J. Elster, 'Marxism, Functionalism and Game Theory, the Case for Methodological Individualism', *Theory and Society*, Vol. 11, 1982, pp. 453–82 and G. A. Cohen, 'Reply to Elster on Marxism, Functionalism and Game Theory', *Theory and Society*, Vol. 11, 1982, pp. 483–95. For a most effective recent critique of this kind of reasoning see J. McCarney, *Social Theory and the Crisis of Marxism*, London, Verso, 1990.

31 Gillian Rose, op. cit., p. 45.

32 Quoted from Scott Meikle, 'Critique of Cohen', unpublished paper given at the journal *Critique* weekend school, April 1980.

33 Cohen, op. cit., p. ix.
34 Sean Sayers, 'Marxism and the Dialectical Method: A Critique of G. A. Cohen', *Radical Philosophy*, No. 36, Spring 1984, p. 4.
35 Such a distinction does go rather in the opposite direction from recent more 'sociological' accounts of Marx's theory, e.g. P. Corrigan, H. Ramsey and D. Sayer, *Socialist Construction and Marxist Theory: Bolshevism and its Critique*, London, Macmillan, 1978.
36 Cohen, op. cit., pp. 28–31.
37 Karl Marx, *Capital*, Vol. I, London, Penguin Books/New Left Review, 1976, p. 103. It is good to be able to note that this is recognised now even by those who were once heavily influenced by Althusser. Richard Johnson for example, can now write that 'The attempt to drive a wedge between Hegel and the "later" Marx is a distinct weakness of Althusserian interpretations and leads to some real travesties of "reading" of the Marx texts themselves', in 'Reading for the Best Marx: History-writing and Historical Abstraction' in *Making Histories: Studies in History-writing and Politics*, Centre for Contemporary Cultural Studies, ed. Richard Johnson, Gregor McLennan, Bill Schwartz, David Sutton, p. 353, note 49, London, Hutchinson University Library, 1982.
38 J. Elster, *Making Sense of Marx*, op. cit.
39 Sayers, op. cit., p. 5.
40 Relevant here are Roy Edgley, 'Science, Social Science and Socialist Science: Reason as Dialectic', *Radical Philosophy*, 15, Autumn 1976; Lucio Colletti, 'Marxism and the Dialectic', *New Left Review*, 93, 1975; Peter Dews, 'Misadventures of the Dialectic', *Radical Philosophy*, No. 18, Autumn 1977; Roy Edgley, 'Dialectic: The Contradiction of Colletti', *Critique*, No. 7, 1976.
41 This is clearly brought out in his book, *Marxism and Hegel*, London, NLB, 1973, and perhaps most pointedly in his interview with Perry Anderson for *New Left Review*, Lucio Colletti, 'A Political and Philosophical Interview', in Gareth Stedman and G. S. Jones, *Western Marxism: A Critical Reader*, London, New Left Review Editions, 1977. Here he says,

> there are two main traditions in this respect one that descends from Spinoza and Hegel and the other from Hume and Kant. These two lines of development are profoundly divergent. For any theory that takes science as the sole form of real knowledge – that is falsifiable, as Popper would say – there can be no question that the tradition of Hume–Kant must be given priority and preference over that of Spinoza–Hegel (p. 325).

42 Peter Dews, op. cit., p. 10.
43 R. Edgley, 'Dialectic: The Contradiction of Colletti', op. cit., pp. 49–50.
44 Scott Meikle, 'Dialectical Contradiction and Necessity', in *Issues in Marxist Philosophy*, Vol. I, *Dialectics and Method*, ed. John Mepham and D. H. Ruben, Brighton, Harvester Press, 1979, p. 20, emphasis added.

45 Ibid., p. 22.
46 Ibid., p. 24. Meikle is careful to point out that Marxist essentialism cannot be simply developed out of Kripke's position (pp. 26–9); his work on the necessary identity of things is rather a necessary but not sufficient condition for this kind of Marxism.
47 R. Rorty, 'Kripke versus Kant', op. cit.
48 Christopher Norris, *The Deconstructive Turn: Essays in the Rhetoric of Philosophy*, London, Methuen, 1983, p. 145.
49 Ibid., p. 151.
50 Christopher Norris's first book, *Deconstruction: Theory and Practice*, London, Methuen, 1982 is an excellent guide to this complex and often bewildering topic.
51 C. Norris, *Deconstructive Turn*, op. cit., p. 152.
52 Rorty, op. cit.
53 C. Norris, *Deconstructive Turn*, op. cit., p. 154.
54 Rorty, op. cit. For Rorty as philosophic deconstructor, see *Philosophy and the Mirror of Nature*, Oxford, OUP, 1980.
55 See, for example, a response to modern liberal Protestant theology: Keith Ward, *Holding Fast to God*, London, SPCK, 1982.
56 Aside from his book *Essentialism in the Thought of Karl Marx*, op. cit., other relevant material by this author, that I have drawn on, includes: 'Dialectical Contradiction and Necessity', op. cit., 'Aristotle and the Political Economy of the Polis', *Journal of Hellenic Studies*, 1979, Vol. XCIX, and 'Marxism and the Necessity of Essentialism' (a review article of G. E. M. de Ste Croix's *The Class Struggle in the Ancient World*), *Critique*, 16, 1984, 'Making Nonsense of Marx' (a review article of Jon Elster's *Making Sense of Marx*), *Inquiry*, Vol. 29, pp. 29–43, March 1986.
57 'Making Nonsense of Marx', op. cit., p. 38.
58 *Essentialism in the Thought of Karl Marx*, op. cit., p. 9.
59 'Making Nonsense of Marx', op. cit., p. 38.
60 Ibid., pp. 38–9. 'Ergon' behaviour of a kind that expresses the essence of the kind of thing it is; see Glossary p. 176, in *Essentialism in the Thought of Karl Marx*, op. cit; see also, on the question of what a law is pp. 171–4, ibid.
61 Ibid., p. 40.
62 Allen Wood, *Karl Marx*, London, Routledge & Kegan Paul, 1981, p. 235. Others who have noted Marx's Aristotelian connection include Richard W. Miller: 'Marx and Aristotle: A Kind of Consequentialism', *Canadian Journal of Philosophy*, Supp. Vol. 7, 1981; and Alan Gilbert: 'Marx's Moral Realism: Eudaimonism and Moral Progress' in T. Ball and J. Farr (eds) *After Marx*, Cambridge, Cambridge University Press, 1984. In addition on the question of the Labour Theory of Value in relation to essentialism, see Diane Elson's 'The Value Theory of Labour' in Diane Elson (ed.) *Value: The Representation of Labour in Capitalism*, C. S. E. Books, London, 1979, especially p. 149 where she is using the Aristotelian concept of potentia to explain Marx's theory. All these seem compatible with Scott Meikle's approach. Also see Hannah Arendt's *The*

Human Condition, Chicago, University of Chicago Press, 1958, the entire book being an exploration of the tradition of thought concerning 'work, labour and activity' which she sees running from Aristotle to Marx. More recently R. N. Berki's *Insight and Vision: The Problem of Communism in Marx's Thought*, London, J. M. Dent, 1983: his understanding of at least the derivation of Marx's thought, as opposed to its viability, is at one with Meikle:

> Marx's connecting capitalism and communism is really not much more than a peculiar and striking adaption of the Aristotelian categories of potentiality and actuality, and it is certainly not an accident that Marx's later theoretical writings (the *Grundrisse* as well as *Capital*) are replete with references to Aristotle, in revealing contrast to the earlier texts. Of course, Marx's immanentist 'Hegelianism' and his increasing reliance on and preoccupation with Aristotle are not in any sort of contradiction: Hegel himself . . . [needs little] . . . analysis for his Aristotelianism to be discovered . . . But again neither Hegel nor Marx is a simple interpreter of Aristotle. Marx's project, and in this he more or less carries further and perhaps culminates the Hegelian philosophical enterprise, is an attempt at a gigantic synthesis of classical and modern thought (pp. 97–8).

This seems to be the basis of Marx's unrepeatable brilliance; it could be said of him what he said of Cobbet, that he was 'the last man of the old world, and the first man of the new'.

63 Meikle, *Essentialism in the Thought of Karl Marx*, op. cit., p. 31.
64 Ibid., p. 32. He is quoting from Hegel's *Reason in History*, p. 24, trans. Robert S. Hartman, New York, 1953.
65 Ibid., p. 33.
66 Ibid., p. 35, quoting Hegel, op. cit., p. 69.
67 Ibid., p. 36.
68 Ibid., p. 36.
69 Quoted in ibid., p. 42.
70 Ibid., p. 44.
71 Ibid., p. 47.
72 Ibid., p. 57.
73 Ibid., p. 58; on this point, see Meikle note 137, p. 58.
74 Ibid.
75 Rorty, 'Kripke versus Kant', op. cit., both Rorty quotations.
76 Important attempts at precisely this have been made by the Marxist political economist Hillel Ticktin working on the fate of Russian Marxism and what the existence of the USSR as a bureaucratic tyranny means for teleology. See especially 'Towards a Political Economy of the USSR', *Critique* 1 and 'Class Structure and the Soviet Elite', *Critique* 9. Ticktin is now applying these same essentialist Marxist categories to modern capitalism in a series of important articles on finance capital, which he sees as both expanding and growing, but also as a declining form of the organism that is capitalism: 'Finance Capital, the Transitional

Epoch and Britain', *Critique* 16, 1984.
77 See *After Virtue*, op. cit., Chapter 15.
78 *After Virtue*, op. cit., p. 152.
79 See *Whose Justice? Which Rationality?*, London, Duckworth, 1988; also *Three Rival Versions of Moral Enquiry*, London, Duckworth, 1990. It is clear from both these works that although MacIntyre is increasingly committed to an Aristotelian-Thomist realism he is at the same time committed to a version of a kind of hisoricist dialectic in which realism may or may not vindicate itself in a variety of social and historical contexts. It would appear that for MacIntyre it is still too early to tell if such a realism can really win out. See especially MacIntyre's ninth Gifford Lecture 'Tradition Against Genealogy: Who Speaks to Whom?' in *Three Rival Versions of Moral Enquiry*, op. cit.
80 *Social Research*, Vol. 45, No. 4, Winter, 1978, p. 683.
81 Ibid., p. 695.
82 Ibid., p. 729.
83 Ibid., p. 730.
84 Ibid., pp. 732–3.
85 Ibid., p. 730.
86 Ibid., p. 735.
87 Alasdair MacIntyre, *Marxism and Christianity*, London, Duckworth, 1968, p. 130.
88 Ibid., p. 130.
89 Ibid., p. 131.
90 Ibid., p. 111.

3 MACINTYRE'S EVALUATIVE HISTORY AND POLANYI'S HISTORICAL SOCIOLOGY

1 Karl Polanyi, *The Great Transformation*, Boston, Beacon Press, 1944.
2 Alan MacFarlane, *The Origins of English Individualism: The Family, Property and Social Transition*, Oxford, Blackwell, 1978. But Mac-Farlane is not alone; his colleague Peter Lasslett in works on the medieval family claiming the long existence of the nuclear family, clearly implied similar conclusions to MacFarlane's, e.g. Laslett, *The World We Have Lost* (2nd edition), Cambridge, Cambridge University Press, 1971.
3 Ibid., p. 199.
4 Ibid., p. 196.
5 Ibid., p. 199.
6 Ferdinand Mount, 'Goodbye to the Peasants', *Spectator*, 17th February 1979, p. 4.
7 A. MacIntyre, 'After Virtue and Marxism: A Response to Wartofsky', *Inquiry*, Vol. 27, Nos. 2–3, July 1984, pp. 253–4.
8 It was the younger Alasdair MacIntyre who made the following point about Marxism:

    As Marx depicts it the relation between basis and superstructure is fundamentally not only not mechanical, it is not even causal. What may be misleading is Marx's Hegelian vocabulary. Marx certainly talks of the basis 'determining' the superstructure and of a 'correspondence' between them. But the reader of Hegel's 'logic' will realise that what Marx envisages is something to be understood in terms of the way in which the nature of the concept of a given class, for example, may determine the concept of the membership of that class . . . the economic basis of a society is not its tools, but the people co-operating using these particular tools in the manner necessary for their use, and the superstructure consists of the social consciousness moulded by and the shape of this co-operation.

Alasdair MacIntyre, 'Notes from the Moral Wilderness I' in *New Reasoner* 7, Winter 1958–9, p. 98.

There may be doubts about the use of this Hegelian philosophy of internal relations in Marxism but it does raise questions about the legitimacy of his rather sweeping criticisms of Marxist formulations as positivistic causal explanations. Indeed, it seems likely that his present formulations are an attempt to salvage, in a revised philosophic mould, much of the methodological substance of the Hegelian-Marxist theory of internal relations (see also Part One).

9 Op. cit., MacIntyre, *Inquiry*, 1984, p. 253.

10 In what follows I draw on a variety of critical commentary about MacFarlane's work including: Keith Tribe's review of MacFarlane in *Social History*, Vol. 4, No. 3, 1979, pp. 520–2; Rodney Hilton's critical remarks in 'Individualism and the English Peasantry', *New Left Review*, 120, March–April 1980, pp. 109–12; and most helpful of all Stephen D. White and Richard T. Vann: 'The Invention of English Individualism: Alan MacFarlane and the Modernization of Pre-modern England' in *Social History*, Vol. 8, No. 2, 1983, pp. 345–63.

11 MacFarlane, op. cit., p. 10.

12 Ibid., p. 13. MacFarlane is here quoting from Teodor Shanin (ed.), *Peasants and Peasant Societies*, London, Penguin, 1971, pp. 203–4.

13 Ibid., p. 15. Once more MacFarlane is quoting Shanin, ibid., p. 241.

14 Ibid., p. 17.

15 Ibid., p. 18; whether this is true is another matter.

16 R. Hilton, op. cit., p. 109.

17 E.g. Rodney Hilton's essay, 'The Peasantry as a Class' in R. Hilton, *The English Peasantry in the Later Middle Ages*, Oxford, Oxford University Press, 1973.

18 S. White and R. Vann, *Social History*, 1983, op. cit., p. 351.

19 K. Tribe, *Social History*, 1979, op. cit., p. 520.

20 Hilton, *New Left Review*, p. 109, op. cit.

21 K. Tribe, *Social History*, 1974, p. 520, op. cit.

22 See most particularly on this G. de Ste Croix's opening chapters of *The Class Struggle in the Ancient Greek World*, London, Duckworth, 1981; also see excursus above.

23 S. White and R. Vann, *Social History*, op. cit., p. 352.

24 Ibid.
25 Ibid., p. 355.
26 MacFarlane, op. cit., p. 86.
27 Op. cit., pp. 356–7.
28 *After Virtue*, op. cit., pp. 36–7.
29 Jürgen Habermas, 'The Public Sphere: An Encyclopedia Article', *New German Critique*, Vol. 3, Fall 1974.
30 However, this process should not be assumed so easily as the emergence, in the 1980s, of a right-wing Tory historiography, under the influence of Maurice Cowling, makes clear; it points to the importance of the concept of a confessional state in England right into the nineteenth century: J. C. D. Clark, *English Society 1688–1832*, Cambridge, Cambridge University Press, 1985.
31 *After Virtue*, p. 36. MacIntyre gives a much more detailed account of the nature and significance of an educated reading public, using particularly the case of Scotland in his paper 'The Idea of an Educated Public' in *Education and Values: The Richard Peter Lectures*, ed. Graham Haydon, Institute of Education, London University, 1987.
32 I draw here on Chapter 5 of *After Virtue*, 'Why the Enlightenment Project had to fail', pp. 49–59.
33 Ibid., p. 50.
34 For detail on this, see Ian Hacking, *The Emergence of Probability*, Cambridge, Cambridge University Press, 1975.
35 *After Virtue*, p. 52.
36 Ibid., p. 53.
37 See the interesting work of Peter Gay, especially *Freud for Historians*, Oxford, OUP, 1986.
38 Oxford, Clarendon Press, 1962.
39 John Dunn, *Western Political Theory in the Face of the Future*, Cambridge, Cambridge University Press, 1979, pp. 38–9.
40 John Dunn, *John Locke*, Oxford, OUP, 1984, pp. 42–3.
41 A. MacIntyre, *Inquiry*, 1984, op. cit., p. 253.
42 Princeton, Princeton University Press, 1977.
43 Paul Piccone (Gonzales), 'Rethinking Radical Politics', *Telos*, 48, Summer 1981, p. 110.
44 Albert O. Hirschman, *The Passions and the Interests: Political Arguments for Capitalism before its Triumph*, Princeton University Press, 1977, pp. 14–15.
45 See J. Huizinga, *Waning of the Middle Ages*, London, Penguin Books, 1955.
46 See Perry Anderson, *Lineages of the Absolutist States*, London, New Left Books, 1974.
47 Calvin and Calvinism of a certain kind perhaps emphasised this view more than any other. However, for qualifications on Calvin's view of non-resistance to authority, Q. Skinner, *The Foundations of Modern Political Thought*, Vol. II, Cambridge University Press, 1978, pp. 191–4.
48 Hirschman, op. cit., pp. 18–19.

49 Ibid., pp. 18–19.

50 Ibid., p. 41.

51 This in itself raises many questions, especially, why the concentration on avarice at this point? Lester Little has pointed to the sudden upsurge of religious movement that emphasised poverty as an ideal in the later Middle Ages, e.g. the Franciscans emerging in the commercial centre of the period, as new social relations threatened the integrity of an older social order and belief systems: Lester K. Little, *Religious Poverty and the Profit Economy in Medieval Europe*, London, Paul Elek, 1978. No one interested in these questions can possibly afford to miss Umberto Eco's excellent novel *The Name of the Rose*, London, Secker and Warburg, 1983, for a wonderful evocation of the cultural conflicts of the period.

52 See Raymond Williams, *Key Words: A Vocabulary of Culture and Society*, London, Fontana/Collins, 1976, p. 143.

53 Hirschman, op. cit., p. 33.

54 Ibid., p. 40, but see MacIntyre's own attempt to rehabilitate the concept in *After Virtue*, op. cit., pp. 99–100.

55 Benjamin Nelson, *The Idea of Usury from Tribal Brotherhood to Universal Otherhood*, Chicago, University of Chicago Press, second enlarged edition, 1968.

56 B. Nelson, op. cit., Appendix, 'Some Remarks on the Parallel Fate of the Ideals of Friendship and Brotherhood in Early Modern Times', pp. 142–3. See also Terry Eagleton's study of Shakespeare for an analysis of the mixture of feudal and capitalist elements, *The Free Dependent: Shakespeare and Society*, London, Chatto & Windus, 1967.

57 B. Nelson, op. cit., pp. 147–8.

58 Ibid., pp. 157–8.

59 Hirschman, op. cit., pp. 41–2.

60 Ibid., p. 42.

61 Ibid., p. 50.

62 *After Virtue*, op. cit., p. 83.

63 Quoted in Hirschman, op. cit., p. 108.

64 Ibid., p. 109.

65 See the interesting essay by Alessandro Pizzaro, 'On the Rationality of Democratic Choice', *Telos*, No. 63, Spring 1985 and C. B. Macpherson, 'The Economic Penetration of Political Theory' in *The Rise and Fall of Economic Justice and Other Papers*, Oxford, Oxford University Press, 1985.

66 Claus Offe, 'Ungovernability: The Renaissance of Conservative Theories of Crisis', p. 82 in *Contradictions of the Welfare State*, ed. John Keane, London, Hutchinson, 1984.

67 In *Primitive, Archaic and Modern Economics: Essays of Karl Polanyi*, ed. George Dalton, pp. 139–174, Boston, Beacon Press, 1971.

68 Ibid., pp. 139–40.

69 Ibid., p. 140.

70 Karl Polanyi, *The Great Transformation: The Political and Economic Origins of our Times*, Boston, Beacon Press, 1944, p. 46.

71 Ibid.
72 'The Economy as Instituted Process', op. cit., in G. Dalton, 1971, p. 148.
73 Ibid.
74 Joel Whitebrook: 'Pre-market Economics: The Aristotelian Perspective', *Dialectical Anthropology*, Vol. 3, August 1978, p. 200.
75 Polanyi, *Great Transformation*, op. cit., p. 57.
76 Jürgen Habermas, *Legitimation Crisis*, London, Heinemann, 1976, pp. 76–7.
77 K. Polanyi, 'The Obsolete Market Mentality' in G. Dalton (ed.) op. cit., p. 66.
78 A. MacIntyre, 'Moral Rationality and Tradition and Aristotle: A Reply to Onora O' Neill, Raimond Gaita and Stephen R. L. Clark, *Inquiry*, Vol. 26, No. 4, December 1983, p. 465.
79 *After Virtue*, op. cit., p. 170.
80 Ibid., p. 171.
81 See the famous discussion of Franklin in M. Weber, *Protestant Ethic and the Spirit of Capitalism*, London, Allen and Unwin, 1976, especially pp. 51–6.
82 *After Virtue*, op. cit., pp. 171–2.
83 Ibid., p. 172.
84 Ibid.
85 Ibid., p. 173.
86 M. Weber, *Protestant Ethic*, op. cit., p. 53.
87 *After Virtue*, op. cit., p. 174.
88 Polanyi, *The Great Transformation*, op. cit., p. 58.
89 Ibid., p. 60.

4 THE MORALITY OF MARKETS AND THE 'CRISIS OF AUTHORITY': NOTES FOR A SOCIOLOGY IN A WORLD AFTER VIRTUE

1 *Whose Justice? Which Rationality?*, London, Duckworth, 1988, pp. 222–3.
2 Ibid., p. 216.
3 Ibid., pp. 216–17.
4 *After Virtue*, op. cit., p. 206.
5 J. A. G. Pocock, *The Machiavellian Movement: Florentine Political Thought and the Atlantic Republican Tradition*, Princeton, Princeton University Press, 1975, p. 341.
6 This vast question can be approached in many ways. J. A. G. Pocock's *The Ancient Constitution and the Feudal Laws*, Cambridge, Cambridge University Press, 1957 is an important source. Much of Tom Nairn's work is concerned with this question; particularly useful is his essay 'The English Literary Intelligentsia' in *Bananas* edited by Emma Tennant, in collected form published by Quartet Books, London, 1977, pp. 57–83, where he develops the concept of a 'synthetic conservatism'. Also extremely relevant is the question

of the ideological use of history: see especially Patrick Wright's *On Living in an Old Country*, London, Verso, 1985.

7 Edmund Burke, *Reflections on the Revolution in France and on the Proceedings in Certain Societies in London relative to that Event*, edited with introduction by Conor Cruise O' Brien, (1790), London, Penguin Books, 1969, pp. 194–5. It is important to note the full title, because Burke wrote the book against English radicalism rather than against the French as such. The second half of the eighteenth century saw a complex relation between England and France with much borrowing of ideas in both directions: see Derek Jarrett, *The Begetters of Revolution: England's Involvement with France 1759–1784*, London, Longman, 1973. See pp. 283–6, on Burke's response to English radicalism.

8 Cited in C. B. Macpherson, *Burke*, Oxford, OUP, 1980, pp. 21–2. Burke wrote a good deal about economics but often for a practical purpose, his fullest theoretical statements are in his 'Thoughts and Details on Scarcity', published in 1795 in *Burke's Works*, London, Rivington, 1815–27.

9 C. B. Macpherson, ibid., p. 63, 'so by Burke's time the capitalist order had in fact been the traditional order in England for a whole century'. Since Burke was born in 1729 I calculate that his 'partnership . . . with those who are dead' stretched to his grandparents at most, but then conservatives like Burke have always been more concerned with preserving capital accumulation than the past.

10 Quoted in Macpherson, ibid., p. 60.

11 Ibid., p. 61.

12 Roy Porter, *English Society in the Eighteenth Century*, London, Penguin, 1982, p. 111.

13 Derek Fraser, *The Evolution of the British Welfare State*, London, Macmillan, 1973, p. 34.

14 Z. Bauman, *Memories of Class: The Pre-History and After Life of Class*, London, Routledge & Kegan Paul, 1982, p. 60. Bauman writes of two forms of power relationship in this context, 'control-through-money' and 'control-through-space', operating on the one hand via landed property and on the other space independent capital: see pp. 44–5.

15 Quoted in H. Perkin, *The Origins of Modern English Society, 1780–1880*, London, Routledge & Kegan Paul, 1969, p. 186.

16 Ibid., p. 182.

17 I draw here freely upon Eugene D. Genovese, especially *The World the Slaveholders Made: Two Essays in Interpretation*, London, Allen Lane, 1970.

18 Ibid., p. 126.

19 Ibid., p. 98.

20 The slave holders were themselves the heirs of the democratic and egalitarian traditions of Jeffersonian democracy, so inevitably there were counter-pressures to the development of paternalist and hierarchical ideologies. None the less the success of the pro-slavery arguments and the loyalty of the non-slave holders to the regime is

a powerful example of the social basis of ideologies.

21 Ibid., pp. 138–9.
22 Ibid., p. 159.
23 Quoted in ibid., p. 160.
24 Ibid., pp. 230–1.
25 Ibid., p. 232.
26 Ibid., p. 242.
27 Op. cit., p. 60.
28 Ibid.
29 Bryan S. Turner, 'Simmel, Rationalisation and the Sociology of Money', *Sociological Review*, Vol. 34, February 1986.
30 Georg Simmel, *The Philosophy of Money*, translated by Tom Bottomore and David Frisby, London, Routledge & Kegan Paul, 1978.
31 Ibid., p. 511.
32 *After Virtue*, op. cit., pp. 182–3.
33 Max Weber, 'The Market: Its Impersonality and Ethics', *Economy and Society*, Vol. 2, New York, Bedminster Press, p. 636.
34 Turner, op. cit., pp. 97–8.
35 Simmel, op. cit., p. 286.
36 Ibid., p. 295.
37 Ibid.
38 Ibid., p. 298.
39 Ibid.
40 Ibid., p. 299.
41 *After Virtue*, op. cit., p. 32.
42 Simmel, op. cit., pp. 300–1.
43 Ibid., p. 301.
44 Ronald Dworkin, 'Right, Left and Centre', *Sunday Times*, 12/1/86, p. 45.
45 Simmel, op. cit., pp. 296–7.
46 Brian Barry, *The Liberal Theory of Justice*, Oxford, Clarendon Press, 1973, p. 166.
47 *After Virtue*, op. cit., p. 233.

5 MANAGERIALISM AND THE CULTURE OF BUREAUCRATIC INDIVIDUALISM

1 Cambridge Mass., Harvard University Press, 1976, p. 119.
2 Alasdair MacIntyre, *After Virtue*, London, Duckworth, 1981, p. 14.
3 Fred Hirsch, *The Social Limits of Growth*, Cambridge Mass., Harvard University Press, 1976, p. 122.
4 See the excellent discussion found in Raymond Plant, 'Hirsch, Hayek and Habermas: Dilemmas of Distribution' and Krishan Kumar, 'Pre-capitalist and Non-capitalist Factors in the Development of Capitalism: Fred Hirsch and Joseph Schumpeter', both in A. Ellis and K. Kumar (eds), *Dilemmas of Liberal Democracies: Studies in Fred Hirsch's Social Limits to Growth*, London, Tavistock, 1983.

5 F. Hirsch, op. cit., p. 138.
6 Bryan S. Turner, *Religion and Social Theory*, London, Heinemann, p. 240.
7 F. Hirsch, op. cit., p. 84.
8 Ibid. The question is discussed in Chapter 5, 'The Economics of Bad Neighbours', pp. 71–83.
9 Ibid., p. 120.
10 Ibid., p. 154.
11 J. H. Goldthorpe, 'The Current Inflation: Towards a Sociological Account' in F. Hirsch and J. H. Goldthorpe (eds), *The Political Economy of Inflation*, Oxford, Martin Robertson, 1978, pp. 199–200.
12 Alasdair MacIntyre, 'Social Science Methodology as the Ideology of Bureaucratic Authority', in M. S. Falco (ed.), *Through the Looking Glass*, Washington, University Press of America, 1979, pp. 57–8.
13 On Weber's analysis in this area, see especially Roger Brubaker, *The Limits of Rationality: An Essay on the Social and Moral Thought of Max Weber*, Allen & Unwin, London, 1984. This book brings out very well the powerful tensions that Weber saw in the modern world, and deeply reflected in his own make-up. As Brubaker puts it: 'the tension between the formal rationality of the capitalist economy and its substantive irrationality from the point of view of egalitarian, fraternal and caritative values. This antagonism is 'one source [quoting Weber] of all "social" problems and above all of the problem of socialism' (p. 38). See also Wolfgang Mommsen, *The Age of Bureaucracy*, Oxford, Blackwell, 1974. But also the criticism of Weber in Leo Strauss, *Natural Right and History*, University of Chicago Press, Chicago, 1953, especially Chapter 2 on the fact and value distinction and also E. B. F. Midgley, *The Ideology of Max Weber: A Thomist Critique*, Aldershot, Gower, 1983; both the latter works have some affinities with what is presented here.
14 Alasdair MacIntyre, 'Social Science Methodology as the Ideology of Bureaucratic Authority', pp. 55–6.
15 The full argument of MacIntyre concerning facts and laws in the social sciences is to be found in Chapters 7 and 8 of *After Virtue*, pp. 76–102. Also see 'Social Science Methodology as the Ideology of Bureaucratic Authority', op. cit.
16 'Is a Science of Comparative Politics Possible?' in A. MacIntyre, *Against the Self-Images of the Age: Essays on Ideology and Philosophy*, London, Duckworth, 1971. 'The Essential Contestability of Some Social Concepts', *Ethics*, 1973–4, Vol. 84, Pt. 1.
17 'The Intelligibility of Action', in J. Margolis, M. Krausz, R. M. Burian (eds) *Rationality, Relativism and the Human Sciences*, Dordrecht, Martinus Nijhoff, 1986, p. 63.
18 *After Virtue*, op. cit., p. 81.
19 Ibid., p. 85. The article is D. J. C. Smyth and J. C. K. Ash, 'Forecasting Gross National Product, the Rate of Inflation and the Balance of Trade: The OECD Performance', *The Economic Journal* 85, 1975. In a much less specific sense than is intended here, it might be argued that social scientists have made predictions that

were accurate, e.g. the work of John Rex and his co-workers at the Ethnic and Race Relations Unit, and Stuart Hall and his co-authors of *Policing the Crisis*, London, Macmillan, 1978, all of whom it might be argued predicted the urban riots of 1981. However, they could not, nor would they claim to be able to have predicted precisely when or where such riots would occur in the manner necessary for an efficient management science to utilise. Nor is it obvious that their various books on racism and the inner city have any cognitive privilege over the work of good community-relations journalists working for the serious press or TV.

20 *After Virtue*, op. cit., p. 89–102.

21 Ibid., p. 92.

22 Op. cit.

23 Donald N. Levine, 'Sociology after MacIntyre', in *American Journal of Sociology*, Vol. 89, No. 3, 1983, p. 702.

24 Alasdair MacIntyre, 'Ideology, Social Science and Revolution', *Comparative Politics*, Vol. 5, No. 3, April 1973. See pp. 332–7 for a detailed response to such a view.

25 Cited in Richard Sennett's 'The Boss's New Clothes', *The New York Review of Books*, 22nd February 1979, p. 44.

26 A. MacIntyre, 'Social Science Methodology', op. cit., p. 55.

27 A good example of an attempt to make the bureaucrat fit this ideal model is A. Downs, 'Decision Making in Bureaucracy' in F. G. Castle et al. (eds) *Decisions, Organisations and Society*, Harmondsworth, Penguin, pp. 59–78.

28 Alasdair MacIntyre, 'Ideology, Social Science and Revolution', op. cit., p. 335.

29 *After Virtue*, op. cit., p. 50.

30 These questions are very complex and controversial. Chapters 4, 5 and 6 of *After Virtue* give some philosophical background in an historical form. David Knowles, *The Evolution of the Medieval Thought*, London, Longmans, 1962 is useful for the medieval context. It is worth mentioning a possible historical precedent for the fact/value distinction, which is the so-called double truth theory of later medievalism (unmentioned by MacIntyre in *After Virtue*). This theory held that something could be true in theology and false in philosophy, a point that seems to have been revived in the Reformation, with Luther's prioritising of faith over or indeed in spite of reason, solved by Luther by the primacy of will in his theology. The tension between faith and reason is present throughout Protestant theology, down to the nineteenth century, Kierkegaard being a distinct product of it, a tension that is passed on in a secularised form to Weber given his pessimism over resolving the tension between formal and substantive rationality: see Midgley, op. cit.

31 An interesting analysis that bears on this question is Peter Berger, Brigitte Berger and Hansfried Kellner, *The Homeless Mind*, Harmondsworth, Penguin, 1974. This and Peter Berger's essay collection, *Facing up to Modernity*, Harmondsworth, Penguin, 1979,

contain interesting comments on the role of intellectuals as carrying through a rationalisation process in which the strict observance of the fact/value distinction is carried through all spheres of life, systematically. The 'liberal' intellectual is an important cultural figure who demands greater sociological attention.

32 *After Virtue*, op. cit., p. 80.
33 Ibid., p. 81.
34 Theo Nichols and Huw Beynon, *Living with Capitalism: Class Relations and the Modern Factory*, London, Routledge & Kegan Paul, 1977, p. 34.
35 He will not use the word ideology because he feels it is part of, in Marx, the very would-be social science of law-like generalisation that he is opposing; see *After Virtue*, p. 104.
36 *After Virtue*, op. cit., p. 104.
37 Ibid., p. 72.
38 On the waste and inefficiency of the Soviet economy, see Hillel Ticktin, 'Towards a Political Economy of the USSR', *Critique*, No. 1, 1972. On the inefficiency of Nazi Germany, see Albert Speer, *Inside the Third Reich: Memoirs*, London, Weidenfeld and Nicolson, 1970.
39 *After Virtue*, op. cit., p. 101.
40 *Social Text*, Winter 1983, p. 151.
41 See for a clear statement of Offe's view his 'Theses on the Theory of the State' in C. Offe, *Contradictions of the Welfare State*, Hutchinson, London, 1984; on p. 120 he states, 'since state power depends on a process of accumulation which is beyond its power to organise, every occupant of state power is basically interested in promoting those political conditions most conducive to private accumulation'. There is nothing in *After Virtue*, that would cause MacIntyre to dissent from this view.
42 Some of the most important items in this literature from which I draw are: Stephen Marglin, 'What Do Boss's Do? The Origins and Functions of Hierarchy in Capitalist Production', *Review of Radical Political Economy*, Vol. 6, No. 2, Summer 1974; Harry Braverman, *Labour and Monopoly Capital*, London, Monthly Review Press, 1974; Sydney Pollard, *The Genesis of Modern Management*, London, Edward Arnold, 1965 and his 'Factory Discipline in the Industrial Revolution', *Economic History Review*, XVI, 1963–4; Dan Clawson, *Bureaucracy and the Labour Process: The Transformation of US Industry 1860–1920*, London, Monthly Review Press, 1980.
43 Peter Sedgwick, 'An Ethical Dance – A Review of Alasdair MacIntyre's *After Virtue*', *The Socialist Register*, London, Merlin, 1982. He writes,

'MacIntyre's life has been a long polemical itinerary, battling against massive and deliberately chosen odds with the weapons of a ruthless honesty . . . But the very intensity and rigour of his adversary role has, over the long series of battles in and outside the political left, tended to isolate him from any base in a collective endeavour . . . [an example of this]. That radical tendency in ideas . . . approximating to MacIntyre's present position – the school of European Critical Theory . . . is never referred to in *After Virtue* except in the surly amalgam we have noted between the Frankfurt School and Managerial Conformity (p. 265).

However, I do not believe Sedgwick's review is adequate to the real importance of *After Virtue*, particularly in regard to the related questions of MacIntyre's Aristotelianism and his critique of individualism. As to MacIntyre's intellectual and perhaps social isolation, it is now the case that MacIntyre's move to the University of Notre-Dame and his acceptance of the Roman Catholic Church marks a most definite form of collective endeavour, though doubtless one, that had Sedgewick lived to see it, he would have deeply disapproved of.

44 See E. P. Thompson, 'Time, Work Discipline and Industrial Capitalism', *Past and Present* 38, December 1967.
45 Anthony Giddens, *A Contemporary Critique of Historical Materialism*, London, Macmillan, 1981. This is perhaps the central element of Marxism that Giddens retains in his social theory.
46 Michael Burawoy, 'Towards a Marxist Theory of the Labour Process, Braverman and Beyond', *Politics and Society*, Vol. 8, No. 3–4, 1978.
47 Ibid., p. 279. On the ideological significance of scientific management for curtailing class conflict and limiting trade unionism, see C. S. Maier, 'Between Taylorism and Technocracy: European Ideologies and the Vision of Industrial Productivity in the 1920s', *Journal of Contemporary History*, Vol. 5, No. 2, 1970; we look at this further below.
48 Burawoy, op. cit., 260.
49 Ibid., p. 264.
50 Ibid., p. 271.
51 Ibid., p. 272.
52 Ibid., p. 279.
53 Ibid., p. 279; Maier's work, see note 47 above.
54 Ibid., p. 280.
55 Cited in Sennett, op. cit., p. 43.
56 Ibid., p. 43.
57 Theo Nichols, 'The "Socialism" of Management: Some Reflections on the New "Human Relations"' in *Sociological Review*, Vol. 23, May 1975, p. 249.
58 Sennett, op. cit., p. 42.
59 Nichols, op. cit., p. 251.
60 MacIntyre, 'Social Science Methodology', op. cit., p. 44.
61 Ibid., p. 44.
62 H. Beynon, R. Hudson and D. Sadler, *A Tale of Two Industries: The Contraction of Coal and Steel in the North East of England*, Buckingham, Open University Press, 1991, p. 75.
63 Ibid., p. 44.
64 Ibid., p. 45.
65 Duncan Gallie, *Social Inequality and Class Radicalism in France and*

Britain, Cambridge, Cambridge University Press, 1983.
66 Scott Lash, *The Militant Worker: Class Radicalism in France and America*, London, Heinemann, 1984.
67 Gallie, op. cit., p. 261.
68 Lash, op. cit., pp. 235–6.
69 T. Adorno, cited in R. Jacoby, 'Review article of H. Braverman's *Labour and Monopoly Capital*', *Telos*, 1976, No. 29, Fall, p. 206.

6 CONCLUSION: NARRATIVE AND COMMUNITIES

1 *After Virtue*, London, Duckworth, 1981, p. 201.
2 S. Lovibond, 'Feminism and Postmodernism', *New Left Review*, 1989, No. 178, p. 7.
3 M. Canovan, 'Economy of Truth: Some Liberal Reflections', *Political Studies*, 1990, Vol. 38, pp. 11–12.
4 *After Virtue*, op. cit., p. 115.
5 Ibid., p. 175.
6 Ibid.
7 Ibid., pp. 175–6.
8 *Three Rival Versions of Moral Enquiry*, London, Duckworth, 1990, p. 194.
9 Ibid., pp. 178–9.
10 Ibid., p. 192.
11 Ibid., pp. 191–2.
12 Ibid., p. 245.
13 *The Monist*, Vol. 60, 1977, pp. 453–72.
14 Ibid., pp. 458–9.
15 M. Bell, 'How Primordial is Narrative?' in C. Lash (ed.) *Narration and Culture*, London, Routledge, 1990.
16 Ibid., p. 174.
17 MacIntyre, 'The Intelligibility of Action', in J. Margolis, M. Krausz and R. M. Burian (eds) *Rationality, Relativism and the Human Sciences*, Dordrecht, Martinus Nijhoff, 1986, pp. 64–5.
18 *Sociology of Health and Illness*, 1984, Vol. 6, No. 2, pp. 175–200.
19 Ibid., p. 175.
20 Ibid., p. 176.
21 Ibid., p. 179.
22 *After Virtue*, op. cit., p. 203.
23 Ibid., p. 204.
24 Ibid., p. 205.
25 W. E. Connolly, *Appearance and Reality in Politics*, Cambridge, Cambridge University Press, 1981. Raymond Williams, *Towards 2000*, London, Chatto & Windus, 1983. Michael Ignatieff, *The Needs of Strangers*, London, Chatto & Windus, 1984. Michael Malzer, 'The Communitarian Critique of Liberalism', *Political Theory*, 1990, Vol. 18, No. 1. Christopher Lasch, *The True and Only Heaven: Progress and its Critics*, New York, W. Norton, 1991.
26 MacIntyre, *After Virtue*, op. cit., p. 244.

27 Connolly, op. cit., pp. 93–4.
28 MacIntyre, op. cit., p. 220.
29 Ibid., p. 221.
30 See A. Fraser, 'The Corporation as a Body Politic', *Telos*, 1983, No. 57, Fall and also his 'Legal Amnesia: Modernism vs the Republican Tradition in American Legal Thought', *Telos*, 1984, No. 60, Summer.
31 Ibid., 'The Corporation . . .', p. 33.
32 A. A. Berle and G. C. Means, *The Modern Corporation and Private Property*, New York, Macmillan, 1947.
33 Fraser, 'The Corporation', op. cit., p. 6.
34 Ibid.
35 Ibid., p. 33.
36 Fraser, 'Legal Amnesia', op. cit.
37 Ibid., p. 52.
38 P. Piccone, 'Federal Populism in Italy', *Telos*, 1991–2, No. 90, Winter, p. 6.
39 Ibid.
40 Huw Beynon, 'The Miners' Strike at Easington', *New Left Review*, 1984, No. 148, p. 107. This piece provides a particularly vivid description of the mobilisation of a whole mining community.
41 Craig Calhoun, *The Question of Class Struggle: Social Foundations of Popular Radicalism During the Industrial Revolution*, Oxford, Blackwell, 1982; see especially Chapter 6, pp. 149–82.
42 *New Statesman*, 11th January 1985.
43 See B. J. McCormick, *Industrial Relations in the Coal Industry*, London, Macmillan, 1979 and, for more generally how this fits into the corporatist aspects of the British state, see Keith Middlemass, *Politics in Industrial Society*, London, André Deutsch, 1979.
44 On this see the important documentation and historical reinterpretation of the role of mining inside the politics of the British working class in Terry Austrin and Huw Beynon, *Master and Servants: Class and Patronage in the Making of a Labour Organisation*, forthcoming, 1993.
45 McCormick, op. cit., p. 47.
46 Huw Beynon and I have documented this process in our 'Decisive Power: The New Tory State Against the Miners' in Huw Beynon (ed.), *Digging Deeper: Issues in the Miners' Strike*, London, Verso, 1985. In this essay we outline the careful strategic planning carried out by the Tories, while in opposition and continued in government. We show how elements of the state were reorganised to face down a large-scale strike. This involved most particularly the organising of those industries and utilities owned by the state, as in effect tools of a clear political strategy. We illustrate the authoritarian potential within those corporatist elements of the state, in the hands of a government determined to break the post-war consensus.
47 Quoted in Huw Beynon's introduction, *Digging Deeper*, op. cit., p. 10.

48 Ibid., p. 13.
49 Quoted in R. J. Holton, 'Syndicalist Theories of the State', *Sociological Review*, 1981.
50 Andre Gorz has wrestled with this problem in his *Farewell to the Working Class: An Essay on Post-Industrial Socialism*, London, Pluto Press, 1982. Gorz suggests the notion of a dual society, in which there would be what he calls a heteronomous sphere which is equated with the continuation of industrial production and all the technical necessities that flow from that. Outside of this there would exist a sphere of autonomous, self-organised activity. On this view unpleasant production cannot be abolished but it can be minimised and subordinated to the realm of freedom. His argument is important, it seeks to insulate spheres of life from market domination and could, perhaps, provide a basis for reconstituted communities. However, it is important to note that his conception of two sectors is not too far away from neo-liberals' models of small-scale self-organised, secondary market sectors, existing outside the main labour market. These liberals wish to introduce this form to relieve the major market and state sectors of the 'surplus' population. This means that for a decent and fulfilling autonomous sphere to exist it would have to be protected and promoted economically and politically, presumably by political and economic organisation directed towards the state. It seems likely then, that the autonomous sector would be in a more or less permanent conflict with the heteronomous sector and its allies in the state. This, of course, raises again the question of politics; who and what groups can be mobilised for such ends and how? See also the interviews with Gorz 'The Limits of Self-Determination and Self-Management' and his article, 'The Reconquest of Time' in *Telos*, 1983, No. 55, Spring and his 'The American Model and the Future of the Left' in *Telos*, 1985, No. 64, Summer.
51 Marx in *The German Ideology*, quoted in D. Sayer, 'The Critique of Politics and Political Economy: Capitalism, Communism and the State in Marx's Writings of the Mid-1840s', *Sociological Review*, 1985, Vol. 33, May, pp. 237–8.
52 Emile Woolf, senior partner in chartered accountants Kingston Smith, writing in *The Guardian*, 10th July 1985.
53 Raymond Williams, 'Mining the Meaning: Key Words in the Miners' Strike', *New Socialist*, 1985, No. 25, March, pp. 6–9.
54 Ibid.
55 R. Williams, *Forward March of Labour Halted*, ed. M. Jacques and F. Mulhern, London, Verso, 1981, p. 151.
56 See Lucio Colletti's introductory essay to *Karl Marx's Early Writing*, Harmondsworth, Penguin, 1975, concerning Marx's debt to Rousseau.
57 Connolly, op. cit., p. 91.
58 Quoted in ibid., p. 118.
59 Ibid., p. 110.
60 Jürgen Habermas, *Legitimation Crisis*, London, Heinemann, 1976,

p. 108; see also his *Communication and the Evolution of Society*, Heinemann, London, 1979. The best overall survey of Habermas is Thomas McCarthy, *The Critical Theory of Jurgen Habermas*, London, Hutchinson, 1978. Also David Held, *Introduction to Critical Theory*, London, Hutchinson, 1980, see especially Chapter 12 for a valuable survey of Habermas's theory of communication. Perry Anderson in his, *In The Tracts of Historical Materialism*, London, Verso, 1983, pp. 57–67, provides a powerful and lucid if brief critique of Habermas's linguistic turn.

61 Anderson, op. cit., p. 66.
62 Jeffrey C. Alexander, Review essay: 'Habermas's New Critical Theory: Its Promise and Problems', *American Journal of Sociology*, 1985, Vol. 91, No. 2, p. 420.
63 Ibid., p. 419.
64 See D. Held, op. cit., p. 331.
65 Alexander, op. cit., p. 421.
66 Connolly, op. cit., p. 111.
67 *Three Rival Versions of Moral Enquiry*, op. cit., p. 234.
68 Donald H. Levine, 'Review Essay: Sociology after MacIntyre', *American Journal of Sociology*, 1983, Vol. 89, No. 3, p. 706.
69 *After Virtue*, op. cit., p. 182.

Bibliography

Note on abbreviations:
OUP   Oxford University Press
CUP   Cambridge University Press
RKP   Routledge & Kegan Paul
NLB   New Left Books

Abercrombie, N. (1980) *Class Structure and Knowledge*, Oxford, Blackwell.
Abercrombie, N., Hill, S. and Turner, B. S. (1980) *The Dominant Ideology Thesis*, London, Allen & Unwin.
Abrams, P. (1982) *Historical Sociology*, Somerset, Open Books.
Abrams, P. (1982) 'History, Sociology, Historical Sociology', *Past and Present*, No. 87.
Ackerill, J. L. (1981) *Aristotle the Philosopher*, Oxford, Clarendon Press.
Albrow, M. (1970) *Bureaucracy*, London, Macmillan.
Alexander, J. C. (1985) Review essay on Habermas, *American Journal of Sociology*, Vol. 91, No. 2, Sept.
Althusser, L. and Balibar, E. (1970) *Reading Capital*, London, NLB.
Althusser, L. (1971) *Lenin and Philosophy and Other Essays*, London, NLB.
Althusser, L. (1977) 'On the Materialist Dialectic', in *For Marx*, London, NLB.
Althusser, L. (1977) *For Marx*, London, NLB.
Altieri, C. (1976) 'Wittgenstein on Consciousness and Language Challenge to Derridean Literary Theory', *Modern Language Notes*, Vol. 91.
Anderson, P. (1974) *Passages from Antiquity to Feudalism*, London, NLB.
Anderson, P. (1974) *Lineages of the Absolutist States*, London, NLB.
Anderson, P. (1976) *Considerations on Western Marxism*, London, NLB.
Anderson, P. (1980) *Arguments within English Marxism*, London, Verso & NLB.
Anderson, P. (1983) *In the Tracts of Historical Materialism*, London, Verso.
Appleby, J. (1984) *Capitalism and a New Social Order*, New York, New York University Press.

Arato, A. and Breines, P. (1979) *The Young Lukács and the Origins of Western Marxism*, London, Pluto Press.

Arblaster, A. (1984) *The Rise and Decline of Western Liberalism*, Oxford, Blackwell.

Arendt, H. (1958) *The Human Condition*, Chicago, University of Chicago Press.

Aristotle, (1948) *The Politics*, Oxford, Clarendon Press.

Aristotle, (1955) *The Nicomachean Ethics*, Harmondsworth, Penguin.

Arthur, C. (1979) 'Dialectics and Labour', in J. Mephan and D. H. Ruben, *Issues in Marxist Philosophy* Vol. 1, *Dialectics and Method*, Brighton, Harvester Press.

Austrin, T. and Beynon, Huw (forthcoming 1993) *Master and Servants: Class and Patronage in the Making of a Labour Organisation*, being Vol. 1 of *Durham Miners and the English Political Tradition*.

Avineri, S. (1968) *The Social & Political Thought of Karl Marx*, Cambridge, CUP.

Ball, T. and Farr, J. (eds) (1984) *After Marx*, Cambridge, CUP.

Barry, B. (1973) *The Liberal Theory of Justice: A Critical Examination of the Principal Doctrines in a Theory of Justice by John Rawls*, Oxford, Clarendon Press.

Bauman, Z. (1982) *Memories of Class: The Pre-History and After Life of Class*, London, RKP.

Bauman, Z. (1983) 'Industrialism, Consumerism and Power', *Theory Culture and Society*, Vol. 1, No. 3.

Beetham, D. (1986) *Max Weber and the Theory of Modern Politics*, Cambridge, Polity Press

Bell, D. (1976) *The Cultural Contradictions of Capitalism*, London, Heinemann.

Bell, M. (1990) 'How Primordial is Narrative?', in C. Lash, *Narration and Culture*, London, RKP.

Bendix, R. (1969) *Nation Building and Citizenship: Studies of Our Changing Social Order*, New York, Doubleday.

Benton, T. (1977) *Philosophical Foundations of the Three Sociologies*, London, RKP.

Berger, P., Berger, B. and Kellner, H. (1974) *The Homeless Mind*, Harmondsworth, Penguin.

Bergner, J. T. (1981) *The Origins of Formalism in Social Science*, Chicago, University of Chicago Press.

Berki, R. N. (1983) *Insight and Vision: The Problem of Communism in Marx's Thought*, London, J. M. Dent & Sons.

Beynon, H. (1984) 'The Miners' Strike at Easington', *New Left Review*, No. 148.

Beynon, H. ed. with an introduction by Huw Beynon, (1985) *Digging Deeper: Issues in the Miners' Strike*, London, Verso.

Beynon, H. and McMylor, P. (1985) 'Decisive Power: The New Tory State Against the Miners', in Huw Beynon (ed.), *Digging Deeper: Issues in the Miners' Strike*, London, Verso.

Beynon, H., Hudson, R. and Sadler, D. (1991) *A Tale of Two Industries*, Buckingham, Open University Press.

Birnbaum, P. (1982) 'The State versus Corporatism', *Politics and Society*, Vol. II, No. 4.

Bloch, E. (1986) *The Principle of Hope*, 3 vols, Oxford, Blackwell.

Block, F. and Somers, M. (1984) 'Beyond the Economistic Fallacy: The Holistic Social Science of Karl Polanyi', in T. Skocpol (ed.), *Broad Visions: Methods of Historical Social Analysis*, Cambridge, CUP.

Bohannon, P. and Dalton, G. (1965) 'Karl Polanyi: 1886–1964', *American Anthropologist*, Vol. 67.

Bosanquet, N. (1983) *After the New Right*, London, Heinemann.

Brenner, R. (1976) 'Agrarian Class Structure and Economic Development in Pre-Industrial Europe', *Past and Present*, No. 70.

Brubaker, R. (1984) *The Limits of Rationality: An Essay on the Social and Moral Thought of Max Weber*, London, Allen & Unwin.

Burawoy, M. (1978) 'Towards a Marxist Theory of the Labour Process, Braverman and Beyond', *Politics and Society*, Vol. 8, Nos 3–4.

Burke, E. (1790) *Reflections on the Revolution in France and on the Proceedings in Certain Societies in London Relative to that Event*, ed. with an introduction by Conor Cruise O' Brien (1969), Harmondsworth, Penguin.

Burke, P. (1980) *Sociology and History*, London, Allen & Unwin.

Calhoun, C. (1982) *The Question of Class Struggle*, Oxford, Blackwell.

Callinicos, A. (1976) *Althusser's Marxism*, London, Pluto Press.

Callinicos, A. (1985) 'Post-modernism, Post-structuralism, and Post-Marxism?' *Theory, Culture and Society*, Vol. 2, No. 3.

Carver, T. (1981) *Engels*, Oxford, OUP.

Castoriadis, C. (1978) 'From Marx to Aristotle, from Aristotle to Us', *Social Research*, Vol. 45, No. 4, Winter.

Cavell, S. (1979) *The Claim of Reason*, Oxford, OUP.

Clark, J. C. D. (1985) *English Society 1688–1832*, Cambridge, CUP.

Clark, S. R. L. (1983) *Aristotle's Man: Speculations upon Aristotelian Anthropology*, Oxford, OUP.

Clarke, S. (1980) *One Dimensional Marxism*, London, Allison and Busby.

Clawson, D. (1980) *Bureaucracy and the Labour Process: The Transformation of US Industry 1860–1920*, London, Monthly Review Press.

Clawson, D. and Fantasia, R. (1983) 'Beyond Burawoy: Dialectics of Conflict and Consent on the Shop Floor', *Theory and Society*, Vol. 12, No. 5, September.

Cohen, G. A. (1978) *Karl Marx's Theory of History: A Defence*, Oxford, OUP.

Cohen, G. A. (1980) 'Functional Explanation, Reply to Elster', *Political Studies*, Vol. 18.

Cohen, G. A. (1982) 'Reply to Elster on Marxism, Functionalism and Game Theory', *Theory and Society*, Vol. 11.

Cohen, J. (1983) *Class and Civil Society*, Oxford, Martin Robertson.

Colletti, L. (1973) *Marxism and Hegel*, London, NLB.

Colletti, L. (1975) 'Introduction', *Karl Marx's Early Writings*, Harmondsworth, Penguin.

Colletti, L. (1975) 'Marxism and the Dialectic', *New Left Review*, No. 93.

Connolly, W. E. (1981) *Appearance and Reality in Politics*, Cambridge, CUP.

Corrigan P. and Sayer, D. (1985) *The Great Arch: English State Formation as Cultural Revolution*, Oxford, Blackwell.

Covell, C. (1986) *The Redefinition of Conservatism*, London, Macmillan.

Crouch, C. (ed.) (1979) *State and Economy in Contemporary Capitalism*, London, Croom Helm.

Crouch, C. (1979) 'The State, Capital and Liberal Democracy', in C. Crouch (ed.), *State and Economy in Contemporary Capitalism*, London, Croom Helm.

Crouch, C. (1983) 'Market Failure: Fred Hirsch and the Case for Social Democracy', in A. Ellis and K. Kumer (eds), *Dilemmas of Liberal Democracies: Studies in Fred Hirsch's Social Limits to Growth*, London, Tavistock, 1983.

Deutscher, I. (1954) *The Prophet: Armed Trotsky: 1879–1921*, Oxford, OUP.

Deutscher, I. (1959) *The Prophet: Unarmed Trotsky: 1921–1929*, Oxford, OUP.

Dews, P. (1977) 'Misadventures of the Dialectic', *Radical Philosophy*, No. 18, Autumn.

Douglas, M. (1966) *Purity and Danger*, London, RKP.

Downs, A. (1971) 'Decision Making in Bureaucracy', in F. G. Castles, D. J. Murray, D. C. Potter and C. J. Pullitt (eds), *Decisions, Organisations and Society*, Harmondsworth, Penguin.

Dunn, J. (1979) *Western Political Theory in the Face of the Future*, Cambridge, CUP.

Dunn, J. (1984) *The Politics of Socialism: An Essay in Political Theory*, Cambridge, CUP.

Dunn, J. (1984) *John Locke*, Oxford, OUP.

Duprie, L. (1983) *Marx's Social Critique of Culture*, Yale, Yale University Press.

Eagleton, T. (1967) *The Free Dependent: Shakespeare and Society*, London, Chatto & Windus.

Eco, U. (1983) *The Name of the Rose*, London, Secker & Warburg.

Edgley, R. (1976) 'Science, Social Science and Socialist Science: Reason as Dialectic', *Radical Philosophy* 15, Autumn.

Edgley, R. (1976) 'Dialectic: The Contradiction of Colletti', *Critique*, No. 7.

Ellis, A. and Kumer, K. (eds) (1983) *Dilemmas of Liberal Democracies: Studies in Fred Hirsch's Social Limits to Growth*, London, Tavistock.

Elster, J. (1976) *Logic and Society*, Chichester, Wiley.

Elster, J. (1980) 'Cohen on Marx's Theory of History', *Political Studies*, Vol. 18.

Elster, J. (1982) 'Marxism, Functionalism and Game Theory, the Case for Methodological Individualism', *Theory and Society*, Vol. 11.

Elster, J. (1985) *Making Sense of Marx*, Cambridge, CUP.

Elzioni-Halevy, E. (1985) *The Knowledge Elite and the Failure of Prophecy*, London, Allen & Unwin.

Ferguson, A. (1767) *An Essay on the History of Civil Society*, Edinburgh, Edinburgh University Press, 1966.

Fischer, N., Patsouras, L. and Georgopoulos, N. (1983) *Continuity and*

Change in Marxism, Brighton, Harvester.

Foucault, M. (1979) 'On Governmentality', *Ideology and Consciousness*, No. 6, Autumn.

Fraser, A. (1983) 'The Corporation as a Body Politic', *Telos*, No. 57, Fall.

Fraser, A. (1984) 'Legal Amnesia: Modernism vs the Republican Tradition in American Legal Thought', *Telos*, No. 60, Summer.

Fraser, A. (1991) 'Populism and Republican Jurisprudence', *Telos*, No. 88, Summer.

Fraser, D. (1973) *The Evolution of the British Welfare State*, London, Macmillan.

Frisby, D. (1981) *Sociological Impressionism – A Reassessment of Georg Simmel's Social Theory*, London, Heinemann.

Frisby, D. (1984) *Georg Simmel*, London, Tavistock.

Frisby, D. (1984) 'Georg Simmel and Social Psychology', *Journal of the History of the Behavioural Sciences*, Vol. 20.

Frisby, D. (1985) 'Georg Simmel, First Sociologist of Modernity', *Theory, Culture and Society*, Vol. 2, No. 3.

Frisby, D. (1991) 'The Aesthetics of Modern Life: Simmel's Interpretation', *Theory, Culture and Society*, Vol. 8, No. 2.

Frisby, D. and Sayer, D. (1986) *Society*, London, Tavistock Publications.

Gallie, D. (1983) *Social Inequality and Class Radicalism in France and Britain*, Cambridge, CUP.

Gane, M. (1984) 'Institutional Socialism and the Sociological Critique of Communism', *Economy and Society*, Vol. 13, No. 3.

Gay, P. (1986) *Freud for Historians*, Oxford, OUP.

Geach, P. T. (1977) *The Virtues*, Cambridge, CUP.

Genovese, E. (1970) *The World the Slaveholders Made*, London, Allen Lane.

Giddens, A. (1971) *Capitalism and Modern Social Theory*, Cambridge, CUP.

Giddens, A. (1979) *Central Problems in Social Theory Action, Structure and Contradiction in Social Analysis*, London, Macmillan.

Giddens, A. (1981) *A Contemporary Critique of Historical Materialism, Vol. I: Power, Property and the State*, London, Macmillan.

Goldthorpe, J. H. (1978) 'The Current Inflation: Towards a Sociological Account', in F. Hirsch and J. H. Goldthorpe (eds), *The Political Economy of Inflation*, Oxford, Martin Robertson.

Gonzales, M. (P. Piccone), (1981) 'Rethinking Radical Politics', *Telos*, No. 48, Summer.

Goodwyn, L. (1991) 'Rethinking "Populism": Paradoxes of Historiography and Democracy', *Telos*, No. 88, Summer.

Gorz, A. (1982) *Farewell to the Working Class: An Essay on Post-Industrial Socialism*, London, Pluto Press.

Gorz, A. (1983) 'The Limits of Self-Determination and Self-Management', *Telos*, No. 55, Spring.

Gorz, A. (1983) 'The Reconquest of Time', *Telos*, No. 55, Spring.

Gorz, A. (1985) 'The American Model and the Future of the Left', *Telos*, No. 64, Summer.

Gouldner, A. W. (1975–6) 'Prologue to a Theory of Revolutionary Intellectuals', *Telos*, No. 26, Winter.

Gouldner, A. W. (1976) *The Dialectic of Ideology and Technology: The Origins, Grammar and Future of Ideology*, London, Macmillan.

Gouldner, A. W. (1979) *The Future of Intellectuals and the Rise of a New Class*, London, Macmillan.

Gouldner, A. W. (1980) *The Two Marxisms: Contradictions and Anomalies in the Development of Theory*, London, Macmillan.

Gouldner, A. W. (1985) *Against Fragmentation: The Origins of Marxism and the Sociology of Intellectuals*, Oxford, OUP.

Grossman, L. (no date) 'Basle, Bachofen and the Critique of Modernity in the Second Half of the 19th Century', *Journal of Warburg & Courtauld Institutes*, Vol. XLVII.

Habermas, J. (1974) 'The Public Sphere: An Encyclopedia Article', *New German Critique*, Vol. 3, Fall.

Habermas, J. (1976) *Legitimation Crisis*, London, Heinemann.

Habermas, J. (1983) 'Neo-Conservative Criticism in the United States and West Germany: An Intellectual Movement in Two Political Cultures', *Telos*, No. 56, Summer.

Hall, S. (1980) 'Review article of Poulantzas's *State, Power, Socialism*', *New Left Review*, No. 119, January/February.

Harrington, M. (1977) *The Twilight of Capitalism*, London, Macmillan.

Hayek, F. A. (1960) *The Constitution of Liberty*, London, RKP.

Hearn, F. (1978) *Domination, Legitimation and Resistance: The Incorporation of the 19th Century English Working Class*, London, Greenwood Press.

Hedman, C. G. (1981) 'Rawls' Theory of Justice and "Market Socialism"', *Radical Philosophy*, No. 28, Summer.

Held, D. (1980) *Introduction to Critical Theory: Horkheimer to Habermas*, London, Hutchinson.

Hill, C. (1969) *Reformation to Industrial Revolution*, Harmondsworth, Penguin.

Hill, S. (1981) *Competition and Control at Work: The New Industrial Sociology*, London, Heinemann.

Hilton, R. (1973) 'The Peasantry as a Class', in R. Hilton, *The English Peasantry in the Later Middle Ages*, Oxford, OUP.

Hilton, R. (1980) 'Individualism and the English Peasantry', *New Left Review*, No. 120.

Hilton, R. (1985) 'Medieval Market Towns and Simple Commodity Production', *Past and Present*, No. 109.

Hindess, B. (1977) *Philosophy and Methodology in the Social Sciences*, Brighton, Harvester Press.

Hirsch, F. (1976) *The Social Limits of Growth*, Cambridge Mass., Harvard University Press.

Hirsch, F. and Goldthorpe, J. (eds) (1976) *The Political Economy of Inflation*, Oxford, Martin Robertson

Hirschman, A. (1977) *The Passion and the Interests: Political Arguments for Capitalism before its Triumph*, Princeton, Princeton University Press.

Hirst, P. (1979) *On Law and Ideology*, London, Macmillan.

Hirst, P. and Wooley, P. (1982) *Social Relations and Human Attributes*, London, Tavistock.

Holland, R. (1977) *Self and Social Context*, London, Macmillan.

Holton, R. J. (1981) 'Syndicalist Theories of the State', *Sociological Review.*

Holton, R. J. (1986) *The Transition from Feudalism to Capitalism*, London, Macmillan.

Holton, R. J. and Turner, B. S. (1986) *Talcott Parsons on Economy and Society*, London, RKP.

Humphreys, S. C. (1969) 'History, Economics and Anthropology in the Works of Karl Polanyi', *History and Theory*, Vol. 8.

Hunt, R. N. (1975) *The Political Ideas of Marx and Engels, Vol. I: Marxism and Totalitarian Democracy 1818–1850*, London, Macmillan.

Ignatieff, M. (1984) *The Needs of Strangers*, London, Chatto & Windus.

Jacoby, R. (1977) *Social Amnesia: A Critique of Conformist Psychology from Adler to Laing*, Brighton, Harvester Press.

Jacoby, R. (1981) *Dialectic of Defeat: Contours of Western Marxism*, Cambridge, CUP.

Jacques, M. and Mulhern, F. (1981) (eds) *The Forward March of Labour Halted?*, London, Verso.

Jameson, F. (1971) *Marxism and Form: Twentieth-century Dialectual Theories of Literature*, Princeton, Princeton University Press.

Jay, M. (1973) *The Dialectual Imagination: A History of the Frankfurt School and the Institute of Social Research 1923–50*, London, Heinemann.

Jay, M. (1984) *Adorno*, London, Fontana.

Johnson, R. (1979) 'Culture and Idology', in M. Barrett, P. Corrigan, A. Kuhn and J. Wolff (eds), *Ideology and Cultural Production*, London, Croom Helm.

Johnson, R., McLennan, G., Schwartz, W. and Sutton, D. (eds) (1982) *Making History: Studies in History-writing and Politics*, London, Hutchinson.

Kamenka, E. (1982) *Community as a Social Ideal*, London, Edward Arnold.

Karnooth, C. (1986) 'Lost Paradise and Regionalism', *Telos*, No. 67, Spring.

Kaye, H. J. (1984) *The British Marxist Historians*, Cambridge, Polity Press.

Keane, J. (1984) *Public Life in Late Capitalism: Essays towards a Socialist Theory of Democracy*, Cambridge, CUP.

Keat, R. (1981) 'Individualism and Community in Socialist Thought', in J. Mephan and D. H. Ruben, *Issues in Marxist Philosophy*, Vol. 4, *Social and Political Philosophy*, Brighton, Harvester.

Keat, R. (1981) *The Politics of Social Theory: Habermas, Freud and the Critique of Positivism*, Oxford, Blackwell.

Keat, R. and Urry, J. (1975) *Social Theory as Science*, London, RKP.

Kilminster, R. (1978) *Praxis and Method: A Sociological Dialogue with Lukács, Gramsci and the Early Frankfurt School*, London, RKP.

Kindleberger, C. D. (1973) Discussion of K. Polanyi's Great Transformation', *Daedalus*, Vol. 103, No. 1, Winter, pp. 45–52.

Kitto, H. D. F. (1951) *The Greeks*, Harmondsworth, Penguin.

Knowles, D. (1962) *The Evolution of Medieval Thought*, London, Longmans.

Kolakowski, L. (1972) *Positivist Philosophy: From Hume to the Vienna Circle*, Harmondsworth, Penguin.

Kolakowski, L. (1978) *Main Currents of Marxism, Vol. 1: The Founders*, Oxford, OUP.

Kolakowski, L. (1978) *Main Currents of Marxism, Vol. 2: The Golden Age*, Oxford, OUP.

Korsch, K. (1970) *Marxism and Philosophy*, London, NLB.

Kripke, S. (1980) *Naming and Necessity*, Oxford, Blackwell.

Kumar, K. (1983) 'Pre-Capitalist and Non-Capitalist Factors in the Development of Capitalism: Fred Hirsch and Joseph Schumpeter', in A. Ellis and K. Kumar (eds), *Dilemmas of Liberal Democracies: Studies in Fred Hirsch's Social Limits to Growth*, London, Tavistock.

Lasch, C. (1980) *The Culture of Narcissism: American Life in an Age of Diminishing Expectations*, London, Abacus.

Lasch, C. (1981) 'Democracy and the Crisis of Confidence', *Democracy*, Vol. 1, January.

Lasch, C. (1985) *The Minimal Self: Psychic Survival in Troubled Times*, London, Pan Books.

Lasch, C. (1986) 'Making America Feel Good about Itself', *New Statesman*, 19th August.

Lasch, C. (1991) *The True and Only Heaven: Progress and its Critics*, New York, W. Norton.

Lasch, C. (1991) 'Liberalism and Civic Virtue', *Telos*, No. 88, Summer.

Lash, C. (ed.) (1990) *Narration and Culture*, London, RKP.

Lash, S. (1984) *The Militant Worker: Class Radicalism in France and America*, London, Heinemann.

Lash, S. and Urry, J. (1984) 'The New Marxism of Collective Action: A Critical Analysis', *Sociology*, Vol. 18, No. 1.

Lepenies, W. (1971) 'Anthropology and Social Criticism: A View on the Controversy between Gehlen and Habermas', *Human Context*, Vol. 3, No. 2.

Levine, D. H. (1983) 'Sociology after MacIntyre', *American Journal of Sociology*, Vol. 89, No. 3.

Levitas, R. (1985) 'New Right Utopias', *Radical Philosophy*, No. 39, Spring.

Little, L. K. (1978) *Religious Poverty and the Profit Economy in Medieval Europe*, London, Paul Elek.

Livesay, J. (1985) 'Habermas, Narcissism and Status', *Telos*, No. 64, Summer.

Lloyd, J. (1985) *Understanding the Miners' Strike*, Fabian Tract, 504, London, Fabian Society.

Lockwood, D. (1964) 'Social Integration and System Integration', in G. K. Zollschon and W. Hirsh (eds), *Explorations in Social Change*, London, RKP.

Lovibond, S. (1987) 'Feminism and Enlightenment', *New Left Review*, No. 178.

Lowry, M. (1980) 'Jewish Messianism and Libertarian Utopia in Central Europe', *New German Critique*, No. 20, Spring/Summer.

Lowry, M. (1985) 'Revolution against Progress: Walter Benjamin's Romantic Anarchism', *New Left Review*, No. 152.

Lukács, G. (1971) *History and Class Consciousness: Studies in Marxist Dialectics*, London, Merlin Press.

Luke, T. (1991) 'Community and Ecology', *Telos*, No. 88. Summer.

McCormick, B. J. (1979) *Industrial Relations in the Coal Industry*, London, Macmillan.

MacFarlane, A. (1978) *The Origins of English Individualism: The Family, Property and Social Transition*, Oxford, Blackwell.

MacIntyre, A. (1953) *Marxism: An Interpretation*, London, SCM Press.

MacIntyre, A. (1955) 'Visions', in A. Flew and A. MacIntyre (eds), *New Essays in Philosophical Theology*, London, SCM Press.

MacIntyre, A. (1958–9) 'Notes from the Moral Wilderness I', *New Reasoner*, No. 7, Winter.

MacIntyre, A. (1959) 'Notes from the Moral Wilderness II', *New Reasoner*, No. 8, Spring.

MacIntyre, A. (1960) 'Breaking the Chains of Reason', in E. P. Thompson (ed.), *Out of Apathy*, London, NLB, Stevens & Sons.

MacIntyre, A. (1967) *A Short History of Ethics*, London, RKP.

MacIntyre, A. (1967) *Secularisation and Moral Change*, Riddell Memorial Lectures, delivered at University of Newcastle upon Tyne, November, Oxford, OUP.

MacIntyre, A. (1968) *Marxism and Christianity*, New York, Schocken Books.

MacIntyre, A. (1968) 'The Strange Death of Social Democratic England', originally published in *The Listener*, republished in D. Widgery (1976) (ed.), *The Left in Britain 1956–68*, Harmondsworth, Penguin.

MacIntyre, A. and Ricoeur, P. (1969) *The Religious Significance of Atheism*, New York, Columbia University Press.

MacIntyre, A. (1970) *Marcuse*, London, Collins.

MacIntyre, A. (1971) *Against the Self-Images of the Age: Essays on Ideology and Philosophy*, London, Duckworth.

MacIntyre, A. (1972) 'Praxis and Action', *Review of Metaphysics*, Vol. 25, June.

MacIntyre, A. (1973) 'Ideology, Social Science and Revolution', *Comparative Politics*, Vol. 5, No. 3.

MacIntyre, A. (1973–4) 'The Essential Contestability of Some Social Concepts', *Ethics*, Vol. 84.

MacIntyre, A. (1975) 'Medicine and Society, How Virtues Become Vices', in *Encounter*, July.

MacIntyre, A. (1977) 'Epistemological Crisis, Dramatic Narrative and the Philosophy of Science', *The Monist*, Vol. 60.

MacIntyre, A. (1979) 'Social Science Methodology as the Ideology of Bureaucratic Authority', in M. S. Falco (ed.), *Through the Looking Glass: Epistemology and the Conduct of Inquiry*, Washington, University Press of America.

MacIntyre, A. (1980) 'Alasdair MacIntyre on the claims of Philosophy', *London Review of Books*, 5–18th June.

MacIntyre, A. (1980) 'The Idea of America', *London Review of Books*, 6–19th November.

MacIntyre, A. (1981) *After Virtue: A Study in Moral Theory*, London, Duckworth.

MacIntyre, A. (1981) 'Dr Kung's Fiasco', *London Review of Books*, 5–18 February.

MacIntyre, A. (1981) Review of V. Descombes' *Modern French Philosophy* (Cambridge, CUP, 1981), in *London Review of Books*, 16th March–6th May.

MacIntyre, A. (1982) 'Philosophy, the "Other" Disciplines and their Histories: A Rejoiner to Richard Rorty', *Soundings*, Vol. 45.

MacIntyre, A. (1982) 'Public Virtues', *London Review of Books*, 18th February–3rd March.

MacIntyre, A. (1982) Review of E. Dipple's, *Iris Murdoch: Work for the Spirit* (London, Methuen, 1982), in *London Review of Books*, 3rd–16th June.

MacIntyre, A. (1983) 'The Magic in the Pronoun "My"', *Ethics*, Vol. 94 October.

MacIntyre, A. (1983) 'Moral Rationality, Tradition and Aristotle: A Reply to Onara O'Neill, Raimond Gaita and Stephen R. L. Clark, *Inquiry*, Vol. 26, No. 4, December.

MacIntyre, A. (1984) 'After Virtue and Marxism: A Response to Wartofsky', *Inquiry*, Vol. 27, Nos. 2–3, July.

MacIntyre, A. (1984) 'Bernstein's Distorting Mirrors: A Rejoiner,' *Soundings*, Vol. 67.

MacIntyre, A. (1984) 'The Relationship of Philosophy to its Past', in R. Rorty, J. B. Schreewind and Q. Skinner (eds), *Philosophy in History*, Cambridge, CUP.

MacIntyre, A. (1986) 'Positivism, Sociology, and Practical Reasoning: Notes on Durkheim's Suicide', in A. Donagan, A. N. Perovich Jr. and M. V. Wedin (eds), *Human Nature and Natural Knowledge*, Boston, Reidel.

MacIntyre, A. (1986) 'The Intelligibility of Action', in J. Margolis, M. Krausz and R. M. Burian (eds), *Rationality, Relativism and the Human Sciences*, Dordrecht, Martinus Nijhoff.

MacIntyre, A. (1987) 'The Idea of an Educated Public', in G. Haydon (ed.), *Education and Values*, London University, Institute of Education.

MacIntyre, A. (1987) 'Past Conflicts and Future Direction', *Proceedings of the American Philosophical Association*, Vol. 61, Supplement.

MacIntyre, A. (1987) 'Relativism, Power and Philosophy', in J. Baynes, H. Bohman and T. McCarthy (eds), *After Philosophy: End or Transformation?*, Cambridge Mass., Harvard University Press.

MacIntyre, A. (1988) 'Sophrosune: How a Virtue can become Socially Disruptive', *Midwest Studies In Philosophy*, Vol. 13.

MacIntyre, A. (1988) *Whose Justice? Which Rationality?*, London, Duckworth.

MacIntyre, A. (1990) *Three Rival Versions of Moral Enquiry*, London, Duckworth.

McLellan, D. (ed.) (1977) *Karl Marx: Selected Writings*, Oxford, OUP.
McLennon, G. (1981) *Marxism and the Methodologies of History*, London, Verso.
Macpherson, C. B. (1980) *Burke*, Oxford, OUP.
Macpherson, C. B. (1985) 'The Economic Penetration of Political Theory', in *The Rise and Fall of Economic Justice and Other Papers*, Oxford, OUP.
Macpherson, C. B. (1985) *The Rise and Fall of Economic Justice and Other Papers*, Oxford, OUP.
Maguire, J. (1978) *Marx's Theory of Politics*, Cambridge, CUP.
Maier, C. S. (1970) 'Between Taylorism and Technocracy': European Ideologies and the Vision of Industrial Productivity in the 1920s', *Journal of Contemporary History*, Vol. 5, No. 2.
Maier, S. C. (1975) *Recasting Bourgeois Europe*, Princeton, Princeton University Press.
Mandel, E. (1977) *The Formation of the Economic Thought of Karl Marx*, London, NLB.
Marglin, S. (1974) 'What Do Boss's Do? The Origins and Functions of Hierarchy in Capitalist Production', *Review of Radical Political Economy*, Vol. 6, No. 2, Summer.
Marx, K. and Engels, Friedrich (1970) *The German Ideology*, edited and with an introduction by C. J. Arthur, London, Lawrence & Wishart.
Marx, K. (1975) *Early Writings*, introduced by Lucio Colletti, London, Penguin/NLR.
Meikle, S. (1978) 'Aristotle and the Political Economy of the Polis', *Journal of Hellenic Studies*, Vol. XCIX.
Meikle, S. (1979) 'Dialectical Contradiction and Necessity', in J. Mepham and D. H. Ruben (eds), *Issues in Marxist Philosophy, Vol. I: Dialectics and Method*, Brighton, Harvester.
Meikle, S. (1984) 'Marxism and the Necessity of Essentialism' (a review of S. G. M. de St Croix's *Class Struggle in the Ancient World*), *Critique* 16.
Meikle, S. (1985) *Essentialism in the Thought of Karl Marx*, London, Duckworth.
Meikle, S. (1986) 'Making Nonsense of Marx' (a review article of Jon Elster's *Making Sense of Marx*), *Inquiry*, Vol. 29, March.
Merquior, J. G. (1986) *Western Marxism*, London, Granada (Paladin).
Middlemass, K. (1979) *Politics in Industrial Society*, London, André Deutsch.
Midgley, E. B. F. (1983) *The Ideology of Max Weber: A Thomist Critique*, Aldershot, Gower.
Miller, J. (1979) *History and Human Existence from Marx to Merleau Ponty*, California, University of California Press.
Miller, R. W. (1981) 'Marx and Aristotle: A Kind of Consequentialism', *Canadian Journal of Philosophy*, Vol. 7, Supplement.
Mommsen, W. (1974) *The Age of Bureaucracy*, Oxford, Blackwell.
Moore Jr., B. (1963) *Social Origins of Dictatorship and Democracy: Lord and Peasant in the Modern World*, London, Allen Lane, Penguin Books.
Moore Jr., B. (1978) *Injustice: The Social Bases of Obedience and Revolt*, London, Macmillan.

Murray, D. (1979) 'Utopia or Phantasy? – A Reply to Ollman on Marx's Vision of Communism', *Radical Philosophy*, No. 22, Summer.

Nairn, T. (1980) 'Internationalism: A Critique', *The Bulletin of Scottish Politics*, No. 1, Autumn.

Nelson, B. (first published 1949) *The Idea of Usury from Tribal Brotherhood to Universal Otherhood*, 2nd edition, Chicago, University of Chicago Press, 1968.

New Left Review (ed.) (1977) *Western Marxism: A Critical Reader*, London, NLB.

Nichols, T. (1975) 'The "Socialism" of Management: Some Reflections on the New "Human Relations"', *Sociological Review*, Vol. 23, No. 2, May.

Nichols, T. and Beynon, Huw (1977) *Living with Capitalism: Class Relations and the Modern Factory*, London, RKP.

Nisbet, R. (1967) *The Sociological Tradition*, London, Heinemann.

Nisbet, R. (1968) *Tradition and Revolt: Historical and Sociological Essays*, New York, Random House.

Nisbet, R. (1973) *The Social Philosophers: Community and Conflict in Western Thought*, London, Heinemann.

Nisbet, R. (1976) *Twilight of Authority*, London, Heinemann.

Nolte, E. (1983) *Marxism, Fascism, Cold War*, Van Gorcum, Assen, Netherlands.

Norris, C. (1982) *Deconstruction: Theory and Practice*, London, Methuen.

Norris, C. (1983) *The Deconstructive Turn: Essays in the Rhetoric of Philosophy*, London, Methuen.

Oakley, A. (1983) *The Making of Marx's Capital: A Bibliographical Analysis*, London, RKP.

Offe, C. (1984) 'Ungovernability: The Renaissance of Conservative Theories of Crisis', in C. Offe's *Contradictions of the Welfare State*, ed. John Keane, London, Hutchinson.

Offe, C. (1984) *Contradictions of the Welfare State*, ed. John Keane, London, Hutchinson.

Ollman, B. (1977) 'Marx's Vision of Communism: A Reconstruction', *Critique*, No. 8.

O'Neill, J. (1972) 'The Concept of Estrangement in the Early and Later Writings of Karl Marx', in John O' Neill, *Sociology as a Skin Trade*, London, Heinemann.

O'Neill, J. (ed.) (1976) *On Critical Theory*, New York, Sesbury Press.

O'Neill, J. (1983) *For Marx against Althusser*, Washington, University Press of America.

Parker, N. (1982) 'What's so Right about Adam Smith', *Radical Philosophy*, No. 30, Spring.

Patton, P. (1978) 'Althusser's Epistemology: The Limits of the Theory of Theoretical Practice', *Radical Philosophy*, No. 19, Spring.

Perkin, H. (1969) *The Origins of Modern English Society 1780–1880*, London, RKP.

Piccone, P. (1969) 'Structuralist Marxism?' *Radical America*, III, No. 5, September.

Piccone, P. (1980) 'The Future of Critical Theory', *Current Perspectives in Social Theory – A Research Annual* 1, pp. 21–30.

Piccone, P. (1983) *Italian Marxism*, California, University of California Press.

Piccone, P. (1991) 'The Crisis of Liberalism and the Emergence of Federal Populism', *Telos*, No. 89, Fall.

Piccone, P. (1991–2) 'Federal Populism in Italy', *Telos*, No. 90, Winter.

Pierson, C. (1984) 'New Theories of State and Civil Society: Recent Developments in Post Marxist Analysis of the State', *Sociology*, Vol. 18, No. 4, November.

Pizzarro, A. (1985) 'On the Nationality of Democratic Choice', *Telos*, No. 63, Spring.

Plant, R. (1978) 'Community: Concepts, Conception and Ideology', *Politics and Society*, Vol. 8, No. 1.

Plant, R. (1983) 'Hirsch, Hayek and Habermas: Dilemmas of Distribution', in A. Ellis and K. Kumar (eds), *Dilemmas of Liberal Democracies: Studies in Fred Hirsch's Social Limits to Growth*, London, Tavistock.

Pocock, J. A. G. (1957) *The Ancient Constitution and the Feudal Laws*, Cambridge, CUP.

Pocock, J. A. G. (1976) *The Machiavellian Movement: Florentine Political Thought and the Atlantic Republican Tradition*, Princeton, Princeton University Press.

Polanyi, K., Lewis, J., Kitchen, D. F. and Needham, J. (eds) (1935) *Christianity and the Social Revolution*, London, Gollancz.

Polanyi, K. (1944) *The Great Transformation: The Political and Economic Origins of our Time*, Boston, Beacon Press.

Polanyi, K. (1971) (ed. George Dalton), *Primitive, Archaic and Modern Economics: Essays of Karl Polanyi*, Boston, Beacon Press.

Polanyi, K. (1971) 'The Economy as Institutional Process', in G. Dalton (ed.), *Primitive, Archaic and Modern Economics: Essays of Karl Polanyi*, Boston, Beacon Press.

Polanyi, K. (1971) 'The Obsolete Market Mentality', in G. Dalton (ed.), *Primitive, Archaic and Modern Economics: Essays of Karl Polanyi*, Boston, Beacon Press.

Polanyi, K. (1971) 'Aristotle Discovers the Economy: Essays of Karl Polanyi', in G. Dalton (ed.), *Primitive, Archaic and Modern Economics*, Boston, Beacon Press.

Pollard, S. (1965) *The Genesis of Modern Management*, London, Edward Arnold.

Porter, R. (1982) *English Society in the Eighteenth Century*, Harmondsworth, Penguin.

Poster, M. (1975) *Existential Marxism in Postwar France from Sartre to Althusser*, Princeton, Princeton University Press.

Przeworski, A. and Wallerstein, M. (1987) 'Democratic Capitalism at the Crossroads', *Democracy*, July.

Ranciere, J. (1982) 'Proletarian Nights', *Radical Philosophy*, No. 31, Summer.

Rieff, P. (1966) *The Triumph of the Therapeutic*, New York, Harper & Row.

Rieff, P. (1970) 'The Impossible Culture', *Encounter*, September.

Rieff, P. (1979) *Freud: The Mind of the Moralist*, 3rd edition, Chicago, University of Chicago Press.

Rieff, P. (1985) *The Fellow Teachers of Culture and its Second Death*, 2nd edition, Chicago, University of Chicago Press.

Robertson, R. (1978) *Meaning and Change: Explorations in Cultural Sociology of Modern Society*, Oxford, Blackwell.

Robertson, R. and Holzner, B. (1981) *Identity and Authority: Explorations in the Theory of Society*, Oxford, Blackwell.

Rookmaaker, H. R. (1970) *Modern Art and the Death of Culture*, London, Inter-varsity Press.

Rorty, R. (1980) *Philosophy and the Mirror of Nature*, Oxford, OUP.

Rorty, R. (1980) 'Kripke versus Kant', *London Review of Books*, Vol. 2, 4th September – 17th September.

Rose, G. (1981) *Hegel Contra Sociology*, London, Athlone.

Rose, G. (1984) *Dialectic of Nihilism: Post-Structuralism and Law*, Oxford, Blackwell.

Sandel, M. J. (1982) *Liberalism and the Limits of Justice*, Cambridge, CUP.

Sandel, M. J. (1984) *Liberalism and its Critics*, Oxford, Blackwell.

Sayer, D. (1979) 'Science as Critique: Marx versus Althusser', in J. Mepham and D. H. Ruben (eds), *Issues in Marxist Philosophy, Vol. 3*, Brighton, Harvester.

Sayer, D. (1985) 'The Critique of Politics and Political Economy: Capitalism, Communism and the State in Marx's Writings of the Mid-1840s', *Sociological Review*, Vol. 33, May.

Sayers, S. (1984) 'Marxism and the Dialectical Method: A Critique of G. A. Cohen', *Radical Philosophy*, No. 36, Spring.

Scruton, R. (1982) *Kant*, Oxford, OUP.

Sedgwick, P. (1982) 'An Ethical Dance – A Review of Alasdair MacIntyres's *After Virtue*', in Martine Eve and David Masson, *The Socialist Register*, London, Merlin.

Selbourne, D. (1985) *Against Socialist Illusions: A Radical Argument*, London, Macmillan.

Sennett, R. (1974) 'The Boss's New Clothes', *The New York Review of Books*, 22nd February.

Sennett, R. and Cobb, J. (1977) *The Hidden Injuries of Class*, Cambridge, CUP.

Sennett, R. (1980) *Authority*, London, Secker & Warburg.

Simmel, G. (1971) *On Individuality and Social Forms: Selected Writings*, edited and introduced by D. H. Levine, Chicago, University of Chicago.

Simmel, G. (1978) *The Philosophy of Money*, London, RKP.

Skinner, Q. (1978) *The Foundations of Modern Political Thought*, Vols. I & II, Cambridge, CUP.

Skinner, Q. (1984) 'The Idea of Negative Liberty: Philosophical and Historical Perspectives,' in R. Rorty, J. B. Schreewind and Q. Skinner (eds), *Philosophy in History*, Cambridge, CUP.

Smith, T. (1979) *The Politics of the Corporate Economy*, London, Martin Robertson.

Speer, A. (1970) *Inside the Third Reich: Memoirs*, London, Weidenfeld and Nicolson.

Stanfield, J. R. (1986) *The Economic Thought of Karl Polanyi: Lives and Livelihood*, London, Macmillan.

Stephens, J. D. (1979) *The Transition from Capitalism to Socialism*, London, Macmillan.

Strauss, L. (1953) *Natural Right and History*, Chicago, University of Chicago Press.

Stuart Hughes, H. (1959) *Consciousness and Society: The Re-orientation of European Social Thought 1890–1930*, London, MacGibbon and Kee.

Sweezy, P. M. (1946) *The Theory of Capitalist Development: Principles of Marxist Political Economy*, London, Dennis Dobson.

Taylor, C. (1979) 'What is Wrong with Negative Liberty', in A. Ryan (ed.), *The Idea of Freedom*, Oxford OUP.

Taylor, C. (1979) *Hegel and Modern Society*, Cambridge, CUP.

Taylor, C. (1984) 'Philosophy and its History', in R. Rorty, J. B. Schreewind and Q. Skinner (eds), *Philosophy in History*, Cambridge, CUP.

Thompson, E. P. (ed.) (1960) *Out of Apathy*, London, NLB, Stevens & Sons.

Thompson, E. P. (1965) *The Making of the English Working Class*, London, Gollancz.

Thompson, E. P. (1967) 'Time, Work Discipline and Industrial Capitalism', *Past and Present*, No. 38.

Thompson, E. P. (1971) 'The Moral Economy of the English Crowd in the Eigteenth Century', *Past and Present*, No. 50.

Thompson, E. P. (1974) 'Patrician Society, Plebian Culture', *Journal of Social History*, Summer.

Thompson, E. P. (1978) 'An Open Letter to Leszek Kolakowski', in E. P. Thompson *The Poverty of Theory and Other Essays*, London, Merlin.

Thompson, E. P. (1978) 'Eighteenth Century English Society: Class Struggle without Class?', *Social History*, Vol. 3, No. 2, May.

Thompson, E. P. (1978) *The Poverty of Theory and Other Essays*, London, Merlin.

Ticktin, H. (1972) 'Towards a Political Economy of the USSR', *Critique* 1.

Ticktin, H. (1978) 'Class Structure and the Soviet Elite', *Critique* 9.

Tilly, C. (1975) *Formation of Nation States in Western Europe*, Princeton, Princeton University Press.

Tribe, K. (1978) *Land, Labour and Economic Discourse*, London, Macmillan.

Tribe, K. (1979) Review of Alan MacFarlane's 'The Origins of English Individualism', *Social History*, Vol. 4, No. 3.

Trilling, L. (1972) *Sincerity and Authenticity*, Cambridge Mass., Harvard University Press.

Turner, B. S. (1981) *For Weber: Essays in the Sociology of Fate*, London, RKP.

Turner, B. S. (1983) *Religion and Social Theory: A Materialist Perspective*, London, Heinemann Educational Press.

Turner, B. S. (1986) 'George Simmel: Rationalisation and the Sociology of Money', *Sociological Review*, Vol. 34, February.

Turner, B. S. (1986) 'Personhood and Citizenship', *Theory, Culture and Society*, Vol. 3, No. 1.

Turner, D. (1978) 'The "Subject" and the "Self"', *New Blackfriars*, Vol. 59, March.

Turner, D. (1983) *Marxism and Christianity*, Oxford, Blackwell.

Turner, R. (1976) 'The Real Self: From Institution to Impulse', *American Journal of Sociology*, Vol. 81, No. 5.

Unger, R. M. (1984) *Passion: An Essay on Personality*, London, Collier/Macmillan.

Walzer, M. (1979) 'Nervous Liberals', *New York Review of Books*, 11th October.

Ward, K. (1982) *Holding Fast to God*, London, SPCK.

Wartofsky, M. W. (1984) 'Virtue Lost or Understanding MacIntyre', *Inquiry*, Vol. 27, Nos. 2–3, July.

Weber, M. (1976) *The Protestant Ethic and the Spirit of Capitalism*, 2nd edition, London, Allen & Unwin.

Weber, M. (1978) *Economy and Society*, 2 vols., California, University of California Press.

Wellmer, A. (1971) *The Critical Theory of Society*, New York, Herder & Herder.

White, S. D. and Vann, R. (1983) 'The Invention of English Individualism: Alan MacFarlane and the Modernization of Pre-modern England', *Social History*, Vol. 8, No. 3, October.

Whitebrook, J. (1978) 'Pre-market Economics: The Aristotelian Perspective', *Dialectical Anthropology*, Vol. 3, No. 3, August.

Williams, R. (1961) *Culture and Society*, Harmondsworth, Penguin.

Williams, R. (1975) *The Country and the City*, London, Paladin.

Williams, R. (1976) *Key Words: A Vocabulary of Culture and Society*, London, Fontana/Collins.

Williams, R. (1977) *Marxism and Literature*, Oxford, OUP.

Williams, R. (1981) *Forward March of Labour Halted* (comments), ed. M. Jacques and F. Mulhern, London, Verso.

Williams, R. (1983) *Towards 2000*, London, Chatto & Windus.

Williams, R. (1985) 'Mining the Meaning: Key Words in the Miners' Strike', *New Socialist*, No. 25, March.

Wilson, B. (1985) 'Morality in the Evolution of the Modern Social System', *British Journal of Sociology*, Vol. 36, No. 3.

Wittgenstein, L. (1958) *Philosophical Investigations*, Oxford, Blackwell.

Wolfe, A. (1974) 'New Directions in the Marxist Theory of Politics', *Politics and Society*, Vol. 4, No. 2.

Wolfe, A. (1977) *The Limits of Legitimacy: Political Contradictions of Contemporary Capitalism*, New York, Free Press.

Wolin, R. (1982) *Walter Benjamin, An Aesthetic of Redemption*, New York, Columbia University Press.

Wolin, S. (1977) 'The Rise of Private Man', *New York Review of Books*, 14th April.

Wood, A. (1981) *Karl Marx*, London, RKP.

Wright, P. (1985) *On Living in an Old Country*, London, Verso.
Young, N. (1977) *An Infantile Disorder? The Crisis and Decline of the New Left*, London, RKP.
Zyderveld, A. (1979) *On Clichés: The Supersedence of Meaning by Function in Modernity*, London, RKP.

Index